MOON PORT PASTOR

REFLECTIONS ON ADRIAN ROGERS AND *MOON PORT PASTOR*

Adrian Rogers was a titan in both the evangelical and Southern Baptist world. The way God used him at the Bellevue Baptist Church in Memphis and in the Conservative Resurgence, the movement that led Southern Baptists back to the Bible, is well known and well documented. However, his ministry at FBC Merritt Island could rightly be described as "the lost years" of his ministry. Not much has been written about these formative and important years. Thankfully, that problem has now been solved as they have been recovered in this excellent book by Phil Kramer. *Moon Port Pastor* will be an inspiration and education to those who want to learn even more about the man of God known as Adrian Rogers. I was wonderfully blessed by it. You will be too!

DANIEL L. AKIN, *President, Southeastern Baptist Theological Seminary*

Adrian Rogers, often called the Prince of Preachers, was probably best known for his iconic ministry at Bellevue Baptist Church and in Southern Baptist denominational life. Not so well known are the years he served as pastor of the First Baptist Church of Merritt Island, Florida. Yet those years were pivotal and foundational to the significance of his later ministry. Phil Kramer's book, *Moon Port Pastor*, highlights his Merritt Island years and demonstrates that they were transformational for him, the church, and consequently to Christian history. I was a contemporary with Adrian Rogers, sharing many personal and ministry experiences with him, but I now know him at a deeper level through this excellent book. After reading *Moon Port Pastor*, I was refreshed and inspired anew in my own spiritual journey. A must read for all, especially pastors.

JIM HENRY, *Pastor Emeritus, First Baptist Church, Orlando, Florida*

Phil Kramer has done a masterful job of capturing the "Moon Port" years of Pastor Adrian Rogers, everyone's favorite preacher. To fully understand the scope of his powerful ministry one needs to embark upon a journey back and ask, "What was it that created such explosive growth spiritually and numerically at First Baptist Church, Merritt Island, Florida?" We discover it wasn't just location, buildings, or budgets—it was Dr. Rogers' commitment to God's Word, soul-winning, and the Spirit-filled life, something that permeated his life-long ministry. I believe Adrian Rogers, while never desiring to call attention to himself, would appreciate that the four sections of this book are alliterated, much like many of his tremendous messages. I love this book to the moon and back!

JAY DENNIS, *Pastor, City Central Church, Lakeland, Florida*

The year was 1970. I was pastor of First Southern Baptist Church in Del City, Oklahoma. Two of our church members were actively on Major League baseball teams, and both had spring training near Merritt Island. These two shared with me many times about this pastor at First Baptist Church in Merritt Island, whom they heard every year during spring training. They brought me tapes of Adrian's preaching. Without doubt, he was a remarkable preacher of the Gospel. In 1979, he became president of the Southern Baptist Convention. I followed him in 1982 as the third president of the convention during the Conservative Resurgence. I have had the privilege of knowing him as one of the greatest preachers I have ever heard, knowing him as an incredible leader of our convention, and knowing him as a cherished friend and fellow minister. Name any quality of great leadership, and Adrian represented the best of that quality. The

Merritt Island years developed him into the global leader he became. At Merritt Island, he followed the leadership of the Holy Spirit and stood tall as he proclaimed the Word of God. Adrian was known and loved for many reasons. My best memory of his ministry came when I preached at Bellevue one Sunday for a missions emphasis. Adrian and I met in his office to pray before the first service. As we exited his office, a little girl about 5 years of age ran up to him, wrapped her arms around his leg, and said, "I love you, pastor!" He knelt down to give her a big hug, then asked her how her parents and siblings were—by name. That moment captured his life and ministry to me. He was a great preacher, pastor, leader, and friend. But his greatness was not just in all the accolades he received, but in the hug he gave that little girl and how he knew the names of her entire family. That is the real measure of his greatness. Merritt Island shaped his ministry as he shaped the ministry of the church. The *Moon Port Pastor* emerged in the shadow of the Space Center, and his leadership has been felt across this land ever since.

JIMMY DRAPER, *President Emeritus, LifeWay*

One day while serving on staff at the great Bellevue Baptist Church, we had a staff luncheon with Dr. Sidlow Baxter. He was one of Adrian Rogers' heroes of the faith and an incredible apologist and author of many books worth reading. I asked Dr. Baxter, "What books should I as a young minister be reading?" He said—and I'll never forget it—"Lad, read the Book...and if you have to read anything else, read the person who writes about the Book." Great advice for a young man or, for that matter, even an old man of God. What you hold in your hand is a book about a man who loved "The Book." His name is Adrian Rogers, and anyone who knows me knows I believe he was the greatest example of what a preacher, a man's man, and a Man of God should be like all at the same time. To me, he was larger than life, and the greatest eight years of my life was having the privilege of being a Pastor on his staff, sitting under his teaching and leadership, and watching everyday a man who walked his walk and talked his talk. Let's just say the tongue in his mouth and the tongue in his shoe went the same direction. He was "the real deal." And we are indebted to Phil Kramer for writing this book, *Moon Port Pastor*, about the earlier years of Adrian Rogers' ministry. We all saw how he ended. He finished well. But how did he start? Well, keep reading. Phil has captured his heart, his sermons, and his philosophy about growing a church, balancing family, and the beginning of a story of a man God was getting ready to use to shake not only a denomination, but cities and churches across the globe. I loved Adrian Rogers. Truthfully, maybe too much. And I miss him. Our entire denomination does. He was a spiritual Dad and mentor to me. But there are many who didn't know him and probably look at us with a quizzical look on their face when we mention his name and his ministry. Well, keep reading. Thank you, Phil Kramer, for making him come alive again in our hearts. We loved Adrian Rogers because he loved Jesus. And after you read *Moon Port Pastor*, you, too, will love him. And for sure you'll know why I did. All I can say, is "Keep reading."

KEN WHITTEN, *National Director of Pastoral Leadership*, NAMB

I don't think I've ever heard a negative word about Adrian Rogers. While some have disagreed with him, they did so from a perspective of deep respect for the man, his integrity, and his preaching. I get it. Adrian Rogers has influenced my life and ministry in so many ways that it would take a book for me to expand upon all of them. I am deeply grateful that Phil Kramer wrote this book about Dr. Rogers' earlier ministry at First Baptist Church of Merritt Island. Those years were formative for him and the global influence he would become. When I attended Adrian Rogers' funeral on November 15, 2005, I spoke with many people who came to honor the man who had been such a powerful influence in their lives. The most common words I heard were, "I will miss him." Those words were prescient. Thousands of us do indeed miss him. In this book, we relive an important part of his life and ministry, and we get to appreciate again the incredible man that he was.

THOM RAINER, *Founder and CEO, Church Answers*

Adrian Rogers was one of the most prominent preachers and communicators of the twentieth century whose preaching transformed countless lives on a deeply personal level. *Moon Port Pastor* unpacks his early life and ministry in Florida that set a solid foundation for his later, more prominent work in Memphis. By examining the contextual history, the ministry commitments, and the interpersonal connections, Phil Kramer has done a masterful job of bringing Adrian Rogers' Merritt Island years to life!

JOHN MARK YEATS, *President, Corban University*

You are going to enjoy *Moon Port Pastor*! Dr. Phil Kramer has done a beautiful job of writing about the life of Dr. Adrian Rogers before and during the eight historic and glorious years he pastored the First Baptist Church of Merritt Island, Florida! If you are a pastor, church leader, or serious student you will learn much by carefully studying Adrian Rogers' leadership style and deep love for Jesus and the Bible. I was Adrian Rogers' Minister of Music for 38 years in Florida and Tennessee. In the 1960s, I began thinking he was the best preacher in Florida. In the 1970s and 1980s, I began thinking he was the best preacher in the Southern Baptist Convention and America. After 38 years, I ended up believing he was one of the greatest preachers of the twentieth century! Adrian's preaching was riveting and life changing! His leadership was astounding! In the years we worked together, I watched him in every kind of stressful situation and joyful victory. He was the same out of the pulpit as he was in the pulpit. He didn't change. He was quick to ask forgiveness when he was wrong. He was quick to pray with people "on the spot" for healing or an answer from God. He was not perfect, but he wanted to be. People have asked me what one word sums up the life of Adrian Rogers. "Integrity" always comes to mind, but "Jesus" would really be my answer. In the first few years of working together, I never heard a pastor use the word "Jesus" so much! His one passion was to preach, love, worship, exalt, share, and obey Jesus, "...that He Himself (Jesus) will come to have first place in everything" (Colossians 1:18).

JIM WHITMIRE, *Minister of Music Emeritus, Bellevue Baptist Church*

MOON PORT PASTOR

PHIL KRAMER

Moon Port Pastor
by Phil Kramer

ISBN 978-0-9859406-6-9

Published by Love Worth Finding Ministries, Inc.
2941 Kate Bond Road
Memphis, TN 38133-4017
(800) 274-5683

Printed in the United States of America
May 2024

Dedicated to Pastor Guy S. Sanders, III, who led me to faith in Jesus Christ and introduced me to the preaching ministry of Adrian Rogers

CONTENTS

FOREWORD

When I was asked by Pastor Phil Kramer to write the foreword for *Moon Port Pastor*, I was both humbled and honored to do so. But as I sit here thinking about what to write, I am at a loss on what to say. *Not because I have nothing to write but because I could turn the foreword into my own book!*

There are simply no words to express the impact and influence that one of the greatest preachers in the history of the Christian church has had on my life and ministry, and I know I am one in a long line of pastors and preachers to this very day that would say the same thing. I have one picture of one pastor/preacher in my office, and it is Adrian Rogers. I have one "go to" pastor when I am preparing messages to see what he had to say about the text I am studying, and it is Adrian Rogers. I have one pastor above all whose life, ministry, and Godly example I have tried to emulate, and that is Adrian Rogers. What any ministerial success I have had by the grace and favor of God is due in so many ways to this man Adrian Rogers.

I frequently and fondly refer to him as "my mentor" for he truly became that in the most momentous event in my life outside of being born again and meeting my wife Teresa. I had never heard of Adrian Rogers when, as a PhD student at Southern Seminary, another student at Southern walked up to me and handed me a cassette tape and said, "You need to hear this man preach." Being a dad of a newborn, immersed in dissertation research, and pastoring a church, I thought nothing of it.

But then one day while studying I took a break and popped the cassette into a player thinking I would listen for 5 minutes and be able to say I did listen...but then I heard *that voice*...and *that message*...and *that anointing.* I took it upstairs and said, "Teresa, you need to listen to this!" Forty-five minutes later, she came down to my basement study, tossed the tape on the table, and said firmly, "Why don't you preach like that?" I said, "I don't know how, but I am going to learn!"

Fast forward four years later after I had graduated and moved to Mississippi. I realized I was only four hours from Memphis, and I wrote Dr. Rogers to ask if could drive up and have an hour of his time. To my amazement, a few days later he invited me to come up and have lunch with him. I went armed with several pages of single-spaced questions thinking I only had one hour. After the hour was up, I started gathering my materials to leave and Dr. Rogers looked at me and said, "What's your rush? I have cleared my calendar, and you can stay until midnight!" Well, I almost did! But over the next several hours I learned more about preaching, sermon preparation, filing systems, leadership, handling conflicts, managing a staff, setting a schedule, walking with God, and being the dad and husband God wanted me to be than I learned in six years at Southern Seminary. Those lessons and that time impacts me to this very day.

All that to say, I am thrilled that Phil Kramer has written this great book about the Merritt Island years, an amazing season in the life and ministry of a man who for sure is in God's Hall of Faith and whose influence continues and will continue for decades if not centuries to come. Thank you dear pastor for this labor of love, and thank you Heavenly Father for giving your church such a great man of God to write about!

James Merritt
Pastor, Cross Pointe Church
Duluth, Georgia
January 2024

AUTHOR'S PREFACE

"Others adore and idolize athletes.
My hero was Adrian Rogers."
PASTOR KEN WHITTEN[1]

As a high school senior in 1991, I traveled with my pastor, Guy Sanders, to the Baptist College of Florida where he was scheduled to preach in chapel. Pastor Guy led me to the Lord one year earlier, and now he was taking me along as a discipleship opportunity. As we departed First Baptist Church of Lake Wales after the Wednesday evening service and headed north, he pulled out a cassette album of sermons on the book of James by a pastor named Adrian Rogers and said, "You need to listen to this guy!" It was the first time I ever heard Adrian's dynamic teaching and commanding voice, but it certainly wouldn't be the last. After high school graduation, I joined the Marine Corps and continued to grow as a new Christian. I frequently listened to Love Worth Finding on the local radio station and began buying cassette tapes. In fact, my purchases were so frequent that one day a fellow Marine glanced over my shoulder at my Visa card statement and—knowing that I was a consistent Christian—asked with surprise, "Fifty dollars to Love Worth Finding?! Kramer, what kind of stuff are you buying?!"

As the years went by and I attended college, seminary, and began pastoring churches, those radio broadcasts and cassette tapes shaped my life tremendously. I did not grow up in a Bible-teaching church or a Christian home, so Adrian's solid preaching greatly assisted me to make up for lost time. Along the way, God provided a vision for the kind of life he wanted me to live, the kind of wife and family he wanted me to have, the type of witness he wanted me to be, and the kind of ministry he wanted me to pursue. In short, I doubt I would be the man I am today were it not for Adrian Rogers' long-distance impact on my life.

In September 2005, my wife and I had the opportunity to attend Adrian's Pastor Training Institute held in Sevierville, Tennessee. I had never personally met Adrian Rogers, and I wasn't going to miss the chance. We drove from Fort Bragg, North Carolina and even brought our three-week-old son, Philip. The night before the Institute began, Adrian preached a stirring message from Romans 2. Even though he was struggling with the effects of cancer treatments, he was absolutely on fire and showed no signs of diminished strength while preaching. Two days later during the Institute, I had my son in a baby carrier in the church lobby, and Adrian and Joyce came walking by. He said, "Who do we have here?" I said, "Pastor, this is my son, Philip." And he replied, "Philip, I want you to know that hell is hot, heaven sweet, sin black, judgment sure, and Jesus saves." It was the first time anyone ever shared the Gospel with my son!

Later that year, not long after Adrian went to Heaven, I read Joyce Rogers' book, *Love Worth Finding*. I already knew something about the Bellevue years, and the book did an excellent job of adding to that. But I knew very little about his life and ministry before going to Memphis, and *Love Worth Finding* introduced me to a younger Adrian Rogers. Among other things, the book included a picture of the First Baptist Church of Merritt Island and a 2,000-person "living cross." I saw it and immediately thought, "What is *that*, and what's the story behind it?" Being a native Floridian with a keen interest in Sunshine State history as well as the space program, I wanted to know more.

As time went by, I picked up bits and pieces here and there about the Merritt Island years, to include a trip to Florida in 2008 to conduct several interviews. Although I believe God placed an undeniable vision for this book on my heart at that time, multiple deployments to Iraq and Afghanistan got in the way of further research and writing. And, to be honest, I was not yet spiritually ready to tell the story. You see, I was still ministering largely in my own strength and had yet to understand the Spirit-filled life—namely, that authentic Christianity is the product of the Spirit's power within us rather than the fruits of our own labors. As we shall see in *Moon Port Pastor*, this was one of Adrian's primary teachings during the Merritt Island years. Thus, as I began to experience the fullness of the Spirit in my own life and ministry, my Merritt Island research began to make more sense, and I finally felt a liberty and boldness to tell the story.

Ultimately, my work on *Moon Port Pastor* has been a labor of love, but it has also been a source of personal growth. Studying the historical data, reflecting on the timeless qualities of powerful Gospel ministry, and hearing from those who experienced it firsthand at First Baptist Church have left a tremendous impression on me. While conducting research and writing, God has repeatedly encouraged and challenged me as a Christian and a Pastor. I pray that many others will experience the same blessings as they read this book and understand why, years later, Jim Whitmire looked back with tears in his eyes and said, "The *glory* was on that church!"[2]

INTRODUCTION

On Sunday, July 20, 1969, at 10:56 PM EDT some 600 million people around the globe gazed at a grainy video image from the lunar surface as the product of untold man-hours, almost-unlimited tax dollars, and mind-boggling technologies manifested itself in a single footprint. By any human measure, this "one giant leap for mankind" eclipsed all other accomplishments to date. President Richard Nixon, with a verbal flourish, described the event as the highlight of "the greatest week in the history of the world since Creation."[1] With a bit more reserve but no less optimism, Queen Elizabeth II said, "On behalf of the British people, I salute the skills and courage which have brought man to the moon. May this endeavor increase the knowledge and well-being of mankind."[2] On the other hand, CBS News correspondent Walter Cronkite, at the time "the most trusted man in America," was simply overwhelmed by the gravity of the lunar landing: "Man on the moon...oh boy...I'm speechless."[3] Words or no words, it was a surreal moment for all humanity.

That morning, only a few miles from the launch pad from which Apollo 11 departed the Earth four days earlier, another man shared his thoughts on the moonwalk that would take place that evening. The energetic, 37-year-old pastor told the hundreds gathered at the First Baptist Church of Merritt Island—many of whom worked at "the Cape" and personally had a hand in the space program—"All of us have our eyes on the skies right now, and I'm just as excited as you are about man going to the moon.

But as you see these things taking place on television later today, I want you to look beyond the glory of the stars. I want you to look to the glory of the Lord Jesus." Then, in conclusion to his challenge, he quoted the hymn "Beautiful Savior":

> Fair is the sunshine
> Fairer still the moonlight,
> And all the stars in the heavenly host;
> Jesus shines brighter,
> Jesus shines purer,
> Than all the angels heav'n can boast.[4]

Like millions of others, the young pastor understood the historic significance of the occasion. But he knew even better his God-given purpose—namely, to "point men beyond the stars." His name was Adrian Rogers, but as the leader of the largest and fastest-growing church in the vicinity of Kennedy Space Center, many knew him as the "Moon Port Pastor."

MOON PORT PASTOR: A STORY WORTH TELLING

Mention the name Adrian Rogers and those familiar with his life of Gospel service will typically think of three things—and rightly so. First and foremost, many will recall his phenomenal thirty-two-year pastorate at Bellevue Baptist Church in Memphis, Tennessee. When Adrian arrived at Bellevue in September 1972, while the church could boast of some 9,000 members on paper, Sunday morning attendance had declined to about 1,300 over the previous decade. Yet only 8 months later, "Miracle Day" attendance on May 13, 1973, shattered all previous records with over 4,500 on campus. Through strong, dynamic preaching, a high view of God's inerrant Word, and a relentless evangelistic focus, "Miracle Day" was just

Newspaper ads for revival services with the "Moon Port Pastor," Adrian Rogers. *Fort Lauderdale News and Sun-Sentinel,* April 20, 1968, 15A; *Orlando Sentinel,* April 16, 1966, 4C.

the beginning of what would happen in the years to come. By 1977, the growing congregation required two morning services in the sanctuary that could seat several thousand. Then a third service became necessary in 1982. Ultimately, under Adrian's leadership, Bellevue relocated to its current 377-acre campus in 1989. When he retired in 2005, Bellevue's membership surpassed 29,000 and Sunday attendance reached nearly 10,000. By all accounts, the Bellevue years were extraordinarily unforgettable as tens of thousands were saved, baptized, and discipled.[5]

Others know Adrian Rogers best through his continuing ministry, "Love Worth Finding." Founded initially in 1985 as "Word for the World," immediate demand for the broadcast led to growth and a rebranding as "Love Worth Finding" in 1987: "People were requesting tapes of the messages, and soon the requests began to grow to the point that we knew God was leading us into a wider ministry."[6] Initially, Love Worth Finding began as a 1-hour television broadcast on 17 stations and a 30-minute daily radio broadcast on 19 stations.[7] Today, by means of television, radio, satellite, and online resources, viewers and listeners can enjoy Love Worth Finding on demand anytime, anywhere in the world. As a result of this enduring ministry, many are led to Christ and discipled through Adrian's teaching to this day—though "he being dead still speaks" (Hebrews 11:4).

Still others will remember Adrian Rogers as a key lynchpin and spokesman for the Conservative Resurgence within the Southern Baptist Convention (SBC) in the late 1970s and 1980s. Leftward theological drift in the twentieth century plagued many Christian denominations, and the SBC was no different. Numerous professors at Convention seminaries embraced higher-critical views on the Bible, and more than a few SBC churches followed suit. These developments grieved pastors and denominational leaders devoted to the pristine inerrancy of the Scripture. Understanding the inevitable outcomes from this denominational drift, a handful of visionaries developed a plan to right the SBC ship, but they needed a leader to galvanize the effort. So, in 1979, a narrow majority of messengers at the SBC Annual Meeting in Houston elected Adrian as Convention President. He served for one year, made key appointments to committees and boards, promoted the importance of conservative theology for evangelism and missions, and generally pointed the SBC back toward its historic roots. Although he declined to run for a second consecutive term, he remained an important voice among conservative SBC leaders for two decades and eventually served two more one-year terms as President from 1986 to 1988.[8] Looking back, Southeastern Baptist Theological Seminary President Danny Akin has said:

> This was a time of serious contention among Baptists and evangelicals due to the infiltration of theological liberalism and neo-orthodoxy that had spread throughout SBC seminaries and churches. Stakes were high. Not only did Adrian Rogers' leadership have a significant impact on the debate over the doctrine of inerrancy, he also modeled biblical conviction and compassion that caused even those who disagreed with him to respect him for his integrity.[9]

But opponents recognized more than just his integrity, noting that the Conservative Resurgence "could not have known its measure of success apart from Adrian Rogers. Three times the president of the SBC in nine years. No other fundamentalist could rival him as preacher, debater, or intransigent believer. He was by far their most capable leader."[10] By his own admission, Adrian saw his role in the Conservative Resurgence as perhaps the most lasting of his life and ministry:

> I look back on my life, and there are a lot of things that have happened: I have written books, pastored churches, and preached on radio and television around the world. But I think the part that God allowed me to have in the turning of the SBC may have the longest-lasting effect and be the most significant."[11]

To be sure, Southern Baptists should well remember Adrian Rogers and his role in rescuing the SBC from the brink of the liberal abyss.

These monumental spiritual impacts cast a long shadow across the American religious landscape, and countless men, women, boys, and girls have experienced God's mercy and grace as a result. Unfortunately, however, the massive scope of Adrian's ministry in the latter half of his life has largely overshadowed the first half. This is understandable given the heights to which he ascended as pastor, religious broadcaster, and denominational leader. But it is also regrettable, not least because in many ways, the first half of his ministry was just as amazing (if not more so) than the latter half, albeit on a somewhat smaller scale. For example, few know about his powerful and anointed service as a student pastor in Florida and Mississippi (1950-1958). Furthermore, not many are familiar with the details of his service as pastor of two churches in Florida after graduating from New Orleans Baptist Theological Seminary and before going to Memphis (1958-1972). Yes, the churches he served then were smaller—in some cases, *significantly* smaller. And, compared to his later notoriety, he was relatively unknown in those days. Nevertheless, the early years of his ministry should not be overlooked.

Of all the churches that Adrian Rogers led prior to Bellevue, the most noteworthy was certainly the First Baptist Church of Merritt Island,

Florida (1964-1972). Located on Florida's Atlantic coast in Brevard County—known in the 1960s as "Moon Port USA"—Merritt Island took center stage in the nation's historic race to the moon in the 1960s. President John F. Kennedy's challenge issued in May 1961 of "landing a man on the moon and returning him safely to the earth" by the end of the decade was the driving force behind a task as monumental as any nation had ever attempted. Situated only a few miles west of Cape Canaveral, Merritt Island—and all of Brevard County, for that matter—experienced an enormous population explosion as thousands of contractors, scientists, construction workers, engineers, and their families flooded the area. As a result, and as one might suspect, the Merritt Island ministry was characterized by incredible numerical growth. In eight years, the church grew from approximately 300 on Sunday morning to 2,000 in attendance, saw over 2,400 people baptized, increased the annual budget from $75,000 to $475,000, and added over $1.5 million in new and innovative buildings.[12] But as we shall see, the story is about much more than numbers.

And it is a story worth telling.

MOON PORT PASTOR: TELLING THE STORY

Beyond the obvious need to tell an intriguing story that has largely gone untold, there are several specific purposes for this book. Ultimately, our intent is to provide a resource for pastors, rank-and-file Christians, and historians alike.

First, for twenty-first-century church leaders, an accessible portrait of Adrian Rogers as pastor offers a great deal of promise for their own contemporary ministries. We say *accessible*, because, by his own admission, few pastors and church leaders could digest Bellevue's immense administrative structure and operational policies that were routine during his pastorate there. In fact, at his Pastor Training Institute in 2005, Adrian remarked, "A church [like Bellevue] is hard to get your mind wrapped around. It would choke most people down if I was to give them the policies and procedures that we have at Bellevue—they couldn't relate."[13] In comparison, at Merritt Island in 1964, he inherited a modest campus, only one associate minister on staff, and a little more than 300 in Sunday morning attendance. Clearly, that scenario offers a much more accessible model for pastors and leaders. And we should not forget that, in our contemporary age when growth-desperate pastors often sacrifice the message for the sake of methods that they *think* will bring crowds and depth of maturity, Adrian had *both* at Merritt Island when he led the church to be "geared to the times and anchored to the rock."[14] Yes, for contemporary pastors and church leaders eager to impact the world around them with the Gospel of Jesus Christ, the story of Adrian's Merritt Island years needs to be told.

Second, there is a timeless, inspirational message to be found when talking about the Merritt Island years. With a priority upon the inerrant Word of God preached in a dynamic and endearing way along with an emphasis upon personal evangelism, the fullness of the Holy Spirit, and an innovative vision for comprehensively ministering to "the whole man...physical, mental, and spiritual,"[15] contemporary readers will feel as though Adrian Rogers once again stands behind the Merritt Island pulpit, challenging them just as he challenged his congregation 60 years ago. Indeed, readers will be hard-pressed to remain uninspired and unchanged after experiencing the timeless story of the Moon Port Pastor.

Third, sustained research and writing about the Merritt Island years must take place because little has been written or said about it. In fact, the story of Adrian's years in Merritt Island thus far has been largely untold. Two key biographical works about him have appeared over the years, but neither has given the Merritt Island years due attention. First and foremost is Joyce Rogers' book *Love Worth Finding*, published in 2005.[16] This volume provides a wonderful biographical overview as well as several intimate details of ministry and family life. But since *Love Worth Finding* was written as a biography with emphasis on the Bellevue years, SBC presidency, and founding of Love Worth Finding, the Merritt

Island years were understandably not highlighted extensively. Likewise, the excellent but largely forgotten 1997 biographical video "Standing on the Promises"[17] is a fantastic resource on Adrian Rogers' life and ministry. But the 52-minute video devotes only 3 minutes to the Merritt Island years, and much of that talks more about human-interest matters than substantive information about the ministry itself. Ultimately, *Love Worth Finding* and "Standing on the Promises" are tremendous primary resources that leave an open door to tell the story of the Moon Port Pastor in greater detail. Therefore, now is the time to research and write about this portion of Adrian's life, both to catalog living testimonies of those years, and also to begin assembling the building blocks that some future author will incorporate into a definitive Adrian Rogers biography.

Now, if this is a story worth telling, how shall we tell it? Maximizing the story requires four parts: (1) the man, (2) the moment, (3) the ministry, and (4) the means. First, we cannot understand Adrian Rogers the pastor without understanding Adrian Rogers the man. Specifically, what key experiences shaped the 32-year-old man who arrived in Merritt Island in August 1964? What key moments did God use to prepare him for the colossal opportunity that Merritt Island presented? In the first section, entitled "The Man," our intention is not to retell in detail the story of the first three decades of Adrian's life. Rather, we will specifically highlight those earlier experiences in childhood, college, seminary, and his first three pastorates that formed the personal and spiritual essence of the man leading up to his Merritt Island ministry.

In the second section, "The Moment," we will consider the unique factors that filled Brevard County and the First Baptist Church of Merritt Island with almost unlimited potential during the 1960s and early 1970s. Driven initially by the missile program that began in 1950 and then by the space program that took its place, multitudes relocated to Brevard County and Merritt Island in the 1950s and early 1960s. When they came, they faced housing shortages, limited infrastructure, and clouds of mosquitos. Yet none of these challenges prevented Brevard from becoming the fastest-growing county in America by 1960. Then, in 1961, President John F. Kennedy challenged the nation to reach for the moon by the decade's end, and Project Mercury stirred the public's fascination with space. As a result, Brevard was flooded with even more people, increased funding, and greater national attention. The days were undeniably electric as the eyes of the nation gazed upon Brevard County—known across America as "Moon Port USA." Meanwhile, the First Baptist Church, founded within months of the missile program's establishment in the area, experienced the ebb and flow of growing pains during its first 15 years of existence. While a new 1,000-seat worship center was built in 1960 to accommodate anticipated growth, the church lacked a dynamic, catalyst leader to spearhead efforts equal to the moment. As we shall see, all these factors set the stage for a mighty movement of God during Adrian's Merritt Island years.

The third section, "The Ministry," will contain the lion's share of the story as we highlight the people, events, strategies, and victories that characterized Adrian's ministry at First Baptist Church from 1964 to 1972. These chapters will chronologically detail the Merritt Island years and demonstrate how the church impacted the local community and how the local community impacted the church. In addition, we will see early signs of the trajectory that ultimately carried Adrian to the highest levels of SBC leadership and influence. In the process, the amazing story of the Moon Port Pastor will become evident to all who read it.

The fourth section, "The Means," will highlight in essay-like manner the timeless spiritual values that made the Merritt Island years so glorious. As the church became widely known across the SBC in the late 1960s and early 1970s, many began to ask Adrian the secret to his success. Typically, he would always highlight the same basic principles: "Let me tell you what has made First Baptist Church of Merritt Island a great church: soul-winning, evangelism, and the Spirit-filled life...taking a stand on the Word of God, and refusing to be drawn off into secondary tangents."[18] Indeed, a high view of the Scripture, Holy Spirit power, dynamic Gospel leadership, and relentless personal evangelism are just as relevant today as they were in the Merritt Island years, and we will highlight these in the fourth section. Some of the methods by which pastors preach, lead, and minister today look different than they did 60 years ago, but the same spiritual means that made the First Baptist Church of Merritt Island a great church are available to pastors and churches today—and in that regard, nothing has changed.

ACKNOWLEDGMENTS

The breadth of this project and the years required to write it represent the time and kindness of a number of helpful brothers and sisters in Christ. First and foremost, I want to thank Joyce Rogers and her children Steve, Gayle, David, and Janice for their hospitality and willingness to open their lives to me. I have been thoroughly blessed to know them, and I will never forget singing "Some Golden Daybreak" with Joyce, Gayle, and Janice at the conclusion of our visit in Memphis.

At Merritt Island, church historians Gene and Norma Baird (now with the Lord) and Lyvonne Burleson shared with me the fruits of their tireless efforts to preserve the story of First Baptist Church. I am especially indebted to Lyvonne, who has fielded many questions and has frequently gone above and beyond to assist my research. Likewise, Jim Whitmire, Nelson and Flo Rutledge, Peter Lord, Joe Boatright, Bill Cochran, Carl and Frances Hicks, Vernon Wise, Virgil Dudit, and Bill Fowler—several of whom are also now with the Lord—all sat for interviews that proved especially helpful.

Numerous archivists, librarians, and scholars provided invaluable assistance. Penny Baumgardner of the Florida Baptist Historical Society assisted in many ways and responded to more requests than I can remember—"Penny, I have just one more question for you." Jeremy Westbrook of the Ohio Baptist Convention, Adam Winters of the Kentucky Baptist Convention, and Eric Dressler of the Arizona Baptist Convention provided key documents about events at which Adrian Rogers spoke in their respective states. At Southwestern Baptist Theological Seminary in

Fort Worth, Jill Botticelli and Emily Blakley of the B. H. Carroll Center for Baptist Heritage and Mission graciously met my every research need. Barry Hankins of Baylor University shared with me his Adrian Rogers interview transcript, and Doug Weaver, also of Baylor, provided keen insights that supplemented his book *Baptists and the Holy Spirit*.

Fellow pastors and associates provided priceless feedback. Many thanks go to Jim Henry, especially for his initial encouragement to devote my best energies to this project. Jay Dennis proved to be an unlimited source of encouragement and insight. My very good friend John Mark Yeats provided encouragement and highly constructive comments. Ken Whitten provided thoughtful comments as well as an admiration for Adrian Rogers that I found particularly inspiring. James Merritt deserves special mention, not only for writing the Foreword but also for sharing ideas that profoundly impacted my thinking and writing. And Michael Catt, now with the Lord, shared some significant thoughts on the Holy Spirit among Southern Baptists in the 1960s and 1970s.

I am especially indebted to Cary Vaughn, Bobby Lewis, and the entire Love Worth Finding team for their partnership in sharing the story of the Moon Port Pastor with the world.

My children, Emma (and her husband, Andrew), Libby, Baur, Lightsey, and Adrian, cheered me on as I spent large quantities of time in research and writing. And most importantly, my wife Shara lovingly encouraged me, prayed for me, read each chapter, and provided affirmative feedback that kept me on the right track. Many women do well, but she surpasses them all!

PART I
THE MAN

1

GROWING IN STATURE AND FAVOR WITH THE LORD (1931-1954)

Born on September 12, 1931 and raised in West Palm Beach, Florida, Adrian Rogers' childhood did not initially forecast the amazing story that God would write. He described his parents as "good, hard-working, salt of the earth kind of people," but God was not part of their priorities: "As a family, we were not anti-God. We were just an average family that was without Christ. As a child, I never heard my father pray. We never had Bible reading in our home, and we did not attend church."[1] Without a healthy spiritual foundation, Adrian frequently skipped school, used foul language, cheated in class, made trouble for his teachers, and fought often: "Before I got saved, among my other bad habits, I liked to fight. And I would get into, on average, about one fight a week."[2]

In spite of their lack of spiritual priority, when Adrian was 14 years old the Rogers family accepted a neighbor's invitation to revival services at Northwood Baptist Church in West Palm Beach, only a few blocks from their home. Much to Adrian's surprise, his father stepped forward to receive Christ during the invitation, and, before fully realizing what was taking place, Adrian followed down the aisle and likewise prayed to receive

Christ: "When Daddy stepped out to give his heart to Christ, that brought me under great conviction, and I thought, 'I need to do the same thing.' So, I went forward and as best as I knew how, I gave my heart to Jesus Christ."[3]

Not long after, those familiar with his troublesome reputation began asking, "What has happened to Adrian Rogers?" Perhaps his sweetheart, Joyce Gentry, was the person most pleased with these developments. Prior to Adrian's salvation, the principal at Northboro Junior High School, Mrs. McCauley, had notified Joyce's mother that her daughter was spending time with the worst boy in the school.[4] But after Adrian's experience with Jesus, everything began to change.

BLESSED ASSURANCE AND HOLY BOLDNESS

Nevertheless, for two years, Adrian struggled with consistency and spiritual confidence. Many of the sinful habits that had characterized his pre-conversion life still appeared from time to time. Looking back, he recalled that he received little follow-up or discipleship after his experience at Northwood Baptist: "I basically had a 'pencil and card' religion. To this moment, I'm not certain if I was saved at that time or not. I rode a spiritual roller coaster for a while. There was a change in my life, but I was fighting a tremendous civil war inside."[5] The battle even brought doubts about his salvation that left assurance out of reach.

Finally, when he was 16 years old, Adrian knew he needed to "get it settled" once and for all. After walking Joyce home one evening, he came to a spiritual (and literal) crossroads at the intersection of 39th Street and Calvin Avenue near his home in West Palm Beach. This episode played a critical role in his life as his own words indicated:

> At 39th Street and Calvin Avenue, I stopped and prayed, "Lord, I don't know if I'm lost and you have me under conviction or I'm saved and the devil's trying to make me doubt it, but I need to get it settled." Then

> I looked straight up into heaven—I didn't bow my head—and I said, "Lord, you told me in your Word that if I would trust you, you would save me. If I have been saved, this won't take it away. But if I have not been saved, I'm going to settle it right now. So, Lord Jesus, now and forever, I trust you to save me. I don't look for a feeling. I don't look for a sign. It is done. Praise your holy name."[6]

This watershed moment gave rise to a bold confidence that marked Adrian's life and ministry until the end of his days. Those familiar with his preaching know that the doctrine of assurance played a significant role in his theology and teaching. And one could easily argue that his own assurance of salvation as well as his unwavering commitment to the doctrine of assurance directly contributed to the significant results of his ministry, especially the evangelistic fruit: "How wonderful it is to tell people that the God who saves them is the God who will keep them. It's a great tool in evangelism—sharing the Lord Jesus Christ."[7]

Not long after Adrian experienced assurance of his salvation, an opportunity to stand for Jesus presented itself, which he described as "the first test I really had as a Christian."[8] In those days, he was an exceptional student-athlete, playing football and basketball, and running track, but as this episode demonstrated, he prioritized his relationship with God. During his junior year, the Palm Beach High School football team was one of the best in the state, and Adrian played quarterback, fullback, and linebacker. Late in the season, as the team remained undefeated, Adrian contracted the mumps. After a period of bed rest, the doctor cleared him to resume normal activities but told him that for a time he could not play football under any circumstances. With another big game coming on Friday night, Adrian found himself in a dilemma, because his church had scheduled revival services for that night: should he go and cheer on his teammates or should he go to church?

> Had I been able to play, I would have been there to play. I wanted to go to that football game so bad I could taste it. But I knew that my

Coach Red Whittington's 1949 Palm Beach Wildcats with #46 Adrian Rogers back row, fifth from left. Courtesy Joyce Rogers.

> loyalty was first of all to my Lord and His Christ. So, I went to the revival meeting on that Friday night. When my coach heard about it, he was furious. He taught a psychology class, and during one class the week after the game he began talking about me even though I wasn't in the room: "Then there's Adrian Rogers. He didn't come to the football game on Friday night; he went to church instead. And when we have Sunday practices, he won't practice on Sundays. Do you see how a man will use religion to get out of something he doesn't want to do?" This got back to me, and I decided it was time I took a stand for the Lord.[9]

Adrian went to see his coach, even though everyone feared him: "I was quivering on the inside because I feared my coach. But I made up my mind to stand for Jesus. I'd never done it before." Walking up to the coach, Adrian looked him in the eye and said, "Coach, I want you to understand something. Jesus Christ means more to me than football or anything else in the world, and I don't appreciate what you said. And furthermore coach, the Lord has laid it on my heart to not play football any more this season." The coach said, "Young man, if you do that, you'll let down your school, this community, your teammates, and your coaches." Adrian responded, "I'd rather let you all down than let the Lord Jesus Christ down—that's it." And for several months, Adrian and the coach did not speak.

As the next season approached, the coach caught up with Adrian in the school hallway and casually said, "Practice starts soon. I'll see you out there," to which Adrian answered, "See you out there." The two had reached an understated truce, but Adrian had earned a certain degree of respect because of his firm stand: "From then on, at the beginning of every game, the coach would say, 'Men, I'm going to ask Adrian to lead us in prayer,' so I was able to pray and witness to my coach. He became my closest friend, and when I graduated high school, he recommended me to several schools for football scholarships. And I learned a lesson: take a stand for the Lord Jesus Christ. Don't fear people. Just fear God."[10]

"A FIRE IN MY BONES"

As a pastor, Adrian was known as much for his evangelistic zeal as anything, and that zeal came early in his Christian experience:

> From the moment that I gave my heart to Jesus Christ, there was a desire to share what I had. I didn't always live the Christian life. As I look back now, I'm ashamed of the weak, carnal life I was living. But there was nevertheless a fire in my bones to share the Gospel of the Lord Jesus Christ.[11]

As a teenager, Adrian went to summer camp at the Ridgecrest Baptist Assembly in Ridgecrest, North Carolina, where he made a public commitment to full-time Gospel service. Additionally, a speaker challenged everyone to lead one person to Jesus over the next year. "I thought he was going to say, 'this month,' but he said, 'this year.' I had never tried to lead someone to Christ, but I put up my hand—*and I meant it.*"[12]

When he returned to West Palm Beach from camp, life went on and he nearly forgot about his pledge. Then, one day he went to a local gas station to buy something, and God presented an opportunity to follow through on his commitment: "I was at the corner of 40th Street and

Broadway in West Palm Beach, and I didn't have any shirt or shoes on—we dressed like that to show off our muscles." At that point, an elderly man approached Adrian with white whiskers on his face and an extension cord in his hand. After he offered to sell the extension cord, he said, "I've been an old fool. I live on a pension check, and when I got my check, I spent all the money on liquor. And now I'm having to sell my tools to get through until next week." With only 16 cents in his pocket, Adrian politely declined and turned to walk away. But then the Holy Spirit reminded him in no uncertain terms of his commitment: "Adrian, speak to that man about his soul." He gave God a few excuses, but once again the Lord said, "Speak to that man about his soul." So, Adrian proceeded to share the Gospel as best he knew how:

> So I turned to the man in fear and trembling and said, 'Mister, are you a Christian, are you saved?' When I said that, his chin started to quiver, and tears began to course down the deep crevices in his face and drip off those white whiskers. He said, "No, son, I'm not a Christian." Then I said, "Do you want to be?" He said, "Yes, if I knew how." I said, "I wish I had a Bible," and he said, "I have one"—and he reached into the lining of his old coat and brought out a Gideon New Testament. With trembling fingers, I found the only verse I knew at the time, John 3:16, and said, "This is how God saved me and how he wants to save you. And if you want to be saved, pray and ask him to save you.' He started to cry and asked Jesus to save him. By that time, I was crying, too, half-hoping that my buddies on that corner wouldn't see me. After he prayed, I said, "Did God save you," and he said, "I believe he did!" Then I turned around to leave and said, "Goodbye, so long"—I didn't know anything about follow-up or anything like that, I just began backing off. But he called me back and said, "Young man, I've been in nearly every one of the 48 states, and you're the first person to ever speak to me about my soul. I'm so glad you did. Thank you.' I walked home leaping and dancing and praising God that he let me be a soul-winner. And from that day to this day, the passion of my heart has been to win men and women to Jesus Christ!"[13]

In the days ahead, Adrian's zeal for souls became more and more instinctive, even though he was still largely ignorant about the Bible—"If someone had told me to look up Phillips 66, I would have started looking."[14] He began witnessing to his family, his friends, and nearly anyone he knew:

> I had a friend who I'd played with and fought with and stole with and cussed with who I was concerned about. So, I went to his house, stood outside, and called to him: 'Hey, David!' He came to his window and said, 'What do you want?' I said, 'Come down here, I want to talk to you.' I imagine I broke every rule in the book so far as soul-winning is concerned. But my friend found Jesus and made a public profession of his faith in our church.[15]

Knowing the full scope of his life's ministry, it is hard to envision Adrian Rogers as anything other than an ardent, exceptionally intentional witness. And clearly, God began to place that burden on his heart at a very young age.

FILLED WITH THE SPIRIT

Perhaps the most profound event in Adrian's young Christian life came as a high school senior on the football field, but not during a much-publicized game or grueling practice session. Rather, it came one night when he was alone, walking back and forth under the stars, talking to God. He had recently committed himself to full-time Gospel service, and the desire to preach and minister was coupled with a burden to be used by God and God alone. At the 2005 Pastor Training Institute, Adrian recalled that night:

> When I was in high school, I went out to the practice football field. It was a summer night, and I went out to pray. Just a kid. I didn't know theology, but I loved God. And I walked up and down that field under that starry night in Florida, and I said, "God, I want you to use me."

> Then I walked up and down and prayed and thought, "Well, that's not enough," so I kneeled and prayed for a while. Then I said, "That's not enough." So, I laid down, spread eagle, put my hands and legs out and my face down, and said, "God, I want you to use me." That didn't seem like enough, so I took my finger, made a hole in the dirt, put my nose down in that hole, and the dirt came up my nostrils. Then I said, "Lord, I am as low as I know how to get." I didn't speak in tongues. I didn't have a vision. I knew no theology about the Holy Spirit. But God moved into my life.[16]

Interestingly, he did not use the words "filled with the Holy Spirit" when describing that momentous occasion in 2005, but he did use that language at other times when describing the same event. For example, as SBC President in 1979, he spoke in chapel at Southwestern Baptist Theological Seminary:

> God filled me with the Holy Spirit as a teenage boy. God called me to preach, and I said, "God, I want you to use me." And I remember, out on the field where I used to practice football, I walked up and down, praying and crying and weeping and saying, "God, I want you to use me." Then I stretched myself out on the ground, put my face in the dirt, and said, "God, please use me." That didn't seem good enough, so I made a hole for my nose and put my nose down in the dirt until the nostrils were filled with dust, and said, "God, I'm as low as I know how to get. I want you to use me." I didn't speak in tongues, I didn't shout, I didn't see any visions. But God moved into my life. And I would preach some theologically and homiletically poor sermons, but when I would give the invitation people would weep and cry and be broken, and they would come and give their lives to Jesus—there was just that plus, that difference.[17]

Years later, during the 1998 SBC Pastor's Conference, Adrian highlighted this experience as one of the "defining moments" of his life:

I wanted God's power in my life. I got out on the football field one night by myself, walking up and down and praying after God had laid his hand upon me for the ministry. My prayer was, "God, I want you to use me." But that didn't seem good enough. So I stopped and got on my knees under those Florida stars, and I said, "Dear Lord, I want you to use me." That didn't seem good enough, so I lay down prone and put my face on the grass, and said, "Dear God, I want you to use me," and that still wasn't enough. So I took my finger and made a little hole in the dirt, and I stuck my nose into that hole until the dirt came up my nostrils. And I said, "God, I'm as low as I can get. I want you to use me." I believe God filled me with the Holy Spirit at that moment. I didn't know anything about the doctrine of being filled with the Holy Spirit; all I knew was the Trinitarian formula, "In the name of the Father, the Son, and the Holy Spirit." But something happened in my life. I didn't see a vision, I didn't speak in tongues, but God moved into my life. I thank God for that, and I would be dishonest if I did not tell you that I believe there is a holy dimension, and I thank God for the fullness of the Holy Spirit.[18]

As high school juniors in 1949, Adrian taught Joyce how to drive in this 1934 Dodge. Courtesy Joyce Rogers.

Looking back, Adrian summed up the impact of his experience in this way: "God graciously released His power into my young heart and life....God's hand was upon my ministry. I know that now by remembrance and hindsight after having seen the Holy Spirit work these many years. God was working supernaturally in the life of a teenage preacher."[19]

Why devote space to three different descriptions of this one event? As we shall see in later chapters, explicit and frequent references to the filling of the Holy Spirit as the means to live the Christian life were a key theme in Adrian's Merritt Island years. Thus, it is important to show that his personal experience with the Holy Spirit informed his teaching about it. This will become even more evident in due time, but for now, it is important to note that Adrian had an initial experience with the Holy Spirit at a relatively young age.

GRADUATION AND NEXT STEPS

As high school graduation approached, Adrian considered his academic options. He was senior class president, participated in numerous sports and extracurricular activities, attended Florida Boys State, and was voted "Most Likely to Succeed."[20] His exceptional performance on the football field made a scholarship likely. Described as "one of the best linebackers in the state," he also played quarterback and blocking back, and as a result, during his senior year, he made the All-Southern Team.[21] As a result, several schools such as the University of Florida, the University of Miami, Baylor University, and the Citadel showed interest. But with his heart set on preparing for full-time Gospel service, he ultimately accepted football and ministerial scholarships from Stetson University, a Baptist institution in Deland, Florida.[22]

Adrian's motives for choosing Stetson were not entirely athletic or ministerial. He and Joyce Gentry had become especially close during their high school years—he often joked, "We got together in the fourth grade, but we didn't get serious until the sixth grade!"[23] Not surprisingly, Adrian and Joyce began to talk of somehow attending the same college. According to Adrian, "Joyce and I had been dating through high school, and I knew that if I went to Stetson University it would seem normal for her to go also since it was our Baptist school. But if I went to one of the other schools and she also went it would seem like collusion."[24] Adrian and Joyce graduated from Palm Beach High School in May 1950 and looked forward to their next steps together at Stetson. Meanwhile, the Northwood Baptist Church licensed Adrian to preach the Gospel on July 30, 1950.[25]

COURAGE ON AND OFF CAMPUS

After arriving at Stetson, Adrian began to sense that something was amiss at the Baptist school. He did not have a deep knowledge of theology and biblical studies at the time—"I didn't know who came first, Abraham or Moses"[26]—but he knew enough to recognize that a number of faculty members at Stetson did not share his basic convictions about the Bible and the Christian faith:

> I began to hear that there wasn't someone named Matthew who wrote the Gospel of Matthew or Luke who wrote Luke or John who wrote John. I heard that Moses didn't write Genesis, Exodus, Leviticus, Numbers, or Deuteronomy—these were put together by a priestly redactor later on. I was told that there is no devil and that Satan is only a personification of evil.[27]

For a brief time, Adrian assumed these ideas must be true. "After all," he thought, "Stetson was a Baptist school supported by Florida Baptist churches." One religion professor described the spectrum of theological thought in this way: "First, you have the fun-damn-mentalists—too much fun, too much damn, and not enough mental. Then there are the modurn'd-ists—those are the Liberals. Then there are the neo-orthodox, and that's what I am."[28] Hearing that, Adrian thought, "Well, then that's what I am, too. This a Baptist college, and I know enough to know that orthodox is good and neo means 'new' so it's the best of both worlds."[29] But still, in his heart, there was what he called a "disquietude," because what he heard in his classes did not align with the Bible he read for himself:

> One day, I had the audacity in a sociology class taught by an ordained minister to witness to my professor. I listened to that man talk about the evolution of mankind and explain away sin, and my heart was grieved. So, after class, I said, "Sir, I don't want to be impertinent, but I want to ask you a question: Are you saved?" That professor said to me, "Well, I'm certain I'm not saved according to your definition of salvation." So, I said, "Sir, what is your definition of salvation?" He said, "Salvation is that experience where man comes to escape the consequences of a maladjustment to his fellow man." Then I said, "Sir, I'm not talking about that. If you were to die right now, would you go to heaven or hell?" He replied, "I don't know there is a heaven or a hell; I've never been to either one." And I thought, "If some church people knew that they were paying this man's salary to teach in a Baptist school, they would be deeply grieved."[30]

Adrian was not the only student burdened by what he heard at Stetson. During one chapel service, a professor unveiled a painting of a baby and said, "Man is basically good." When that happened, a young man named Joe Boatright got up and started walking out in total disagreement with the professor's remarks. As he did, he noticed another young man doing the same thing from the other side of the chapel—it was Adrian. They met at the back door. Adrian said, "Why did you get up and leave?" Joe replied, "I didn't want to be there when the judgment of God fell on the place," to which Adrian said, "I left for the same reason!" Adrian and Joe quickly became friends and remained exceptionally close for the rest of their lives.[31]

Adrian (right of center) and good friend Joe Boatright (far right) meet with Billy Graham in the early 1950s. Courtesy Joyce Rogers.

In addition to his on-campus courage in the face of Stetson's theological climate, Adrian boldly pursued God's call on his life off campus. During his freshman year, he preached to people in all manner of places: "When I was in college, I stood on the street corner and preached, I stood on the bus bench and preached, and I went to bar rooms and preached and handed out tracts. When the movies would let out I'd preach to the people coming out of the movies. Sometimes I preached for pay, and sometimes I preached for nothing but the joy of preaching."[32]

On one occasion, Adrian's courageous preaching established a relationship that would one day prove monumental during the Merritt Island years:

> One time in college, I was standing on a bus bench preaching in Daytona Beach, and about twenty people had gathered. When I talked about praying and asking people to receive Christ, the crowd kind of scattered. But there was one man who just stood there. He was dressed in a grey flannel suit—he was a very striking-looking man—and was standing in front of a hotel. He didn't leave, so I thought, "Maybe he's

> interested." I said, "Sir, may I have a moment?" And he said, "Yes." I said, "Sir, are you a Christian?" He said, "Yes, I know the Lord Jesus. But who are you?" I said, "I'm Adrian Rogers. I'm a student at Stetson." He said, "Who sent you over here? Do they know you are here?" I said, "No, and they probably wouldn't like it if they did know that I was over here." So we began to talk. As it turned out, his name was Doyle Carlton, a very well-known man in Florida, and he owned that hotel. He said, "I want to get to know you better."[33]

As we shall later see, Doyle Carlton proved to be a stellar layman, faithful soul-winner, and dear friend to his pastor in Merritt Island.

THE FIRST, LAST, AND ONLY BAPTIST CHURCH

At the end of his freshman year, on April 29, 1951, Adrian accepted the call to become the pastor of the First Baptist Church of Fellsmere, Florida—the "first, last, and only Baptist church in that town of about 500 people." He dropped his football scholarship in order to make time for the pastorate as well as the 230-mile round trip drive from Deland to Fellsmere each weekend. The congregation numbered only several dozen people when Adrian came. The church building was made of unpainted cinder blocks with cement floors and rough tar paper roof. The pews consisted of crude benches made of two wooden two-by-eight boards held together by a metal bracket. Bare light bulbs hung from the ceiling.[34]

Adrian considered himself "utterly untrained," but he also discovered that God honors the preaching of his Word:

> I would preach some of the worst sermons you've ever heard—no outline, no illustrations, no introduction, no conclusion—but God honored it and there would be tears and souls would be saved. I learned the power of the Word of God there in Fellsmere."[35]

Adrian and Joyce at the First Baptist Church of Fellsmere, Florida in 1951. Courtesy Joyce Rogers.

Indeed, God began rapidly to bless the young pastor's ministry. His dynamic preaching and relentless personal evangelism energized the small congregation, and a number of people came to faith in Christ and followed in Believer's baptism. In fact, the first year of his pastorate the church saw 51 baptisms—the highest number for the Indian River Baptist Association that year.[36]

The first of those baptisms was especially memorable for the young pastor. He had led a young lady named Willie Vereen to Christ and encouraged her to follow in Believer's baptism. But the church had no baptistery—and no running water, either. So, in "one of the great memories of my life," Adrian gathered the congregation along the banks of Canal A near one of Fellsmere's citrus groves:

> Everyone stood on the banks of the canal, and we slithered down into the water. It was a cold day for Florida, and I can remember as I took Willie into that cold water she went "sssshhhhhh" like her breath was being taken away. And I buried her in the likeness of Jesus' death and raised her in the likeness of his resurrection.[37]

As he stood on the banks of that same canal nearly 50 years later, reminiscing about that day, Adrian said, "Thank God we've seen multiplied thousands baptized since then, but there will never be another baptism like the one we had at Canal A in Fellsmere, Florida."[38]

UNLESS THE LORD BUILDS THE HOUSE

As they entered their sophomore years at Stetson, Adrian and Joyce were married on September 2, 1951, at the Northwood Baptist Church. Adrian discovered early in their marriage that right priorities lead to healthy families. First, he and Joyce settled on the supremacy of Jesus above even one another: "My wife knows that she is number two in my life, and she doesn't mind being number two—she'd rather be number two, because she knows that I can love her far more when she's number two than I could ever love her if she was number one." Second, Adrian endeavored never to prioritize the church above his marriage and children: "As a young preacher, I had to learn that the church did not come before my family....The church is Jesus' bride, not my bride."[39]

Adrian and Joyce lived in a 25-foot house trailer in a Deland campground. With no private bathroom facilities, they utilized the community bathhouse and laundry located in the campground—Adrian recalled, "We had a path, not a bath."[40] But the simple austerity of newlywed life was a joy to the young couple. Even the weekly commute to Fellsmere where they would stay with various church families for the weekend before returning to Deland was also a joy.

Seeking the Lord's blessing on having children, Adrian and Joyce—after two previous miscarriages—welcomed their first child, Stephen Michael Rogers, on February 26, 1954. Adrian felt a profound sense of gladness but also the burden of responsibility and leadership as a new father:

> There was a tremendous impact on my life when God gave us our first son. I remember going to the hospital in Deland and seeing that beautiful little baby. Joyce stayed at the hospital, and I remember going home and getting by the couch in the little mobile home we lived in. And I buried my face in that couch and crying and saying, "Oh God, if I never do anything else good, God if I never pastor a successful church, God if I never have any money, God if I never make an impact in this world, dear God I want to be a good daddy. I want to live so that this boy will believe in the God and the Christ that his daddy believes in!"[41]

A few months after Steve's birth, Adrian graduated from Stetson on June 7, 1954. Shortly after that, the Rogers said farewell to their growing Fellsmere church family and moved to New Orleans where Adrian would attend the New Orleans Baptist Theological Seminary. After three years of Adrian's leadership, the church had added running water, a baptistery, wooden theatre seats, upgraded lighting, and a finished ceiling.[42] But most important, a photograph of a packed auditorium on Adrian's final day as pastor in June 1954 shows the real fruit of his ministry—namely, the many who had been led to Christ, baptized, and discipled in the little church while he had led the congregation.

2

NONE OF HIS WORDS FELL TO THE GROUND (1954-1964)

Adrian, Joyce, and baby Steve arrived in New Orleans in the Fall of 1954 to begin seminary studies, hopeful and optimistic about preparing for Gospel ministry. Adrian chose New Orleans Baptist Seminary, both for its location in the southeast and for the tremendous spiritual need he sensed in "the city that care forgot." Additionally, Adrian saw New Orleans as the one Southern Baptist seminary least infected with the same problematic theology he encountered at Stetson, although—as he discovered—even New Orleans was not without its issues:

> The school I attended, New Orleans Baptist Theological Seminary, was much more conservative than the other Southern Baptist schools, and, for a while, was like a breath from heaven because at least we began our classes with prayer, and we were more and more studying the Word of God. But part was good, and part was bad. Again, I was taught to see the Bible as some sort of composite, human instrument, it seemed to me, rather than the divine, holy, inspired, inerrant, infallible, Word of God.[1]

The little family lived in seminary housing for six months, and Adrian took several odd jobs to provide income.

Then, in January 1955, just as their savings ran out, Adrian preached at the Waveland Baptist Chapel in Waveland, Mississippi, and was called as pastor. Although the church had no more than two dozen members with far less in attendance on an average Sunday, Adrian and Joyce gladly and faithfully ministered to the small congregation. Not long after beginning his Waveland ministry, the Rogers moved into a small apartment on the Gulf coast, and Adrian commuted 120 miles per day, four days a week, to and from classes in New Orleans. While Adrian was gone from 7:00 AM to 7:00 PM each of those four days per week, Joyce spent the day with Steve taking long walks, reading to him, and teaching him Bible songs. Joyce remembered, "He could sing twenty little songs by heart when he was just two years old."[2]

Times were tight for the small church. The congregation met entirely in one modest building with large curtains drawn across the room to create separate spaces for Sunday School classes. Ministering in a predominantly Roman Catholic area proved challenging, but Adrian kept his hand on the plow and did not look back. The congregation began to grow slowly, and Adrian did his best to help the people see their need for nursery and education space. Although not everyone in the church caught the vision, Adrian eventually secured plans from the Southern Baptist Convention and led the people to build the needed space.[3]

While in New Orleans, Adrian met Peter Lord, a fellow seminarian originally from Jamaica. Like his friendship with Joe Boatright at Stetson, Adrian and Peter shared many similar convictions about the Bible and Gospel ministry. In fact, as time went by, Adrian, Peter, and Joe became fast friends and eventually all led powerful ministries in Brevard County, Florida.[4]

The Rogers family was also growing. In June 1956, a tropical storm swept the area to the west of Waveland just days before Adrian and Joyce welcomed a baby girl into their family. Gayle Christine Rogers was born on June 16, 1956, and she and Steve quickly became playmates. Then, on

Pastor Adrian Rogers of the Waveland Baptist Chapel (1955-1958). Courtesy Joyce Rogers.

February 26, 1958—Steve's fourth birthday—the family welcomed a baby boy, Philip Gentry Rogers.[5]

THIS IS A TEST

As graduation in early 1958 drew near, Adrian and Joyce reflected on their days in New Orleans and Mississippi. The small church's membership had grown from 25 to 75 in an experience of authentic Gospel momentum. Their family had grown, too. And now they began to pray about their next step in God's plan.

Adrian initially received letters from two small churches in Florida, one in Melbourne and another in Fort Pierce (the town where Joyce was born). Both churches asked him to consider coming as their pastor. At first, he did not believe he was to go to either church. But the Fort Pierce congregation, the Parkview Baptist Church, persisted in writing Adrian about coming. Still, Adrian continued to wonder if God was truly directing him to Fort Pierce:

> When God called me to [Parkview Baptist Church], I didn't want to go there—I really didn't want to go there. The church had been there since 1924, but the average length of a pastorate was only 18 months, and that frightened me. It was a preacher's graveyard. It had a run-down building on a postage stamp piece of property. They had lots of trouble and fighting and feuding. I said, "Lord, don't make me go to that church." But He said, "You go."[6]

So, on a Sunday morning in March 1954, Adrian notified the Waveland congregation that God had called him to Florida, and he did so in dramatic fashion: "A nail-pierced hand has pointed to Florida, and I must follow."[7] He had not yet informed Parkview Baptist Church of his acceptance, but as far as the people in Waveland were concerned, Adrian was going to Florida.

But that afternoon, as Joyce prepared lunch, the phone rang. Adrian answered the phone and heard these words: "Hello, I'm Mr. Graham. I'm from the First Baptist Church of Miami, Florida, and I'd like to talk to you about becoming our pastor." Then he began to tell Adrian about the church and about the staff and about the minister of music and minister of education and about the facilities and the salary—which was more than three times what Parkview Baptist had offered. But almost immediately, Adrian sensed the Holy Spirit convicting him, and he "knew as if it was written on the wall from floor to ceiling and wall to wall, 'THIS IS A TEST.'" So he said, "Mr. Graham, thank you, Sir. But I cannot talk to you anymore. I'm honored you would ask. But I'm going to Fort Pierce, Florida"—and without another word, he hung up the phone. Looking back, Adrian reflected: "I don't know what would have happened to me had I said, 'Forget the nail-pierced hand. Now I've got a bigger offer.'"[8]

TRAGEDY AND TRANSFORMATION

With his integrity intact, Adrian (along with Joyce, Steve, Gayle, and baby Philip) arrived in Fort Pierce and began ministry at Parkview Baptist Church in mid-April 1954. The challenge was everything Adrian expected. The church had slightly more than 100 people in Sunday morning attendance and the annual budget was little more than $15,000. In addition, there was minimal nursery and education space, and the little pastorium, located adjacent to the church, was barely adequate.[9] In fact, on their very first Sunday, one family who typically arrived early for church let themselves into the pastorium's back door for a visit with the new pastor—Joyce recalled, "We never left the door unlocked again."[10] Still, Adrian immediately caught a vision for what the church could be, and he energetically applied himself to the task at hand.

Parkview Baptist Church, Fort Pierce, Florida. Pastorium (and later "Babyland") immediately adjacent to the right. Courtesy Joyce Rogers.

But on May 11—Mother's Day—the unthinkable happened. It was his third Sunday as pastor, and Adrian had just preached a stirring message on the glories of a Christian home. After church, the Rogers retired to the pastorium for lunch. Adrian fed baby Philip, then Joyce put him to bed. After lunch, Joyce went to check on Philip and immediately knew something was wrong:

> I glanced toward the baby's bed and saw blood on the sheet. In alarm, I called [Adrian], and he ran in. Numbly, I asked, "Is he dead?" He picked up the little body and found the pacifier lodged in his mouth. Apparently the obstruction had ruptured a blood vessel. He frantically rushed the baby to the hospital. I called the hospital to tell them he was coming. Then I prayed...Little Steve had gotten out of bed in the confusion, and we prayed together. I quoted that psalm of great comfort, "The Lord is my shepherd." Oh, for the simple trust of a little child. He offered me comfort, "Let's ask God to make Philip well, Mommy." Then he would plead, "Don't cry, Mommy."[11]

Meanwhile, Adrian drove with Philip to the hospital "through blinding tears." Upon arrival, he ran into the emergency room and shouted, "Somebody come and help me!" After a nurse came and took the baby, Adrian fell on his knees in the hall and prayed—"I didn't care who saw me on my knees." Then, after a few minutes, a doctor emerged, laid his hand on Adrian's shoulder, shook his head, and said, "I'm sorry, son, he's gone."[12]

As Adrian pulled his car into the driveway and returned home, Joyce, Steve, and Gayle met him at the door. Joyce asked, "Is he dead?" But by the look on Adrian's face, she didn't need an answer. Joyce recalled:

> A flood of grief and agony went through my heart. I had never lost a close loved one, had never known the meaning of, "Blessed are they that mourn, for they shall be comforted." I who had walked in the sunshine all of my life was now in "the valley of the shadow of death." Could I endure it?[13]

Later that afternoon, Joyce's parents arrived from West Palm Beach to take Steve and Gayle with them, which allowed Adrian and Joyce time to be alone and drive themselves to West Palm Beach. As they departed the pastorium, they could hear music coming from Parkview's Sunday evening services: "No, never alone, never alone. He promised never to leave me, never to leave me alone." During the 90-minute drive, Scriptures and songs flooded their hearts and minds, with one song standing out in particular: "What a friend we have in Jesus, all our sins and griefs to bear."[14]

In the days and weeks following Philip's funeral, Adrian and Joyce took stock of their priorities and determined to seek the Lord in a deeper way. The tragedy had rocked their realities, but the God who somehow infuses everything with purpose began to accomplish a work of spiritual transformation. Specifically, they began to understand more meaningfully the presence and work of the Holy Spirit as their source of spiritual life and strength.

Philip's death had a profound impact on Adrian, in particular. Although he had experienced a powerful filling of the Holy Spirit as a teen accompanied by anointed preaching and ministry in high school and college, he had begun to lose sight of the Spirit's power and began to rely on himself:

> I went off to seminary, and by that time I had gained some reputation as a preacher. But I got a little arrogant, wanting to argue with my professors about some things. I got cold and lost that blessing that I had as a teenager. Now, you would never have convinced me of it at the time, because if I compared myself with others I was still doing alright—you know, as you measure yourself by the wrong measuring stick.[15]

As a result, while he had gained theological knowledge, he had lost spiritual strength. He increasingly relied more on "clever methods and human ability" than on God's power in and through him. The desperate teen who paced up and down the practice football field had become the self-reliant seminarian and pastor:

> I knew more in my head, but the same power from God was not in my heart. Looking back, I see for a period a brash, self-assured young man who felt maybe that he had all the answers. Theology is a wonderful thing, but it is no substitute for anointing. One could know theology and not experience the power of the Holy Spirit.[16]

Baby Philip's death jolted Adrian out of his self-reliant stupor: "The death of my son caused me to reflect and get things in sharper spiritual focus. My life and ministerial priorities were deepened through the death of our son....While I would not want to go through that pain again, I would not take ten million dollars for the experience we had with the Lord through that season."[17]

Times of refreshing and spiritual depth followed. Evangelist Mike Gilchrist came to Parkview Baptist Church for a series of services and preached on abiding in Christ and the fullness of the Holy Spirit. For someone accustomed to laboring tirelessly for God—albeit in his own strength—these powerful messages resonated deeply with Adrian. The themes of "stop trying and start trusting" and "let Jesus do in you and through you what you have been trying to do for him" drove Adrian to a reliance and abandon he had not known for quite some time.[18]

In addition to Mike Gilchrist's influence, Adrian read *The Saving Life of Christ* by Major Ian Thomas. This devotional classic placed a strong emphasis upon the life of Christ inthe Christian, working and producing results that the Believer could never manufacture in his or her own strength. The book opened Adrian's eyes to a profound truth shared by Ian Thomas:

> Have you ever come to the place where you realized that all you can produce, at your best, is ashes? Did you ever come to the place where you presented yourself for what you are—*nothing*—to be filled with

> what He is—*everything*—and step out into every new day, conscious that the eternal I AM is all you need, for all His will!...The sad thing is that even a Christian may be so impressed with himself and with his own ability that even though he gives lip service to the fact, he may still see no personal relevance in the indwelling presence of Christ. It will smack to him of mysticism; he will consider such teaching to be exaggeratedly subjective and will pride himself on being a practical man of action rather than abiding in Christ.[19]

Thomas' book also introduced Adrian to a powerful reading of the Old Testament illustrating the Spirit-filled life. According to Ian Thomas, God portrayed from Exodus to Joshua three kinds of people: life in Egypt depicted the unsaved man or woman, life in the Wilderness depicted the saved-but-carnal man or woman, and life in Canaan depicted the Spirit-filled man or woman.[20] As we shall see in due course, this interpretation would underscore much of Adrian's ministry during the Merritt Island years.

In many ways, Gilchrist's and Thomas' teachings about the fullness of the Spirit, reliance on the Spirit, and the Spirit-filled life were novel for Adrian. Having been saved, discipled, and educated in Southern Baptist circles, these were relatively new ideas for him:

> Either when I was a young Christian I was deaf, or preachers did not preach the fullness of the Spirit. I *never heard it*. I was born again in a Southern Baptist Church, went to a Southern Baptist college, went to a Southern Baptist seminary, and yet I was out and preaching for about five years before I understood how to be filled with the Spirit—that God does not want me to do anything for him; rather, he wants to do something in and through me.[21]

It is difficult to overstate the importance of this transformational season for Adrian and Joyce. For Adrian, it resulted in a synergy between theological truth and experiential power based on the fullness of the Holy Spirit:

> The experience of God's fullness in me that I received [following baby Philip's death] was the same power I had received as a young preacher who prayed that night on the football practice field. This new dimension was really an old dimension. What I discovered then was what I had as a teenage boy—that which I did not even know how to name. I had the experience of the Holy Spirit, then gained the theology but lost the experience. Then I gained the experience back with the theology, and that was the beginning of my pilgrimage of learning to depend upon the Holy Spirit.[22]

At that point, so to speak, the spiritual circuit closed, and Adrian stood ready for powerful days of ministry ahead, ready for God to do something remarkable in and through him. And that is exactly what happened at Parkview Baptist Church.

DAYS OF POWER AT PARKVIEW

The hallmarks of Adrian's ministry—a high view of Scripture, dynamic preaching, relentless personal evangelism, and visionary leadership—electrified the small church in Fort Pierce. If the people of Parkview Baptist did not fully understand at first what they were getting in Adrian Rogers, they quickly discovered that they had called a God-anointed man of faith. And as with every church he would subsequently pastor, Parkview Baptist quickly experienced a move of God shortly after his arrival.

Over the summer and fall of 1958, dozens and dozens of people united with the church, mostly through salvation and baptism. Due to a lack of space for the growing number of babies and children, Adrian proposed that the church convert the pastorium into a nursery and build a new pastorium. (Not surprisingly, Joyce asked that it not be located immediately adjacent to the church!) So, after Adrian had been pastor only seven months, the church dedicated its new pastorium at 1714 Ponce de Leon Prado on December 21, 1958. Meanwhile, the conversion of the old pastorium to "Babyland" for use

Old Fashioned Day at Parkview Baptist Church, Fort Pierce, Florida. Courtesy Joyce Rogers.

as a nursery and children's Sunday school space was described as "one of many steps planned in the enlargement of the facilities."[23] At the end of 1958, Parkview Baptist had already grown from a little over 100 attendees on Sunday mornings to almost 300.[24]

In March of the next year, as part of revival services led by Adrian's friend, Peter Lord, he conducted his first Old Fashioned Day—an event which would become a signature Adrian Rogers event for years to come. To demonstrate the timelessness of the Gospel, Parkview members were encouraged to dress in late-nineteenth and early twentieth-century attire while enjoying dinner on the grounds. Adrian explained to a local reporter, "The purpose of this day is to remind people in a visible way that the need of this modern world is nothing other than the message of an old-fashioned

Savior who can save an old-fashioned sinner from an old-fashioned hell to an old-fashioned heaven."[25]

Another first was Adrian's early-morning, 15-minute radio broadcasts called "Daybreak" from 6:45 AM to 7:00 AM. Through the local airwaves, Adrian began to see the power of a broader influence, both in terms of how it impacted the ministry of his church as well as the Gospel's potential to reach well beyond his immediate church field. However, even during these earliest days of his broadcast ministry, he never lost sight of the fact that he was first and foremost a pastor. It was a priority he would always protect throughout his ministry.[26]

By July 1959, membership surpassed 600 with over 200 additions to the church since Adrian arrived 14 months earlier. God continued to bless the congregation and its Spirit-filled pastor. The "Meet Your Minister" section of the local newspaper noted that Adrian's "eyes sparkle and...he bubbles over with vitality" when speaking about reaching the people of Fort Pierce: "I feel that God has called me to preach, and I just couldn't be happy doing anything else."[27]

In 1960, Adrian led the growing church to conduct a $75,000 bond drive for the construction of a much-needed educational building. The church had already purchased two adjacent homes and converted them to Sunday school space as well as three empty lots behind the church for additional parking. But the need exceeded even those additions. Ultimately, "Babyland" was demolished to make way for the new building.[28] Meanwhile, Adrian and Joyce experienced their own "babyland" season with the births of two more children: David was born on July 30, 1960, and Janice was born on December 4, 1961.[29]

For Adrian, personal evangelism was paramount, and many souls were won during his Parkview years. If one example stands out, it would be when "the meanest man in town" was saved—which actually involved the marvelous conversion of two men. In those days in Fort Pierce, the "town drunk" was a man named Al Cross. Al worked for the power company, and on payday he would take his check and "lay it on the bar and drink until he fell off the barstool." Friends often carried Al from the bar and put him next to a citrus packing warehouse for the night where he would sleep among the rats and the roaches until morning. Everyone knew him as a "pathetic drunkard." But one day, by the grace of God, Al went to see Adrian and said, "I need God." So Adrian took his Bible, shared the Gospel with him, and Al received Jesus.

> From that moment, Al became a new creature; he became a child of God. The next day, we had workday at the church to demolish a building. When I got there, he had already been out there working, early and by himself. He was already lathered in sweat, working for the Lord. And Al never, ever slowed down serving the Lord. He became one of the most godly, compassionate, soul-winning men I have ever known.[30]

Not long after Al Cross was saved, Adrian and a handful of men (including Al) began meeting for early morning prayer at the church after the Daybreak radio broadcasts. One morning, a man asked, "How can we see revival happen in our town?" Another man answered, "I've heard that if you get the meanest man in town saved, that's a good way to have revival." So the men discussed it, and they unanimously nominated a particular man. He was a known moonshiner, gambler, and barroom brawler—one time he even stole a hog out of the game warden's truck. He had a bullet lodged in his hip that the doctor was reluctant to remove. How did he get that? His girlfriend had shot him out of jealousy because he was spending too much time with his wife! He was universally known in Fort Pierce as "a bruiser and the brawler." So, the men began to pray for the man by name every day. Eventually, they agreed it was time to visit this man, so Adrian went to his house.

> I went by the man's house—I'd never met him. His wife met me at the door and said, "May I help you?" I said, "I'm Adrian Rogers, I'm a Baptist preacher, and I'm here to see your husband." She said, "They're in the back room drinking, gambling, and fighting. I don't think you ought to go back there"—so I didn't.[31]

Not long after that, the man got sick and had to spend some time in the hospital. Adrian saw his opportunity, prayerfully went to the hospital, and walked into the man's room:

> I didn't beat around the bush. I knew his reputation, so I said, "Sir, my name is Adrian Rogers and I'm a Baptist preacher. I've come to talk to you and tell you how to be saved. Would you like that?" Do you know what he said to me? He said, "If I thought God could do for me what he did for Al Cross, I'd want to be saved." I said, "Al Cross has been praying for you. And you can be saved, too." And I led that man to Jesus—he fell off into my hands like a ripe apple. The meanest man in town came to faith in Jesus Christ.[32]

Parkview continued to grow under Adrian's energetic leadership, and ultimately hundreds came to faith in Jesus. In addition, many other Christians united with the church for membership. By the pastor's sixth anniversary in April 1964, significant numbers represented lives changed and disciples made: 1,338 additions to the church, 652 by baptism and 686 by transfer of membership letter; 650 in average Sunday morning attendance; an increase in the annual budget from $15,000 to $90,000; and $54,000 in missions giving with 22 percent of the annual church budget marked for the Southern Baptist Cooperative Program. Indeed, over those six years, God had transformed the "preacher's graveyard" into a "great soul-winning and loving church."[33]

A NAIL-PIERCED HAND POINTS TO MERRITT ISLAND

In late April 1964, Adrian received a letter from Anne Hicks, Secretary of the Pastor Search Committee from First Baptist Church of Merritt Island, Florida. The church's pastor had resigned in February 1964, and a committee had been appointed to search prayerfully for a new pastor. The committee's letter spoke to Adrian of their interest in him as a candidate, and also highlighted the needs and opportunities of the hour: "Merritt Island is located in the fastest growing county (Brevard) in the country, population now 170,000—by 1970, 250,000, located six miles from Cape Kennedy...The challenge of the area is second to none, and a man of vision and dedication is needed."[34]

Adrian was no stranger to the Merritt Island leaders, as God had previously orchestrated multiple points of contact. First and foremost, Doyle Carlton served as a key layman at First Baptist Church and was also a member of the search committee. He had never forgotten his initial meeting with Adrian over ten years earlier in Daytona Beach, and he had kept up with the young pastor's ministry in Fort Pierce. In addition, Adrian's friend Joe Boatright was serving a church in Mims, Florida (just 30 miles north of Merritt Island) and knew some of the church leaders through the local Baptist association. Not surprisingly, Joe strongly recommended Adrian to the committee. Also, another member of the search committee, Vernon Wise, had a connection with Parkview Baptist in Fort Pierce: his mother attended church there, and he was familiar with Adrian's ministry and preaching. Last, but not least, Adrian spoke in 1963 at a First Baptist Church bond drive event in Merritt Island, so at least those in attendance had a taste of his abilities as a communicator.[35]

Initially, Adrian had no interest in leaving Parkview Baptist and said so to the Merritt Island committee. He and Joyce were contentedly serving in Fort Pierce, and, in fact, Parkview's average Sunday attendance was notably higher than the Sunday attendance at First Baptist Church. But the committee persisted, and on May 10, Mother's Day, they visited Parkview Baptist and heard Adrian preach. Prior to that visit, committee members desired to hear several candidates both from Florida and outside Florida. But after that visit, according to one man on the committee, "They didn't want to go nowhere else"—Adrian was their unanimous choice.[36] Nevertheless, he continued to express reluctance to leave Fort Pierce.

Yet, Adrian and Joyce could not deny Merritt Island's need for dynamic, godly leadership and the profound opportunity there. Thus, they began to prayerfully seek God's will for their lives on the matter. As part of that search, they drove to Merritt Island one weekday to get a better sense of the need. Years later, Adrian related the trip to the congregation:

> We drove up here one day, hoping that no one would see us—I turned my collar up and sneaked around. I didn't even want you to know I was interested. I really wasn't interested. I just wanted to see what was here. We tip-toed around the auditorium to check it out. You know, I felt so guilty just looking at this church. I felt like a man looking at another woman who wasn't his wife. I thought, "If the folks at Parkview knew I was here—man, I hope nobody sees me!"[37]

Guilty feelings or not, Adrian nevertheless sensed God speaking during his clandestine visit. After he had come as pastor, Jim Whitmire, the minister of music who had arrived at First Baptist Church in December 1962, asked Adrian, "This church was smaller than Parkview. Why did you come?" Adrian told him that during his secret visit, he noticed the remnants of a church social event the night before which included "turned-over trash cans on the sidewalk where dogs had gotten into the garbage and scattered it all over...a jury-rigged water fountain made from an old refrigerator, a pipe, and a funnel...and other similar things all over the church." Seeing that, Adrian said, "My heart broke, and I heard God say, 'This church needs a shepherd.'"[38]

On Sunday, June 21, 1964, Adrian preached at First Baptist Church as a candidate for pastor. God moved in a notable way through his stirring message, and a number of people came forward to receive Jesus Christ as Savior and Lord at the end of the morning service.[39] As Jim Whitmire related to Adrian in a letter the next day, "The spirit in our church [yesterday] was as fine as I have ever experienced" and "that was the largest Sunday attendance we've had in a great while."[40]

After a special church business meeting the following Wednesday night where attendees unanimously voted to call Adrian as pastor, the search committee chairman, Robert Pullin, wrote Adrian to inform him of the unanimous vote: "We await your acceptance and coming with great anticipation and with confidence that the great potentials of this area will be developed toward the ongoing of His Kingdom."[41] Adrian responded immediately with confidence and faith that God had opened a tremendous door of Gospel opportunity:

> After much prayer on our part and yours, we feel that a nail pierced hand is pointing to Merritt Island. ...When I come it will be to invest my life, my strength, all that I have for the glory of our Savior. I will expect great faith and great sacrifices from you people. Merritt Island is not the place nor is this the time for a normal, usual, luke-warm church. I have no desire to pastor such a church. May God help us to be a Spirit-filled, anointed people. I am challenged, thrilled, and excited as I think of the victories that can be ours as we march under the banner of the King. If God is in our plans, we must plan big.[42]

Adrian might have said more than he knew in his challenge to the Merritt Island congregation. But one thing was certain: Adrian Rogers was God's man to lead God's church in one of the most unique moments in American history.

PART II
THE MOMENT

3

FOR SUCH A TIME AS THIS (1949-1960)

One could argue that the story of the Moon Port Pastor began as early as the year 1865 when Jules Verne selected Florida as the lunar mission launch site for his science-fiction novel, *From the Earth to the Moon*. Although Verne chose "Tampa Town" rather than Florida's east coast, his basic criteria were otherwise sound: situated near a large body of water, sparsely populated, and located between the equator and the 28th parallel where the earth rotates at the greatest speed. Never mind that Verne's narrative was far more fiction than science, *From the Earth to the Moon* clearly foreshadowed Florida's role in the missile and space programs.[1]

Nearly a century later, on July 24, 1950, Florida fact replaced Vernian fantasy when a "flaming arrow soared into the heavens from Cape Canaveral and climbed into the stratosphere"—the first-ever missile launch from the recently-named Joint Long Range Proving Ground on Florida's east coast.[2] The two-stage rocket, consisting of a captured German V-2 booster and a US-made second stage, marked the transition of the emerging missile program from White Sands, New Mexico to Cape Canaveral. Seven previous launches had occurred at White Sands. However, when an errant V-2 rocket veered off course, flew directly over El Paso, Texas and Juarez, Mexico, then crashed into the Tepeyac Cemetery, U.S. and Mexican officials agreed that the program needed a new home. In concert with this move, the Naval Air Station (NAS) Banana River became Patrick Air Force Base and headquarters of the Joint Proving Ground.[3] In the midst of these limited beginnings, the die had been cast for Brevard County's giant leap forward, both technologically and demographically.

While the missile program relocated to Cape Canaveral, local Baptist leaders had already recognized a need for Gospel work in central Brevard and especially Merritt Island, an unincorporated town at the center of the island with the same name. In late June and early July 1949, Pastors from First Baptist Church of Cocoa and Orsino Baptist Church partnered to bring the Reverend E. J. Daniels to conduct tent revival meetings behind the Merritt Island fire station. From that series of services, a small congregation of 19 members named the First Baptist Church of Merritt Island began gathering weekly in the upstairs room at the firehouse.

Easter Sunday 1950 and a new sanctuary for First Baptist Church. Courtesy of Lyvonne Burleson.

By September, the church had its first pastor, Bob Lambert, a student from the Florida Baptist Institute in Lakeland. Eager to reach the people of Merritt Island, during the first week of October 1949, Reverend Lambert visited 76 homes on Merritt Island in four days—all on foot. By the end of the year, the initial 19 charter members had grown to 26 committed members. Services on Easter Sunday 1950 saw 125 in attendance as well as the dedication of a new church building, a simple 32' x 54' block structure. By the end of 1950, membership had grown to 81 while the population of Merritt Island had grown to approximately 2,300.[4]

GROWING PAINS

As the missile program and related industries began growing, more and more people relocated to Brevard County, the population of which in 1950 was roughly 23,600. Upon arrival, new residents discovered that living in "missile land" included several challenges. For instance, clouds of pesky mosquitos enthusiastically greeted the newcomers. Brevard County, at nearly 72 miles long (north to south) and only a few miles wide (east to west), sat adjacent to "water, water everywhere." With the Atlantic Ocean, Indian River, Banana River, and Mosquito Lagoon touching its shores and with the Saint John's River immediately to the west, Brevard featured the perfect breeding grounds for both freshwater and saltwater mosquitos. The mosquito problem was such that it was not uncommon for homeowners to meet guests at the door with a brush to remove mosquitos from guests' clothes before entering the house. Meanwhile, the rapid influx of new residents heavily taxed the county's roads and narrow bridges, many of which were drawbridges that gave priority to shipping along the intercoastal waterway even during morning and evening rush hours. At the time, State Roads 3, 520, and A1A as well as U.S. 1, the county's main vehicular arteries, were all two-lane roads. As a result, in a day with no air-conditioned cars, commutes that could have been minutes with better road networks lasted hours. In addition, new residents struggled to find suitable housing. Some workers lived temporarily in their cars, and, in one extreme circumstance, a handful of workers lived in an unused section of sewer pipe, sleeping on newspapers as mattresses.[5]

Several of the new residents who eventually united with First Baptist Church of Merritt Island experienced firsthand the challenges of Brevard County in the 1950s. Bill Cochran arrived with his wife and small children in 1954 and worked at Cape Canaveral as an RCA contractor with the Air Force. For three years, they lived in a small trailer due to shortages of adequate housing, and "there was very little for family life"—for example, blue jeans and children's clothing had to be bought through Sears & Roebuck mail order or by traveling to Orlando. In 1956, Nelson Rutledge and his family moved to the area where he worked as an engineer on the Atlas rocket. Like others, his family struggled to find suitable housing, settling finally in an old Army barracks-type dwelling in the small town of Eau Gallie. The dwelling featured a plywood wall down the middle to divide the small building between two families: "The closets were full of mold, and mosquitos were all over the doors; showers consisted of about three drips of water per person. It was terrible." His daily commute from Eau Gallie to the Cape took 90 minutes, one way, and by the time he arrived in his non-air-conditioned car, his clothes were "wringing with sweat." Gordon Burleson and his wife Lyvonne arrived in 1959 and remembered far more mosquitos than people "by the millions."[6]

First Baptist Church of Merritt Island also experienced its own growing pains. Pastoral tenure quickly became a challenge as five pastors came and went between 1952 and 1957: Bob Lambert (September 1949 to April 1952), Carl Herzberger (January 1951 to September 1951), Hubert Barnes (July 1952 to December 1952), Jack Epps (February 1953 to February 1954), and Ben Haddox (May 1954 to September 1957). Meanwhile, the church added an educational building as well as a pastorium in 1952, incurring debt to do so. By 1955, the combination of frequent pastoral turnover and new debt hindered the church's ability to pay its pastor, pay its bills, service its debt, and maintain a positive bank balance. In short, the "finances were sick" for much of the 1950s.[7]

TURNING THE CORNER

In spite of the challenges in Brevard, conditions began to improve. Across the county, multifaceted mosquito control efforts slowly addressed the pesky problem. Initially, spraying mosquito breeding areas with pesticide and applying an oily film to stagnant waters produced some results. Better yet, Brevard leaders purchased a large mechanical dredge in 1953 for $64,700. This device solved two problems in one: dredging deepened stagnant saltwater marshes, thus limiting the mosquitos' eggs' opportunity to mature. Dredging also created new real estate by filling in some marshy areas with soil dredged elsewhere. These efforts were so successful that they became a model for other areas across Florida.[8]

Meanwhile, the county issued building permits in record numbers as construction slowly began to meet demands for housing and commercial needs. Several of the government-contracted missile and rocket companies even financed their own housing developments—for example, Fairchild Aircraft Corporation resourced a 150-home subdivision at Cocoa Beach (it was filled in less than six months). In 1956 alone, 82 new developments appeared in central Brevard County.[9]

At the same time, local leaders united in efforts to solve one of the area's other pressing needs—namely, roadways capable of handling chronic traffic congestion. One study suggested that upwards of 60 percent of the population was "constantly annoyed" by traffic congestion. In 1958, the Brevard County Civilian-Military Relations Council was formed by Air Force Major General Donald N. Yates and the mayors of Titusville, Cocoa, Cocoa Beach, Eau Gallie, Indialantic, Melbourne, Melbourne Beach, and Rockledge. The Council sought to expand A1A and U.S. 1 to four lanes. Similarly, the State Road Department projected the completion of a highway from Orlando to Port Canaveral, which would eventually become State Road 528.[10]

First Baptist Church also began turning the corner in several ways. First, in the midst of short pastoral tenures and church financial struggles, a couple named Doyle and Alma Carlton intentionally moved their membership from First Baptist Church of Cocoa to First Baptist Church of Merritt Island in order to provide additional lay leadership. Doyle Carlton, a local banker, businessman, citrus owner, and member of Florida's prominent Carlton family was also an outstanding church layman whose priority on Jesus and the Gospel never wavered. Joe Boatright recalled, "Doyle was the finest layman I ever met."[11] His wise leadership, generosity, and soul-winning example along with his wife's musical talent and relentless volunteer spirit provided much-needed stability to First Baptist Church. As one example among many, longtime First Baptist member J. R. Burgess recalled:

> One Sunday morning in September 1954, my wife and I attended First Baptist Church, Merritt Island. That same Sunday afternoon, Doyle Carlton and Pastor Haddox visited with us in our home. They thanked us for visiting FBCMI and said they would like to discuss our relationship with the Lord. Doyle asked me the most important question: "If I died tonight, was I sure I'd go to heaven." My answer was, "No." Doyle explained the plan of salvation from the Scripture on how to be saved. He asked me if I would like to be saved. I said, "Yes." He led me in a sinner's prayer, and I asked Jesus to come into my heart and save me—and He did! Doyle Carlton was a Christian role model and life-long friend then on for me and my family.[12]

Doyle's wife, Alma, was a talented musician who led the church music program during those years. Both Doyle and Alma served tirelessly and brought a degree of stabilizing leadership that First Baptist Church desperately needed. And as we have already seen, not long after coming to First Baptist Church, Doyle also met Adrian Rogers in Daytona Beach. After that meeting, Doyle thought to himself, "Someday he's going to be my pastor."[13] In the years to come, God would create a powerful partnership between the two men.

Another key win that helped First Baptist Church turn the corner occurred in October 1957 when Jiles Lunsford became pastor. As a

The 1950 sanctuary along with the recently-added, single-story 1952 education wing. Courtesy Lyvonne Burleson.

Soldier serving in the European Theatre during the Second World War, Jiles was wounded during the Battle of the Bulge and taken captive in December 1944. He spent five months in Stalag XIII, a prisoner-of-war camp near Hammelburg, Germany, where he dwindled from 210 pounds to 130 pounds before being liberated.[14] A pre-war graduate of Stetson University, after the war Jiles earned two master's degrees from the Southern Baptist Theological Seminary. Prior to his arrival in Merritt Island, he was the pastor for Lake Forest Baptist Church in Jacksonville, Florida for eight years.[15]

Jiles proved to be a loving, "people's pastor." Lyvonne Burleson recalled that after her first visit to First Baptist Church in November 1958, she ran into the pastor a few days later in the grocery store, and he called her by name: "That a pastor could remember a visitor's name several days later really impressed me."[16] As pastor, Jiles also leveraged his love for cooking as he ministered to the congregation, often bringing fresh baked pies and cakes when he visited his flock. Jim Whitmire recalled, "Jiles was a wonderful man whose gift was service. If you were sick, he would bake you an entire meal and take it to you."[17]

The 1960 sanctuary, a "striking, contemporary house of worship," seated over 800 and was located immediately adjacent to the old block sanctuary and, by that time, a two-story education wing. Courtesy Lyvonne Burleson.

Shortly after Jiles became pastor, Sunday morning attendance exceeded capacity in the small block church building, and a second service at 8:00 AM became necessary. Further growth soon followed, and, in addition to purchasing several lots adjacent to the existing campus, church leaders began planning for a new sanctuary that would seat over 800. In late 1958, an initial loan of $15,000 followed by a $130,000 bond drive began the efforts. Then in September 1959, ground was broken for the new building. Finally, on April 24, 1960, the congregation occupied the new "striking, contemporary house of worship" with some 600 people in attendance.[18] The new building, along with the smaller block sanctuary and an educational wing that now featured two stories, postured the congregation to move forward into the 1960s prepared for anticipated growth.

MISSILE CULTURE BECOMES SPACE RACE

As the 1950s progressed, the missile culture became increasingly prominent in Brevard County, and the July 15, 1957 issue of Time magazine featured an article entitled, "Life in Missile Land." The write-up gave Americans everywhere a glimpse into an otherworldly lifestyle: "Brevard is a land of piercing shrieks and thunderous roars, and when the shrieks and the roars combine in one nerve-racking racket, housewives, office workers, and school children rush outdoors to watch another missile on its way." Some became accustomed to the sights and sounds, but for others the experience never quite became normal. One woman remarked: "I've never gotten used to it, and I never will. Every time I hear a roar that isn't a jet, I break my neck getting outdoors." Meanwhile, a Cocoa Beach hotel manager noted, "We've all got rocket fever here. Everything centers on the Cape. We look at it and live with it every day. We rent 70 of our 87 units to missilemen from Convair, North American Aviation, Bell Laboratory, and A.C. Sparkplug." In the late 1950s, Brevard residents experienced first-hand the ups and the downs of the missile program—such as the launch of the first big Atlas rocket in June 1957, which thundered upward, tumbled sideways, and blew up in the air as thousands of spectators stood speechless.[19]

Then on October 4, 1957, missile program momentum gave way to the space race as the Soviet Union launched Sputnik 1, followed soon thereafter on November 3 by Sputnik 2. On a national level, shocked Americans wondered how the Russians had advanced beyond their own technological progress: "No event since Pearl Harbor set off such repercussions in public life."[20] As if Cold War America needed additional cause for panic, Sputnik provided it: "If the Russians can put a satellite in orbit, what's to keep them from sending nuclear weapons over American cities?" For politicians scrambling to provide leadership on space, the resulting crisis of confidence meant one thing: policy and funding, and lots of it. While an American satellite, Explorer 1, finally found its way into space on February 1, 1958, its weight of 30 pounds hardly matched the weights of Sputnik 1 and 2 at 180 pounds and 1,100 pounds, respectively. President Eisenhower, facing flagging poll numbers reflecting public doubt in his leadership against Russian space efforts, created the National Aeronautics and Space Administration (NASA) on October 1, 1958.

One month later, on November 26, America's manned space initiative had a name: Project Mercury. And by April 9, 1959, NASA revealed the names of the seven Mercury Astronauts. With a nod to the past and optimism for the future, Time magazine described them as "seven men cut of the same stone as Columbus, Magellan, Daniel Boone, Orville and Wilbur Wright."[21] Brevard became a home away from home for the Mercury Astronauts. The Cocoa Beach Holiday Inn often hosted them when they were in town for work at the Cape. Scott Carpenter, John Glenn, and Gus Grissom often ran on the beach, and John Glenn frequented a local church on Sundays. Additionally, Glenn purchased the 35mm camera he eventually carried into space at a drugstore in Cocoa Beach.[22]

THE CENTER OF AMERICA'S FASTEST GROWING COUNTY

By decade's end, fueled by mass migration of missile men, space scientists, and their families, Brevard found itself the fastest-growing county in America. In 1950, 23,653 people called Brevard home; by 1960, that number had rocketed to 111,435—an increase of 371 percent. In comparison, during the same ten years, the state of Florida's population grew by 79 percent while the national population grew by only 19 percent.[23] Most newcomers brought their children also: in 1950, approximately 4,100 students attended 13 schools across the county; in 1960, some 25,000 students attended 30 Brevard schools.[24] Newcomers arrived from across the United States: 20 percent came from elsewhere in Florida, 40 percent came from other Southern states, 20 percent came from the Midwest, and the rest came from the farthest reaches of the country.[25]

Unlike Houston or Huntsville (the other two major hubs of the space program), Brevard lacked a centralized urban core, so newcomers settled across the county primarily in four towns: Titusville in the north, Cocoa in the center, Eau Gallie and Melbourne in the south—with Merritt Island located in the center of it all. In fact, nearly all main roads led to or through Merritt Island: Highway 3 ran north to south, Highway 520 ran east to west, and the two intersected in Merritt Island only a few hundred yards from First Baptist Church. Meanwhile, State Road A1A and U.S. 1 brought traffic from across the county to the center.

As with the rest of Brevard, Merritt Island also experienced phenomenal growth in the 1950s. At the beginning of the decade, nearly 2,300 called Merritt Island home; by 1960, that number had climbed to over 9,000. In ten years, the landscape had changed from a multitude of citrus groves to a landscape interspersed with new neighborhoods, improved roads, and a handful of businesses. But there was still plenty of room to grow. And grow it would.

4

FROM MERRITT ISLAND TO MOON PORT USA (1960-1964)

As Brevard County and the First Baptist Church entered the 1960s, both could sense that multitudes of newcomers stood poised to flood the area, and some experts were already suggesting the county's population would surpass 250,000 by 1970. Brevard had largely conquered the mosquito problem, prioritized road improvement, and finally begun to address the need for adequate housing. Meanwhile, First Baptist Church had nearly 700 members, a brand new 800-seat sanctuary, a season of pastoral continuity, and optimism about the future. Of particular importance to the area, the space program gathered momentum toward the first manned flight with anticipation of far greater goals beyond. On top of that, the nation elected a young, vibrant John F. Kennedy who would ultimately cast a sweeping vision for space exploration, the impact of which would stretch from Brevard County to the lunar surface.

NATIONAL CHALLENGES

As early as 1959, NASA leadership discussed a lunar landing's feasibility. NASA's Space Task Group agreed that it was possible and, in February 1961, also agreed that it could happen by decade's end at a cost somewhere between $26 billion and $38 billion.[1] But many steps stood between the present and the moon, not least of which was Soviet space race dominance. More broadly, Cold War realities raised the stakes and added complex challenges to the task at hand.

In February 1961, the newly-inaugurated John F. Kennedy was not, at first, a champion for the space program nor did he cast himself in fierce competition with the Russians. In fact, in his earliest national addresses—his inauguration and his first State of the Union speech—he suggested some degree of collaboration between the American and Russian space programs.[2] Some have even speculated, "Had the balance of power and prestige between the United States and the Soviet Union remained stable in Spring 1961, it is quite possible that Kennedy would never have advanced his moon program, and the direction of American space efforts might have taken a radically different course."[3]

Then on April 12, 1961, the Soviet Union sent its Cosmonaut Yuri Gagarin into orbit, the first human in space. It was another win for the Russians, much to the embarrassment of the U.S. space program. New York Times journalist Hanson Baldwin wrote at the time of the accomplishment, "Even though the United States is still the strongest military power and leads in many aspects of the space race, the world—impressed by the spectacular Soviet firsts—believes we lag militarily and technologically."[4] President Kennedy publicly downplayed the accomplishment, but privately he was "gravely concerned" and recognized that "it was more urgent than ever to define U.S. space aims."[5]

But at that precise moment, Kennedy had other burdens on his mind. Less than a week after Gagarin's flight, Cold War tensions hit an embarrassing flash point on April 15-19 in the abortive Bay of Pigs invasion. Since 1959, Fidel Castro's Communist government in Cuba had developed deep ties with the Soviet Union. Much to the dismay of the United States, only 90 miles to the north, Russian economic and military resources flooded the island nation. In March 1960, President Eisenhower authorized a CIA plan to train and equip Cuban exiles to invade the island, overthrow Castro, and establish a new government friendly to the United States. When Kennedy took office, he authorized the invasion itself, but the execution was doomed almost from the start: Communist agents in Miami learned of the plan, the landing site for the 1,400 Cuban exiles at the Bay of Pigs was poorly chosen, and the Cuban people failed to embrace their "liberators" as anticipated. Instead, a Cuban force of 20,000 easily defeated the 1,400 invaders. American involvement was obvious, which caused tremendous embarrassment to Kennedy personally and to his administration. Publicly, the President attempted to put a positive spin on the failed invasion: "There's an old saying that victory has 100 fathers and defeat is an orphan. I'm the responsible officer of the Government. We intend to profit from this lesson."[6] Privately, a perplexed Kennedy sincerely wondered what went wrong:

> There were 50 or so of us, presumably the most experienced and smartest people we could get, to plan such an operation. But five minutes after it began to fall in, we all looked at each other and asked, "How could we have been so stupid?" When we saw the wide range of the failures we asked ourselves why it had not been apparent to somebody from the start. I guess you get walled off from reality when you want something to succeed too much.[7]

In the wake of Gagarin's spaceflight and the Bay of Pigs fiasco, NASA scored a much-needed American victory when, on May 5, 1961, Alan Shepherd became the first American in space. Shepherd's flight was not a small milestone, to be sure. Yet, it paled in comparison to the Russian efforts: Shepherd's flight lasted 15 minutes and never achieved orbit, Gagarin flew for one hour and 48 minutes and orbited the earth;

Shepherd's Freedom 7 capsule weighed only 2,900 pounds, Gagarin's Vostok 1 capsule weighed nearly twice that. There was still much to do.

For Kennedy, America needed something bigger and something bolder than a sub-orbital flight—or anything Project Mercury had to offer, for that matter. The Nation needed something that would galvanize its purpose, direction, and motivation and guarantee first place on the world stage. But what could it be? Putting a space station of some kind in orbit? Sending a spacecraft to orbit the moon and return? Landing Americans on the moon? The President considered all options with his advisors, but

On May 25, 1961, President John F. Kennedy boldly challenged the Nation to reach for the moon by the end of the decade. Library of Congress.

in an April 21 press conference, Kennedy showed his cards: "If we can get to the moon before the Russians, we should."[8] Advisors believed it was possible within the decade. Wernher von Braun, director of NASA's George C. Marshall Space Flight Center in Huntsville, Alabama reported, "We have a sporting chance of sending a 3-man crew around the moon ahead of the Soviets and an excellent chance of beating the Soviets to the first landing of a crew on the moon. With an all-out crash program, we could achieve a landing by 1968."[9] With those kinds of assurances, despite the incredible financial cost, Kennedy decided to go for broke.

A MOST SERIOUS TIME

On May 25, 1961, just three weeks after Alan Shepherd's sub-orbital flight—and nearly nine months before an American Astronaut would even orbit the earth—President Kennedy addressed a joint session of Congress regarding "Urgent National Needs." Describing the previous months as "a most serious time," he highlighted several needs along various lines: economic and social progress at home and abroad, partnerships for self-defense, the nation's military and intelligence shield, civil defense, and disarmament. But the last need mentioned—space—captured the lion's share of national attention. After mentioning the highs and lows in recent days, President Kennedy began to point to the future: "Now it is time to take longer strides—time for a great new American enterprise—time for this nation to take a clearly leading role in space achievement, which in many ways may hold the key to our future on earth."[10] Kennedy then called for setting long-range goals, an urgent time schedule, and bold management to ensure all would be accomplished. While acknowledging the "head start obtained by the Soviets," he reminded his listeners of America's responsibility to "make new efforts on our own." Then the President called the Nation to action with this memorable challenge:

> I believe that this nation should commit itself to achieving the goal, before this decade is out, of landing a man on the moon and returning him safely to the Earth. No single space project in this period will be more impressive to mankind, or more important for the long-range exploration of space; and none will be so difficult or expensive to accomplish. ...In a very real sense, it will not be one man going to the

> moon—if we make this judgment affirmatively, it will be an entire nation. For all of us must work to put him there.[11]

In addition to massive Congressional applause, Kennedy also received a pledge for additional Congressional funding in the sum of approximately $550 million. As time would tell, it was just a drop in the bucket.

In spite of Kennedy's best rhetoric, Americans were initially divided about this bold vision. In fact, a Gallop poll taken after the speech revealed that 58 percent opposed the priority and cost of a lunar landing.[12] Some

John Glenn, Gus Grissom, and Alan Shepherd—the first three Americans in space. *Life* (March 3, 1961).

argued that monies would be better spent on domestic needs. Others argued that the space program's technological needs would distract from military research and development. Still others wondered if the political and national need to beat the Russians was all that important. But the President and his best public-relations assets, the Mercury 7 Astronauts, remained steadfast in emphasizing the benefits again and again. Ultimately, of course, the groundswell of public opinion gained more and more momentum following the President's speech in May. But winning popular support—and the funding that would go along with it—would take time. And the clock was already ticking.

Another small victory came on July 21, 1961, when Virgil "Gus" Grissom became the second American in space. Like Shepherd, his was only a sub-orbital flight. And, unfortunately, the capsule was lost at sea when, after splashdown in the Atlantic Ocean, the hatch inexplicably blew off and the craft flooded with seawater. Still, the bigger picture continued to develop. In the second half of 1961, after Congress approved Kennedy's request for additional funding, NASA began awarding massive contracts for Apollo projects. On August 9, the Massachusetts Institute of Technology received the Apollo navigation and guidance contract. Meanwhile, by November, contracts for the three stages of the massive Saturn V launch vehicle went respectively to Boeing, the Rocketdyne Division of North American Aviation, and Douglas. And North American received the exceptionally-important command and service module contract on November 28—the "largest peacetime contract awarded by the U.S. Government up to that time."[13]

Brevard County began also to reap benefits from the outlay of Apollo funding as Cape Canaveral was officially designated as a vehicle assembly and launch site. In every way, the infrastructural needs would dwarf those required by Mercury: new control rooms and administrative facilities, massive new launch pads and gantries, a gigantic assembly building, and even a colossal mobile platform for moving the Saturn V rocket from the assembly building to launch pad. Eventually, NASA would also add a visitor's center that would receive over a million guests by 1967. Of course, with the additional funding, construction, and administrative support came the men and their families who would make it all happen.

MOVING FORWARD IN 1962

In 1962, NASA began to take larger strides. On February 20, after ten failed attempts over three months, John Glenn became the first American to orbit the earth. Glenn's mission began to answer some key questions for American scientists, not least of which was, "How will micro-gravity and zero-gravity conditions affect the human body?" But the intangible victory of public optimism was perhaps the biggest payoff: "Colonel Glenn's trip was considered by most observers to have gone a long way toward erasing the nation's 'second best' look in space."[14]

In August 1962, Russia's Vostok 3 and Vostok 4 spacecrafts accomplished another first for the Soviets: they were the first two ships to orbit the earth simultaneously. Although they did not rendezvous and dock, they came within 4 miles of each other—another win for the Russians, another lost opportunity for Americans to be first. As a result, President Kennedy determined to rally the nation with a speech at Rice University on September 12, and he did not disappoint. Before a crowd of over 35,000, Kennedy reminded Americans of the pioneer spirit that characterized the nation's history and that "there is new knowledge to be gained." Then he issued an electric challenge both to those gathered and to the entire nation:

> Why, some say, the moon? Why choose this as our goal? And they may well ask, why climb the highest mountain? Why, 35 years ago, fly the Atlantic? Why does Rice play Texas? We choose to go to the moon. We choose to go to the moon in this decade and to do the other things, not because they are easy but because they are hard, because that goal will serve to organize and measure the best of our energies and skills,

> because that challenge is one that we are willing to accept, one we are unwilling to postpone, and one which we intend to win. It is for these reasons that I regard the decision last year to shift our efforts in space from low to high gear as among the most important decisions that will be made during my incumbency in the office of the President.[15]

Among others, CBS journalist Dan Rather was in attendance and remembered that the speech was "without apologizing, a thrilling moment." And Rice University journalist Sam Byrd recalled, "For a mere 20-minute talk, the speech captured the zeitgeist of a nation and ignited America's commitment to planting its flag on the lunar landscape."[16]

First Baptist Church of Merritt Island also made some significant advances in 1962. Much to the delight of its members, the church installed air conditioning and heat in its new sanctuary. But on a more strategic level, the church called James "Jim" Whitmire as Minister of Music and Youth in December of that year.

Jim Whitmire, originally from Atlanta and a graduate of Stetson University, was a student at Southwestern Baptist Theological Seminary in 1962. His wife, Linda Dooley from Rockledge, Florida—just across the Indian River from Merritt Island—occasionally returned to her home church, First Baptist Church of Cocoa, as guest vocalist. Through these contacts, Jim met Doyle and Alma Carlton. Jim recalls:

> Doyle knew my wife, Linda Dooley, from First Baptist Church, Cocoa, and he said to her, "We need a minister of music. I understand your husband is studying to be a minister of music?" So they brought me to visit and basically hired me on the spot—so, really, they hired me because they knew Linda![17]

The timing and irony of the hire, looking back, was not lost on Jim: "It's interesting how God works because at the time I was liberal in my thinking and theology. So I had to be hired so that Adrian Rogers would inherit me. Adrian would have never hired me in a million years."[18]

In July 1964, just prior to Adrian's arrival, the former pastor, Jiles Lunsford, said to Jim, "I know you and I know Adrian Rogers and the two of you will never last six months together." Once again, Jim recalled, "[Jiles] said that because Adrian Rogers was very conservative, and I was a liberal."[19] But God knew exactly what He was doing.

TRAGEDY AND CONTINUITY IN 1963

In May 1963, Project Mercury concluded when Gordon Cooper completed 22 orbits in his capsule Faith 7. Following his flight, he and the other astronauts lobbied members of Congress for the $5.7 billion that NASA had requested for 1964. In addition, the Astronauts lobbied President Kennedy directly for an additional Mercury flight—at a cost of $10 million—to fill the 18-month publicity gap between Cooper's flight and the first manned Gemini mission scheduled for late 1964 or early 1965.[20] Although Kennedy didn't bite, his enthusiastic support for NASA's goals never wavered.

The colossal Vehicle Assembly Building (VAB) under construction along with the Apollo Launch Control Center (bottom left). Projects such as these brought millions of dollars and thousands of technicians and their families to Brevard County. Courtesy NASA.

In August 1963, the newly-created Canaveral District of the Army Corps of Engineers began construction on the massive Vehicle Assembly Building (VAB). Intended for assembly and final check of the 363-foot-tall Saturn V launch vehicle, the VAB would ultimately become (at the time) the largest building in the world, enclosing 128 million cubic feet of space. Rising to a height of 525 feet and covering eight acres, the building would feature 4,200 steel piles, each driven 160 feet below the surface. All told, the VAB cost over $100 million to complete. One cannot underestimate the impact such a project had on Brevard County, both in terms of resources and manpower.[21]

But in November 1963, tragedy struck as Apollo's political champion was cut down in Dallas, Texas by a deranged, Communist assassin. In the wake of Kennedy's death, more than a few wondered if the race to the moon would continue, at least along the President's ambitious timeline. But proponents of Kennedy's goal need not have worried, because another champion took his place—who, in fact, had supported the space program long before John F. Kennedy gave it any thought whatsoever. His name was Lyndon B. Johnson, and his first space-related act as President was to assign by executive order the name "Cape Kennedy" to the NASA Launch Operations Center at Cape Canaveral on November 29, 1963, one week after Kennedy was slain.

Johnson's interest in the space race began as early as October 1957 when the Russians launched Sputnik 1. Motivated at least in part by a desire to undermine Republican credibility on the issue, as Chairman of the Preparedness Subcommittee of the Senate Armed Services Committee, Johnson concluded that the U.S. must invest heavily in the fledgling space program. He quickly became a key stakeholder in the effort, whether by using his immense influence in Congress to push for funding, strongly supporting legislation that created NASA, or representing President Eisenhower at the United Nations to deliver a rousing call for space exploration. When Johnson became Kennedy's Vice President, he chaired the National Space Council and, in many cases, stood behind the scenes supporting if not orchestrating several of the President's major commitments to beating the Soviets. In fact,

Johnson counseled Kennedy to label any politician not supportive of his goals as "soft on Communism."[22] And when some questioned why America must win the lunar space race, Johnson answered flatly, "What American wants to go to bed by the light of a Communist moon?"[23] Indeed, Johnson provided vigorous continuity for Kennedy's vision when he entered the White House in November 1963—so much so that following the Apollo 11 landing in 1969, Walter Cronkite called him, "The Father of the Program."[24]

Those living and working on Merritt Island knew well the support that President Johnson gave to the space program, mostly in terms of funding and resources—in some cases, for reasons beyond their immediate concern or comprehension. For example, some have argued that Johnson saw the space race as a vehicle for his broader social agenda: "He envisioned it as an economic engine, particularly for the South. That's a big reason why NASA has major facilities in places like Huntsville, Alabama, Merritt Island, Florida, Hancock County, Mississippi, and, of course, Houston."[25] Regardless of Presidential motivation, Merritt Island benefited tremendously from the infusion of millions of space dollars and thousands of space workers.

A STIRRING IN THE AIR

By 1964, Merritt Island was well on its way to becoming the center of something very big and very special. Thousands of people migrated to the area, an enormous amount of funding flooded the island, and the eyes of the nation repeatedly sought a glimpse of what was happening at America's "moon port." In order to feed the nation's appetite for information, the Florida Development Commission produced a short, promotional movie entitled "Florida: Moon Port USA," which provided a comprehensive and exciting picture of life in Brevard County.[26] At the local level, everyone knew that they were living in a unique and almost magical time. Jim Whitmire recalled, "There was a stirring in the air in those years. People were moving to the area in leaps and bounds. And God saw this, too."[27]

At First Baptist Church, the stage was nearly set for a great move of God. The church was growing, but not in pace with the rapid expansion of the area. When Pastor Jiles Lunsford resigned in February 1964, church leaders began to pray that God would send a dynamic, catalyst leader to maximize the incredible opportunity. Six months later, in August 1964, that leader arrived.

PART III

THE MINISTRY

5

LIFTOFF!

(1964-1965)

On August 2, 1964, "Brother Rogers"—as members came to know him—officially began his ministry as Pastor of First Baptist Church. Immediately, momentum was on his side as the congregation and the community recognized the new minister's extraordinary preaching ability. Internally, Adrian began thinking and praying about the next strategic steps to maximize the unique opportunities that Merritt Island offered. He knew that the time for action was at hand. Ultimately, pastor and people sensed that great days were ahead.

"I CANNOT BELIEVE WHAT I JUST HEARD"

Adrian's dynamic and confident preaching with its evangelistic zeal and emphasis on assurance of salvation instantly electrified the congregation. In fact, on August 2 no less than 34 people came forward to receive Jesus Christ as Savior and Lord—"I gave the invitation and one after another they came down the aisle giving their hearts to Jesus Christ, I'll never forget it. The power of God was so thick you could cut it with a knife, and I praise the sweet Lord for it."[1] Most sat spellbound as if a spiritual lightning bolt had struck, and several members thought, "I cannot believe what I just heard—that was almost unbelievable. Is he really real?"[2] They heard the powerful message and saw the undeniable results, yet they wondered if the man would live up to what he said so persuasively. But as Bill Cochran, who would eventually lead Merritt Island's cassette tape ministry, recalled, "There are some preachers you can hear on the radio or television that you still have questions about. With Adrian, there was no question. We learned after a very brief period of time that he was a very real person."[3]

Beyond that first Sunday, Adrian continued to preach the Bible with boldness, clarity, certainty, humor, and a laser-like focus on evangelism, assurance, and eschatological hope. Jim Whitmire recalled:

> I never heard anyone talk so much about the cross, the blood, victory, and the name of Jesus. When Adrian first came, I had never heard a preacher who was more assured of what he said: "This is it, because this is what the Bible says; do this, because this is what the Bible says." At Stetson—and even at Southwestern Seminary—I had heard professors say, "We suppose" and "We think" and "It might be." So I came out of that thinking, "These guys know which parts of the Bible are true and which aren't, and I'm not smart enough to know that." As a result, I even became leery of reading my Bible for lack of certainty. So when Adrian came with his certainty, I initially thought, "The arrogance of this guy. Where does he come off being so sure about what he's saying?!" But then I eventually realized, as he backed up everything with Scripture, that he was simply preaching the Bible.[4]

Bill Cochran remembered that Adrian's preaching appealed to many people, not least because his "unashamedly pre-millennial" messages gave listeners a profound sense of hope. And Norma Baird remembered his preaching as clear, direct, and easy to follow; and that many people began taking notes regularly when Adrian came to First Baptist Church.[5]

Members and guests alike also quickly discovered that the remarkably-godly man behind the preaching was also especially warm and down to earth. Lyvonne Burleson recalled, "He laughed a lot and had a love of life that made it a joy to be around him." Nelson Rutledge remembered that "Adrian was an intellectual who didn't lose touch with his grounding, with his humor, and with his athletic ability—he remembered those things, and it made him very appealing to many people. Men especially flocked to him." Others noticed that "he had a way of making you feel as though you were the most important person to him, and he never forgot a name."[6]

Nevertheless, while humble and accessible, Adrian also possessed an undeniable magnetism that set him apart from other people: "If you were in a room with your back turned toward the door, and Adrian walked in the room, you would immediately know that something changed." Jim Whitmire recalled, "I saw quickly that he was the kind of guy who walked in the room and sucked the oxygen right out of it. He always dominated the room when he came in, not because he wanted to but simply because his personality was like that."[7]

ADRIAN AND DOYLE: NITRO MEETS GLYCERIN

As we have seen, God arranged for the paths of Adrian Rogers and Doyle Carlton to cross in the early 1950s. During that brief but meaningful visit, neither man could have imagined where that early touchpoint would lead. But by the fall of 1964, their partnership was solidified, and both men quickly caught God's vision for First Baptist Church amidst the waves of growth crashing upon Brevard County.

Doyle Carlton had a heart to see the church embrace the phenomenal local growth with strategic ministry and adequate facilities. Through his bank leadership, citrus holdings, and various commercial pursuits, God had graciously given him both the wherewithal to proactively move on every opportunity as well as the spiritual gift of giving. For example, even before Adrian became pastor, when a key piece of property became

Doyle Carlton, "the finest layman I ever met." Courtesy Joyce Rogers.

available, if the church failed to vote on purchasing it or did not have the means at the time, Doyle would often buy it himself and then hold it until the church could buy it—or else he would simply give it to the church. Jim Whitmire reflected on those days, "God knew the time and he knew the man who needed to be there at that church, a man who knew the high stakes of finance, and so he put Doyle there and blessed Doyle."[8]

When Adrian arrived at First Baptist Church, he noted that the campus, while blessed with a relatively-new 800-seat sanctuary, consisted otherwise of modest structures with limited potential. Meanwhile, the land immediately surrounding the church contained numerous old frame houses and trailers as well as a few vacant lots. Steve Rogers has noted, "My dad immediately saw those adjacent properties and said, 'Who owns those and how can we buy them?'"[9] Such sentiment was right in line with Doyle Carlton's heart, and in September 1964, the church formed a long-range planning committee that included Doyle Carlton, Carl Hicks, Richard Hicks, Cecil Houston, John Hurdle, Sylvia Leitner, Mickey Moore, Charles Parker, Jim Whitmire, and Vernon Wise. Not surprisingly, one month later, the church moved quickly to purchase three small lots, three additional properties that included small houses, and one larger lot for future development, the total cost of which was over $100,000. Early momentum made such purchases necessary and justifiable: by mid-October, after only 10 weeks as pastor, the church had already seen 143 additions.[10]

What did Adrian and the long-range committee have in mind? First and foremost, the church needed more space for its increasing worship attendance and Christian education needs. But the church also needed a certain kind of space, an unconventional space that would connect with people beyond the traditional church gatherings. And, as God would have it, Adrian arrived at Merritt Island with a sense of that kind of space already in mind. Just a few years earlier, while driving cross country with his family to the 1962 Southern Baptist Convention Annual Meeting in San Francisco, the Rogers family visited the First Baptist Church of Dallas, Texas. In addition to hearing the Baptist legend W. A. Criswell preach, the family also took note of the unique recreational facilities at the historic

Doyle and Adrian enjoyed many outings together, including this successful hunt in the Ocala National Forest. Courtesy Joyce Rogers.

downtown church that included a bowling alley, roller skating rink, and exercise equipment—all extremely rare for a church in that day. Adrian was intrigued: "Why build buildings to use one day a week when, with only 20 percent additional cost, the buildings can be used to reach people for Jesus all seven days?"[11] So, in the fall of 1964, Adrian casted vision by taking a group from Merritt Island to visit the First Baptist Church of Pompano Beach, which was one of the few churches in Florida at that time with comparable recreational facilities. The team consisted of deacons and other lay leaders, to include Doyle Carlton, Nelson Rutledge, Gene Baird, and Carl Hicks.[12] The idea of reaching the people of Merritt Island for Jesus by means of similar facilities fascinated the team, and they returned with a broader vision of what their expanding campus could and would look like.

Meanwhile, Adrian kept the preaching fires hot both at the Merritt Island campus as well as the church's Cape Canaveral Baptist Mission where he led a "Soul Stirring Evangelistic Crusade" on November 1-7, 1964.[13] The new year saw continued growth as First Baptist Church conducted a four-week "Prove Your Love" campaign leading up to Easter Sunday, April 18, 1965. On the campaign's first Sunday, March 28, the congregational attendance goal of 701 was shattered when 860 attended services that day—in fact, the subsequent weekly goals of 801, 901, and 1001 were all surpassed. The four-week emphasis culminated with "The Greater Merritt Island Crusade for Christ" during Easter week, April 11-18. These nightly, pastor-led meetings featured dynamic messages with intriguing titles such as "The Devil's Religion" and "The Man From Outer Space—The Second Coming of Jesus Christ" as well as "The Teenage Playboy's Payday." Local papers advertising the crusade pointed out the "unusual growth" at First Baptist Church with "over 400 additions to the church in the past seven months."[14]

Throughout 1965, as more and more new members united with the church, Adrian sensed the need for additional pastoral leadership. Jim Whitmire's scope of work had included music, education, and youth, but the expanding participation in his growing number of 13 multi-generational choirs with a total enrollment of 482 limited his ability to lead across multiple ministry areas. In addition, the rapid congregational growth presented the need for strategic educational leadership. So, in May 1965, the Personnel Committee began searching for a Minister of Education. Three months later, the church called Tom Clayton from Terry Parker Baptist Church in Jacksonville, Florida.[15]

Meanwhile, the church continued to purchase additional property, and the acquisition of the "Jobe Building" came first. In 1961, Doyle Carlton had signed a contract with the building's owner, Mr. Jobe, for first right of refusal when the property became available. When that time arrived in August 1965, Doyle loaned the church the funds to make the purchase in exchange for church bonds at a later date. The "Jobe Building," as it would continue to be known, provided much-needed office and educational space. Then, in September 1965, the church purchased key properties

The front half of the "Jobe Building," located across the street from the sanctuary, became office space for the church staff. Adrian's 1960 Volkswagen is pictured here. Courtesy Joyce Rogers.

belonging to Mrs. Ethel Johnson immediately to the south and west of the campus. All told, in August and September, the church added properties valued at nearly $100,000.[16]

By the end of September, with Adrian's first church year complete, First Baptist celebrated its remarkable advances since his arrival. God had blessed with some 630 additions by baptism or membership as well as the acquisition of multiple strategic properties that would make way for visionary facilities. In every way, the church stood poised to take its next giant steps.[17]

GEMINI CLOSES THE GAP AND THE CAPE EXPANDS

As First Baptist Church experienced non-stop growth, the space program likewise continued its march toward the moon. Project Gemini, the series of orbital missions intended to bridge the gap between Mercury and Apollo, began in 1965. The multi-day flights would, among other things, test rendezvous and docking procedures as well as assess the limits of human sustainability in the two-man Gemini capsules. In March, Gemini 3, the first manned flight, carried Gus Grissom and John Young into orbit. Then, in June of that year, Astronaut Ed White became the first American to conduct an extra-vehicular activity (EVA)—a "spacewalk"—as part of the Gemini 4 mission. *Time* magazine reported:

> White stood on top of his spaceship's white titanium hull. He touched it with his bulky thermal gloves. He burned around like Buck Rogers propelling himself with his hand-held jet. He floated lazily on his back. He joked and laughed. He gazed down at the earth 103 miles below, spotted the Houston Galveston Bay area where he lives and tried to take a picture of it. Like a gas station attendant, he checked the spacecraft's thrusters and wiped its windshield.[18]

After the EVA, White described himself as feeling "red, white, and blue all over."[19]

In December, when Gemini 6 and Gemini 7 executed the first orbital manned rendezvous of two spacecraft, prospects for reaching the moon before the Soviets looked as promising as ever. *Time* magazine, noting that the splashdowns of both capsules were televised live, gave this optimistic assessment:

> Now the moon itself seems nearer and definitely accessible. Man's technical talents have brought a lunar visit down out of the realm of science fiction. The Apollo program, with its planned lunar landing before the decade runs out, no longer seems a fanciful goal for overambitious scientists. From the scorched launching pads of Cape Kennedy to the lonely tracking ships in the Pacific, Gemini has pumped new life into U.S. space work.[20]

Meanwhile, at the Cape, government space funds continued to pour in at the tune of some $1.75 billion. In addition to new gantries and launch facilities, the massive VAB began to take shape, the epitome of American assembly-line ingenuity on a gigantic scale. Time magazine observed, "The result is a landscape of the future, so endlessly and rapidly renewing itself that it is almost beyond the capacity of ordinary mortals to keep up."[21]

"COLORBLIND FROM THE GET-GO"

In early August, in addition to hosting its own on-campus Vacation Bible School, dozens of First Baptist volunteers, in partnership with the Greater Mount Zion Missionary Church, conducted its "Negro Vacation Bible School" (as it was called then) in the North Tropical Trail African American neighborhood. Each day, upwards of 125 children attended and heard the Gospel with many making professions of faith in Jesus. This was an annual ministry under Adrian's leadership.[22] "My parents were colorblind from the get-go," Steve Rogers recalled.[23] Indeed, Adrian made it a point to boldly challenge the congregation about unconditional love and compassion across racial lines early in his ministry at Merritt Island:

> I don't care what you believe about segregation or what you believe about integration, but if you're a Christian you must believe that we must love all people everywhere regardless of their color and regardless of their race. If you don't believe that, you do not have the right to wear the label "Christian."[24]

Then, without "stutter, stammer, or equivocation," he issued a strong exhortation about unconditional love for all people:

> I'm going to say something that you might not like, especially if you're from Georgia or South Florida like me. One way to live the Gospel is to have goodwill toward all men regardless of the color of their skin. When you are filled with racial hatred and bigotry, you play right into the hands of the devil. As long as I'm the pastor of this church, our door is open to any human being who can walk through it if he comes to worship. If you don't like that, you can get another pastor.[25]

This bold statement was characteristic of Adrian Rogers' commitment to multi-ethnic ministry. It was a non-negotiable for him, from Merritt Island to Memphis.

THE BIG PICTURE QUICKLY EMERGES

In late 1965, Adrian began making significant visionary overtures to his Merritt Island congregation. The November 2 edition of *The Link*, the weekly church mailer, prominently featured news that O. K. Houstoun, an architect from Coral Gables, Florida would begin drafting the master plan for a multi-phase campus expansion. To accompany the big news, Adrian shared a sweeping vision statement in The Link that captured both the spirit of the age and the incredible opportunities at hand:

> MY PEOPLE, God has placed us in the focal point of the world. Cape Kennedy, Washington, Moscow, Berlin—these and a few other geographical nerve centers are in men's minds, on their lips, and the front page of all newspapers. I HAVE A DREAM. Here at the nation's moon port, we need to build for the glory of our Christ a strong New Testament Church. This church cannot be a normal church. It should be large and strong. It should be attractive and exciting. It should be abreast of the times and should in many respects compare favorably with the dynamic spirit of this area and age. We must not be a "horse and buggy church" in a "jet age." YET THIS CHURCH MUST BE TRUE TO THE PURE GOSPEL. We must unashamedly proclaim the Old Book, the New Birth, the Precious Blood, and the Blessed Hope. Lukewarm, modernistic churches abound everywhere. We need to be distinctly different. In my heart and mind, I envision a church that will be "geared to the times and anchored to the rock." If this is done, I believe we can make an impact on the world for Jesus. To this end we must pray 'til the tears come, work 'til the sweat comes, and give 'til it hurts.[26]

Later that month, Adrian unveiled the new weekly mailer that would set the tone for much of his Merritt Island ministry, the title of which was *The Thrust*. The new mailer also contained a new slogan: "The Church Where Everybody is Somebody and Jesus is Lord."[27] Long before days of e-mails and social media, *The Thrust* would be a primary source of communication, especially the weekly "Pastor's Paragraphs" article.

In December, Adrian kept the vision before the people in a message about the Church in Philadelphia from Revelation 3:7-13. Highlighting the incredible open door that God set before the Merritt Island congregation, Adrian reminded the people:

> Jesus is saying to the First Baptist Church of Merritt Island, "I have set before you an open door, and no man can shut it." If there was ever a church that had an open door, it's our church. We are located in the focal point of the free world. We have people coming here from all over the world. The eyes of the nation are upon us. We're in the heart of the fastest-growing county in the United States, and I want you to take into consideration that God has blessed the First Baptist Church miraculously—we're one of the fastest-growing churches in the world. Every Sunday, we have 30, 40, 50, or 60 visitors, and we've had hundreds and hundreds and hundreds of people walk these aisles making professions of faith and uniting with our church. God is blessing in an unusual way—we're seeing things that very few people get to see. ...I believe that God has given our church a golden opportunity, and may Heaven help us if we don't reach it. I'd rather be Peter, James, and John asleep in the Garden of Gethsemane than be the First Baptist Church of Merritt Island asleep in these times in which we live.[28]

In the same message, Adrian went on to share more thoughts about how the church would reach its community for Jesus Christ through an innovative campus and creative ministries:

We need to build some buildings—I mean, some big buildings, some fine buildings. We need to build some buildings that will be second-to-none in this community as a monument to Jesus Christ with educational facilities that will help us to reach all of the prospects that it is the duty of this church to reach. And we need to include in our buildings a program for character training and recreation where we'll take boys and girls off the streets and bring them down here seven days a week so they can have fellowship together and play together and we can tell them about Jesus Christ.[29]

In the December 19 edition of *The Thrust*, Adrian announced news of more proactive acquisitions—"FIRST BAPTIST CHURCH TAKES ANOTHER GIANT STEP. Last Wednesday night we voted to purchase Beck's Used

Car Lot which occupies the corner of Grove Street and the Merritt Island Causeway. This is a strategic piece of property. At the present rate, over 30,000 cars a day pass this corner."[30]

By the end of 1965, Adrian had repeatedly cast a compelling vision for the future, and Merritt Island members' hearts were on board with their dynamic pastor. As we shall see, 1966 saw their hands and feet—and checkbooks—follow their hearts. The best was yet to come.

6

A SPACE AGE CHURCH (1966)

January 1966 ushered in a season of action and transformation. Under Adrian's dynamic preaching and leadership, the 900-plus men, women, boys, and girls attending weekly services strained the campus infrastructure, yet there was no letup in the number of guests visiting *and* joining. Plans for expansion were forthcoming and, all agreed, could not come soon enough. Nevertheless, no amount of spatial inconvenience could dampen the prevailing excitement and momentum. God was on the move.

"A SPACE AGE CHURCH"

On February 2, at a specially-called congregational meeting, Carl Hicks, Long Range Planning Committee Chair, introduced architect O. K. Houstoun to the congregation and presented detailed plans for "Unit 1," a sizeable, two-story "Elementary Building" that would include space for "9 nursery, 6 beginner, 9 primary, and 4 intermediate departments" and up to 800 people. The Committee also unveiled the master campus plan, which, in addition to Unit 1, would include "Unit 2." The second unit would feature an activities building with a full-size gymnasium, bowling alley, snack bar, and large mall area that could accommodate 600 guests for fellowship meals and other gatherings. In addition, the second unit would include a remodeled sanctuary that would bring capacity to nearly 1,350 (which included a 240-seat overflow area) as well as a new pastorium. All told, the plan would cost a projected $1.3 million—a significant sum in 1966. Most in attendance were already aware of the presentation's general details, as Adrian and the Committee had previously shared information with key leaders across the congregation. Not surprisingly, then, after every question was answered with detailed transparency, members unanimously approved the plan.[1] Local newspapers, in articles such as "Merritt Island First Baptist is Space Age Church," described the campus design as "strikingly modernistic in design" and a "striking example of modern architecture."[2]

The winning bid for Unit 1 came in at $260,995, and on May 22 the church voted to borrow $250,000 so that construction could begin right away—Doyle Carlton's senior-executive role at the local bank helped make it possible. Later in the year, members would purchase church-issued bonds that would pay the mortgage. Then, on May 29, ground was broken with the projected completion of Unit 1 on October 31, 1966. That week's edition of *The Thrust* also featured detailed plans for the much-anticipated activities building, from the full-size gymnasium on one end to the renovated sanctuary on the other and everything in between.[3]

As building plans progressed, the press became increasingly interested. *The Daily Times* in a lengthy article entitled "Space Age Church Anchored to the Rock," remarked that "Few churches anywhere have undertaken a program with such a large scope." Throughout the piece, Adrian shared his vision for the facilities that would become core talking points as the buildings and ministries became reality:

> We are in the center of the space capital of the world—where men are trying to go to the heavens—and we want to bring heaven to the hearts of men. Many families come here for a short stay and move on to other parts of the world. If we can touch their lives, then they can

Adrian Rogers, Doyle Carlton, Tom Clayton, Jim Whitmire, Sylvia Leitner, Cecil Houston, Carl Hicks, Mickey Moore, Ethel Johnson, and Kelly Brinson at the groundbreaking for Unit 1 (Elementary Building). Courtesy Joyce Rogers.

> influence others in many other places. ...The biggest waste of money is putting thousands of dollars into a facility which is used only one day a week when an additional 20 percent cost can make the building useable all seven days. ...We will call it the Family Activities Building. We believe that not only should families pray together—they should play together. We need to minister to the whole man—socially and physically as well as spiritually. There is a crying and desperate need for a renewal of family life![4]

Then, emphatically pointing out that the facilities would be only a means to a Gospel-centered end—and giving a nod to the Merritt Island space culture—Adrian spoke boldly about the opportunities at hand and his ardent commitment to pursuing them:

> These buildings are only tools. They must never be ends to themselves. Our buildings are to be "spiritual launching pads." Our desire is to minister to the people of this dynamic area with the all-sufficient message of Jesus. The need is tremendous, the hour is late, and the opportunities are golden![5]

REACHING THE "AVALANCHE OF HUMANITY"

In the March 27 edition of *The Thrust*, Adrian reminded the congregation of the pressing need to reach the "avalanche of humanity" coming to Brevard:

> The hospitals say they will greatly enlarge to care for men's bodies. Will we neglect their souls? The supermarkets are springing up to provide food. Are we making adequate preparation to distribute the Bread of Life? Roads and bridges are being constructed to facilitate travel. Are we ready to teach about Christ, God's Bridge from Sin to Salvation, and the only Road to Heaven? Dear People, will you join me in a venture of faith for Jesus? Let's not let the people of the world show more faith than the people of God![6]

The strategy to reach the masses included revival services led by some of the best preachers of that day. For example, in March, Moody Adams delivered eight nights of dynamic sermons that left their mark on those in attendance and culminated with 66 new additions to the church—55 of which by baptism—and over 1,100 in attendance the following Sunday morning.[7] Nevertheless, in spite of these revival-driven results, Adrian never lost sight of the priority of personal evangelism in the community:

> All the evangelistic crusades in the world will not replace personal evangelism. This is the only form of evangelism that will reach every human being on Merritt Island. ...The purpose of our church is to take the Gospel into every house in town. We are to evangelize this island by going to all the homes![8]

Indeed, intentional visitation and personal evangelism throughout the year, not seasonal revivals, maintained the incredible Merritt Island momentum in those days, and Adrian kept this message before the people as often as possible:

> I am sure you have heard of a master key. Most large buildings have one key that fits every door. It is called the master key. In the building of a church, there are many keys to various activities and ministries, but there is one key to everything. And that key is VISITATION. Visitation is the master key to growth and enrollment and attendance in our Sunday School, Training Union, and worship services. Visitation is the master key to revival and to evangelistic outreach and to successful soul-winning. Dr. Leo Eddleman, President of our Seminary in New Orleans said, "If one-quarter of the members of our church were truly filled with the Holy Spirit, we would not have to announce revival or visitation. They would be out knocking on doors without prospect cards."[9]

With that kind of consistent messaging, the First Baptist Church experienced a robust, outward-focused culture that produced noteworthy, God-blessed results on a regular basis. As Lyvonne Burleson recalls, "It was not unusual to have 10, 15, or 20 individuals responding to the invitation each Sunday in 1966."[10]

June 1966 saw the introduction of a new prayer emphasis on Wednesday nights that flipped the traditional prayer meeting order. The new concept saw the congregation gathered first for 30 minutes of collective Bible study "to warm our hearts and let God speak to us." Attendees then divided into smaller groups that allowed for greater prayer participation as well as a kneeling prayer posture. While promoting the new format, Adrian reminded the congregation of its benefits: "Our praying will not be so stiff and formal—our church can only move forward on its knees." In *The Thrust*, Adrian was quick to point out, "Our people are excited, and many have come with glowing reports of the new method of praying on Wednesday nights."[11]

In late July, the church celebrated Adrian's second anniversary as pastor with some God-sized reports of growth and expansion over the course of 24 months: 1,196 additions, 481 of which by profession of faith and baptism; acquisition of approximately $212,750.00 in additional property; and an annual budget increase from $85,000.00 to $229,000.00.[12]

The THRUST
of the
First Baptist Church
Magnolia at S. Grove Street
Merritt Island, Florida
"The Church where Everybody is Somebody and Jesus Christ is Lord"
Vol. 2 August 21, 1966 No. 34

★ SATAN DEFEATED AGAIN!

- 931 IN SUNDAY SCHOOL!
- GREAT HOSTS PRESENT AT ALL THREE SERVICES.
- 12 ADDITIONS!
- MORE THAN 200 CAME FORWARD TO MAKE SOUL-WINNING COMMITMENT.
- 7 BAPTIZED!
- 253 PRESENT IN TRAINING UNION.
- $4,703.17 OFFERING RECEIVED!

★ REACH NEW HEIGHTS FOR CHRIST
COUNT DOWN CONTINUES —
— "WEEK THREE" AND COUNTING

GOAL THIS SUNDAY — 951

The Thrust declares, "Satan Defeated Again!" as part of the New Heights Campaign. Courtesy Lyvonne Burleson.

On the heels of that glowing report, and without resting on past successes, the church entered its "New Heights Campaign" in August and early September. The campaign featured four Sundays of attendance goals: 901 on August 14; 951 on August 21; 1,001 on August 28; and 1,051 on September 4. In addition, during the week of August 15-19, Adrian hosted morning and evening "Soul-Winning Clinics" to accommodate members' schedules and provide maximum opportunities to receive basic training in sharing their faith. The following week, Adrian then promoted "A Week of Soul-Winning" in the 7 days leading up to the August 28 to September 4 evangelistic crusade led by Paul Meigs, the Secretary of Evangelism of the Florida Baptist Convention. As always, he kept intentional visitation in front of the people: "Your cooperation has been stupendous thus far. The real test is before us. There is no substitute for visitation."[13] Such engagement ultimately led to 1,102 attending services, 54 additions to the church (29 of which for profession of faith), and a bold banner headline in *The Thrust*: "Satan Defeated Again!"

"THE JAI ALAI LIE"

In late September, Adrian used his column in *The Thrust* to highlight the emerging organized gambling issue in Brevard County, specifically parimutuel betting on Jai Alai. The sport, which originated in Western European and Latin American countries, had gained popularity in South Florida in the mid-twentieth century. As promoters sought new markets, Brevard's growth made it an easy target and plans for a $1.5 million Jai Alai fronton in Brevard began to develop. Without hesitation, Adrian put his finger on the issue:

> The Jai Alai Lie is working to brainwash Brevard. Thoughtful citizens must expend great time and effort to protect ourselves from the menace of certain greedy promoters of parimutuel betting. Their approach will be to pretend that any opposition to gambling is by a few religious pressure groups. They would like to shrug the whole thing off as a "religious tempest in a teapot."[14]

Adrian's opposition was on more than religious grounds, pointing out the sociological, economic, and governmental dangers: "Gambling produces nothing and adds nothing to the economy of our nation." In short, he rallied his people with this challenge: "Few counties have so many undeveloped resources as Brevard. Let us develop these. Let these promoters of Jai Alai, who are from out of town, stay out. We don't need or want them!"[15] Ultimately, the following year, the issue would go to a historic county-wide referendum in which Adrian's voice and leadership would play a key role.

"THE KEY WORD IS EVANGELISM"

The new church year began on October 1, and Adrian challenged the congregation to make it all about winning souls for Jesus Christ—it was to be an absolute priority:

> THIS YEAR AS EVER THE KEY WORD IS EVANGELISM. Soul-winning is the nearest and dearest thing to the heart of God. If you are a Sunday School teacher and you are not interested in winning souls, please resign. You have no business teaching for you know nothing about basic New Testament Christianity.[16]

Had he not cultivated a loving and genuine relationship with his people, such blunt-force challenges could have easily driven people away. But, as Joe Boatright recalled, Adrian's "silk and steel" approach was quite effective. The people never doubted his authentic love for them or his zeal for winning souls—his goals were God's goals, and that was good enough for them:

> I want us to set some goals that will be humanly impossible to meet and then meet them in the all-sufficient grace and power of our Lord. When a church is Spirit-filled, it will believe the incredible, seek the invisible, know the unknowable, and do the impossible.[17]

Two weeks later, he reminded the congregation about the evangelism priority: "HAVE YOU FORGOTTEN SO SOON? Many of you have made solemn promises before God about the matter of soul-winning. Beloved, this is the crux of the whole matter—winning the lost to Jesus. Endeavor to bring a lost friend forward this Sunday."[18]

JIM WHITMIRE'S TRANSFORMATION

Adrian's consistent priority on evangelism with a crystal-clear emphasis on assurance of salvation not only spurred conversions among newcomers, it also brought many church members to a new place of salvation and assurance. Nelson Rutledge recalled, "It seemed as though half of the 'church members' got saved and re-baptized. But many of them had never heard preaching like that, and a number of people realized they had never been saved."[19] As a result, many sought to get their baptism "on the right side of their salvation"—most notably, Jim Whitmire.

Jim had made a public profession of his faith at age 10 and was baptized. Then at age 15, he made a commitment to full-time Gospel service while assisting at a Vacation Bible School in Piketon, Ohio. But in the fall of 1966, as Adrian preached with tremendous conviction and clarity on 1 John 5:13—"These things I have written to you who believe in the name of the Son of God, that you may know that you have eternal life"—Jim began to wonder, "Am I truly saved? Lord, am I in this church, working for Adrian Rogers, and not saved?"

> I had left the church to go home, eat, and get dressed for the evening service. It was five o'clock and I was stopped at a red light. I had been repeating [1 John 5:13] over and over, and then said, "Lord, if I've never accepted you as my Lord and Savior, I do it right now." Well, the light was still red, and I didn't feel anything, so I said, "God, if you didn't save me, then you're a liar!" Suddenly, as I drove away from that light, I got the greatest peace. And I realized that when I had called God a liar, I had accepted him at his Word—I had thrown myself on him and his Word.[20]

In the days after, Jim began to wonder, "When was I saved? Was I saved at 10 years old when I walked the aisle and was baptized? Or was I saved at 15 when I surrendered to the ministry? Or was I saved that day at the red light?" As he reflected, he remembered his experience as a

15-year-old boy in Piketon, Ohio. When the pastor extended the invitation for children to be saved, Jim went forward to commit himself to full-time Gospel ministry. But in the process, he had surrendered himself to Jesus as Savior and Lord—"That day, when I left that little mission church, I said, 'Lord, I feel so clean; I always want to feel this clean." Later, going through college and seminary, he had not grown in his faith. "At Merritt Island, I realized that I had been baptized at 10 before I was saved at 15."[21]

So, in October 1966, Jim walked forward during a service and told Adrian he wanted to be baptized. What did the pastor think about baptizing one of his key staff members? "Adrian was thrilled that I would take that step of faith." And once he did, "There was a boldness there that I'd never had. Before that, there was a weakness in my life. I was saved, and I could see God answering my prayers from 15 onward, but once I was baptized [in 1966], that marked a significant change in my life."[22]

Beyond providing clarity about his own salvation and an increased boldness in his faith, Adrian also influenced Jim Whitmire's music ministry. For example, Adrian was known to say, "It's alright to have an anthem every once in a while, but we need to sing, 'What a wonderful change in my life has been wrought, since Jesus came into my heart.'"[23] Yet, when Adrian came to Merritt Island, the music often included an air of formality, as an episode in December 1965 illustrates. During the Sunday evening performance of a Bach Christmas cantata, Jim had the choir proceed into the service down the center aisle, holding candles, and singing in Latin—to which Adrian responded less than enthusiastically. The next day, Adrian gave some brief instruction to Jim along the lines of, "Don't ever do that again." While Jim acknowledged the admonition, he could not help but poke back just a bit in *The Thrust* the following weekend by including a small piece of clip art featuring a man asking an annoyed Johann Sebastian Bach to play "something folks can whistle while they work"—and he added the initials "JW" over Bach and "AR" over the other man. As the years went by, Adrian and Jim could laugh together about the incident, but the truth was that both men evolved over time as they found common ground in making much of Jesus Christ through a variety of musical means and genres.[24]

Adrian's priority on preaching and speaking to the human heart with a healthy emphasis on experiencing God's glory shaped every Merritt Island ministry, including the music. Overall, Adrian's impact on Jim's life, as with many other aspects of the Merritt Island years, demonstrated that affecting change best occurs through facilitating transformation in the lives of those in leadership.

Jim Whitmire had a little fun with Adrian in the December 19, 1965 edition of *The Thrust*. Courtesy Jim Whitmire.

PAYING FOR THE SPACE AGE CHURCH

Just as sending man to the moon required astronomical funding, building a space-age church likewise called for the commitment of significant resources. As we have already seen, the projected cost of all new buildings was upwards of $1.3 million. In order to secure those funds, the church borrowed the money with the intent to pay off the loan through a church-wide bond program. Such a strategy required the church to amend its charter, which included a "limit of indebtedness" that the building program would significantly surpass.[25]

After the church approved such an amendment, a brochure appeared that outlined the bond program: "Invest Now in the Future." Nelson Rutledge led the campaign steering committee, and members were encouraged to purchase bonds in denominations of $100, $250, $500, $1,000, $2,000, $5,000, or $10,000. For those members who did not have immediate cash to purchase bonds, arrangements were made with the First National Bank of Merritt Island for members to borrow funds equal to the bond purchase at the same six percent rate of return.[26]

The bond program kicked off during "Victory Week," November 13-20. The church was divided into two divisions with 100 teams each, every church family was assigned to a team, and each team was asked to buy for themselves (or sell to others) $4,000 in bonds. Three nightly bond rallies marked the week's events. Adrian spurred the congregation:

> The First Baptist Church is at the crossroads. We will embark on a spiritual quest for souls without parallel in this area and in few places in the world. Victory Week will require our best. Prayer is the key. Without God's help, we cannot succeed. With His help, we cannot fail.[27]

As a result of his leadership, Victory Week was indeed victorious, as *The Thrust* announced on November 27: "WOW!!!! $906,400.00 in Bonds Sold in One Week!" As a result, Adrian highlighted the multiple wins from the program: "The bond program has been one of the more wonderful things that have come to our church. We have gained a new sense of unity by working together, souls have been saved as a result of our witness during the program, the church is being provided money to build needed buildings, and God's people are being blessed spiritually by investing in God's work."[28]

The bond program launch gave increased momentum to the already progressing construction of Unit 1, the two-story Elementary Building. Originally scheduled for completion by October 1, contractors experienced delays that meant the building would not be ready until early 1967. In spite of the delays, members eagerly anticipated the opening of this first phase of their space-age campus. A story in the local newspaper titled, "Here We Grow Again," asked the question that everyone in the community was asking: "How much bigger can one church get?" Answering its own question, the article stated, "The First Baptist Church of Merritt Island is going all out" and featured a picture of Adrian and Carl Hicks standing before the half-completed Elementary Building.[29]

With all the talk of buildings and bonds, Adrian never lost focus on the main point behind it all, and he used his column in *The Thrust* to reinforce his priorities for the church:

> Budget, Building, Bonds and so forth are all necessary and good, but all of these need to be subservient to prayer, praise, and soul-winning. The thing that makes and will make our church distinctive is not fine buildings and a well-oiled program. Other churches have these.

"Here We Grow Again." Adrian and Carl Hicks, Building Committee Chairman, at the Unit 1 (Elementary Building) site. Courtesy Joyce Rogers.

> The crying need in America is for churches that love Jesus and love the lost. ...DO YOU HAVE A SACRIFICIAL LOVE FOR SOULS? There is no cheap, easy, or lazy way to witness. If you are a teacher in our Sunday School and you are not concerned about the lost, you need to resign. It makes no difference how much of the Bible you know—you have a deadening influence on your class. ...There is no substitute for prayer, evangelism, Bible study, and the power of the Holy Spirit. These are our priorities. They must always be so![30]

BOLDNESS AT THE FLORIDA BAPTIST CONVENTION

During the Merritt Island years, Adrian always devoted his absolute best energies to his calling as pastor, but his concern for Southern Baptist allegiance to the Bible as the inerrant, infallible Word of God was never far from his mind. His experience at Stetson University had left a negative impression on his heart, specifically regarding what he considered a fraudulent use of Baptist dollars by a school that did not represent the conservative theological beliefs held by the churches that supported it. As a Florida Baptist, he was grieved to know that funds from his church went to an institution that had increasingly abandoned its ties to the pristine Word of God.

Stetson's share of the $3.3 million 1966-1967 Florida Baptist State Convention (FBSC) annual budget was $149,820, or 4.54 percent, whereas the previous year's budget allocated $269,700, or 8.7 percent for the school.[31] Although the decrease was noted, as far as Adrian was concerned, any amount sent to Stetson by Florida Baptists was too much. So he traveled to the FBSC annual meeting November 8-10 at the First Baptist Church of Pensacola with plans to address the issue with the messengers in attendance.

At the Tuesday evening session, the Stetson University Glee Club presented music, then Professor Clark H. Pinnock of the New Orleans Baptist Theological Seminary delivered a message to the Convention from

2 Corinthians 4:3 about "the sure hope which the Christian has to offer the world because of the resurrected Christ."[32] Before Adrian shared his own motion regarding Stetson's funding, another motion appeared regarding the school. It mandated that "any institution or agency of the Florida Baptist State Convention, including Stetson University, which receives federal grants shall immediately cease receiving Cooperative Program funds."[33] The previous year, Stetson had received some $844,000 in Federal dollars for the construction of a new science building. That motion passed, 517 in favor and 358 against. Then, Adrian stepped to the microphone and made his motion to altogether "delete allocation granting Stetson University 4.54 percent in the 1966-1967 budget." After "much discussion" and "heated debate," Adrian's motion was defeated with 60 percent of messengers against and 40 percent of messengers in favor.[34] Although unsuccessful, the motion further galvanized conservative resolve among Florida Baptists and identified Adrian as a leading voice among them.

While many others clearly agreed with Adrian's sentiments, no one had previously advanced such a bold and sweeping motion. He received strong verbal support from, among others, Homer Lindsey, Jr., pastor of Northwest Baptist Church of Miami. However, at least a dozen other speakers—most of whom were Stetson graduates—vocally opposed his motion. After the meeting, one state leader told Adrian that if he did not learn to compromise, he would ultimately go down "unwept, unsung, and unhonored."[35] Steve Rogers described this episode by saying, "To call out Stetson by name was practically heresy in Florida at that time. But from the very beginning, my dad was never afraid to sit tall in the saddle and take slings and arrows."[36]

One Convention attendee took time personally to encourage Adrian and affirm his strong stand for God's Word. In a letter from New Orleans dated December 13, Clark Pinnock wrote these uplifting words:

> I recall with joy the clarity of your resolution on the floor of the Convention and the firmness of your stand for conservative theology. I want you to know that in my view we need in every state and

> association men of precisely your convictions and ability to state them articulately. The evangelical cause is so often discredited by spokesmen who have not done their homework, and who are shown to be ignorant by scholastic liberals. Our position is more rational, historic, and Biblical than theirs. We must commend it authoritatively and intelligently to men. ...Keep up your strong testimony.[37]

Adrian's boldness certainly foreshadowed days of national leadership when God would use him at a strategic level to point the entire Southern Baptist Convention back to its Biblical roots.

CHRISTMAS MUSIC AND CHRISTMAS BELLS

With the approaching 1966 Christmas season, Jim Whitmire led the full scope of the First Baptist Church music enterprise to worship the newborn King, capping off a year in which the Adult Choir alone presented over 300 pieces of music at church services, revivals, and other gatherings. First, he led the Senior High Choir on a mini-tour to Jacksonville on December 10 and 11. Then, the Children's Choirs presented Christmas songs on Wednesday, December 14. On December 16, the Adult Choir enjoyed its Christmas Banquet two days before partnering with the Adult Handbell Choir to present "The Glory of Christmas" in lieu of Sunday night services. Then, on Wednesday, December 21, the Junior and Handbell Choirs performed "Lo, A Star" for the congregation. Finally, on December 25, the Senior High and Adult Choirs combined to present "An Evening Service of Carols." In addition, both "stereo and hi-fi" records of the Adult and Handbell Choir's recording of "The Glory of Christmas" became available for purchase, which was the second record produced by the Adult Choir under Jim Whitmire's leadership at Merritt Island.[38]

The 1966 Christmas season was especially meaningful for First Baptist Church musicians as a full 37-piece set of new handbells arrived as a result of generous gifts, large and small, from across the congregation.[39] In the years to come, as his pool of musicians dramatically increased, Jim would maximize these instruments for God's glory in amazing ways.

"AND NOW APOLLO"

The space program reached an important milestone in late 1966 when the two-man crew of Gemini 12 splashed down in the Atlantic Ocean on November 15, thus completing all scheduled missions of the program meant to bridge the gap between Mercury and Apollo. Over the course of the ten manned Gemini flights, astronauts rendezvoused between two capsules or target vehicles ten times, docked nine times, and set several endurance records. The entire Gemini program had been a resounding success as it tested multiple maneuvers and items of equipment that would make the Apollo missions possible.

With the conclusion of Gemini, optimism was at an all-time high. NASA was well ahead of its Russian counterpart program, and executives and engineers alike believed reaching the moon in keeping with President Kennedy's mandate was very likely. In fact, Time magazine, in a buoyant article entitled "And Now Apollo," forecasted that "U.S. astronauts can now turn their full attention to Apollo, which will make its first three-man orbital flight during the first quarter of 1967 and may carry U.S. astronauts to the moon as early as 1968."[40] But no one anticipated the tragedy that awaited just around the corner.

7

LAUNCHPAD TRAGEDY AND GOSPEL MOMENTUM (1967)

If NASA could optimistically enter 1967, First Baptist Church members had a similar reason for positivity. Adrian forecasted in *The Thrust* on January 1: "OUR GREATEST YEAR IS AHEAD. 1967—I can hardly wait! We will move into our lovely Children's Building. We will break ground on our fabulous Family Activities Building and remodel our auditorium. If this doesn't excite you, you must have callouses on your soul!"[1] The church had every reason to anticipate the completion of these buildings, as consistent growth strained available space: "Have patience! You have been so good as you have been pushed from pillar to post. We have been trying to [gather] 1,000 people in space designed for 400. Our crowded condition will be cured with the opening of our beautiful new building."[2]

POWERFUL PREACHING

January featured powerful preaching, both at the annual Florida Baptist Evangelistic Conference in Orlando and also in revival services on Merritt

Island. In Orlando, in his first appearance at the state-level conference, Adrian delivered an inspiring, soul-winning challenge to pastors and laity alike. On Merritt Island, nationally recognized evangelist Eddie Martin conducted a week of preaching services that electrified the congregation.

The Evangelistic Conference, held January 10-12 at First Baptist Church of Orlando and billed unofficially as a "preachers revival," saw over 2,000 attendees from across Florida. According to the *Florida Baptist Witness*, it was "the largest attendance ever witnessed at the conference."[3] Keynote speaker, W. A. Criswell, from the First Baptist Church of Dallas, Texas, brought several messages, to include "The Moral Life of the Man of God" and "The Word of God for Today's World."[4]

Adrian, an "up-and-coming" voice among Florida Baptists, delivered an energetic message entitled, "The Church—A Task Force for Evangelism." The bold sermon from Acts 5:42 reminded listeners that Christians have "the greatest mission—evangelism; the greatest message—the Gospel; the greatest Master—Jesus; and the greatest motive—the 'love of Christ constraineth us.'" Furthermore, Adrian exhorted listeners regarding the power to witness: "Your witnessing is in vain without the power of the Holy Spirit...Do you want the power of the Holy Spirit in your life? I want that power in my life—and I would rather die than preach without the power of God in my life." He likewise pointed out that "evangelism in the New Testament was not [primarily] an eight-day meeting where some high-powered evangelist came in." On the contrary, "In the New Testament, they reached souls through a day-in, day-out effort—they never ceased witnessing for the Lord Jesus Christ."[5]

State leaders offered enthusiastic affirmation, both publicly and privately. W. G. Stracener, *Florida Baptist Witness* Editor, remarked in his January 26 conference recap, "How encouraged we were for the future of our work by the scripturally rich, intelligently prepared, enthusiastically delivered, Holy Spirit implanted message by Adrian P. Rogers. No more effective single message was delivered at the conference, and we are grateful to this young pastor for it."[6] By way of private correspondence, Paul Meigs, Florida Baptist Secretary of Evangelism, wrote, "Words are inadequate to tell you how much I appreciate the wonderful message that you brought.... Yours was one of the greatest messages [on the topic of evangelism] in the last ten years."[7] Similarly, John Maguire, Florida Baptist Convention Executive Secretary-Treasurer, wrote to thank Adrian for his noteworthy sermon. Additionally, Maguire offered this encouragement: "Adrian, I do not know a man anywhere within the bounds of the Southern Baptist Convention who has a greater opportunity and is making more use of that opportunity than you, and how I do rejoice at every victory won there for our Lord and Savior."[8]

In addition to preaching at the Evangelistic Conference, Adrian rallied his congregation to prepare for Eddie Martin's revival services at First Baptist Church scheduled for January 22-29. In his January 8 "Pastor's Paragraphs" column, Adrian directed hearts and minds toward spiritual preparation:

> The key to revival, the key to salvation of multitudes, the key to another Pentecost is in the hands of God's people. The greatest need of our churches today is burdened, broken-hearted Christians. It is not great preachers. It is not advertising. It is not singing. The need in our churches is ceaseless, day and night, earnest, weeping prayer for a great sin-convicting, soul-moving revival![9]

Beyond a challenge for humble, fervent prayer, Adrian also laid down a pointed challenge concerning the upcoming services:

> WE ARE PRAYING FOR 100 SOULS. That's right—100 precious people for Christ is our goal. I'm asking every deacon, teacher, staff member, secretary, and mission pastor to lead at least one soul to Christ during the Crusade. Many have already promised. Don't fail![10]

This all-out emphasis on evangelism was wholly in keeping with Eddie Martin's heartbeat. Known as "the Soul-Winning Evangelist," Eddie Martin embodied the same style of evangelism that Adrian embraced. Personally, he challenged himself to share the Gospel with three people each day of his life. In addition, as part of every week of revival services he conducted, Eddie insisted that the pastor of the host church accompany him on house-to-house evangelism in the afternoons prior to the evening services. To no one's surprise, Adrian was happy to participate and to lead many First Baptist Church members to do likewise.[11] As prayed for, the week of services saw over 100 men, women, boys, and girls make professions of faith in Jesus. Adrian took time to celebrate God's goodness accordingly: "The flood gates of blessing have opened, and Eddie Martin has forcefully, faithfully, and frankly preached the Word—and the music was enough to make heaven's angels envious."[12]

"FIRE IN THE COCKPIT!"

Sadly, the victories of the Eddie Martin crusade overlapped with a tragedy that rocked America's Moon Port and sharply tempered the optimism with which NASA began the new year. Stepping into 1967, space program executives had every reason to believe the best was yet to come. In addition to the successful completion of Project Gemini and the subsequent shift to Apollo, going into 1967 NASA also enjoyed Congressional funding totaling nearly five percent of the entire federal budget. That level of mind-boggling resources not only allowed for the development of the most sophisticated technology the world had ever seen, but it also tangibly demonstrated political and public support for the goal of reaching the moon by decade's end. But that was before America lost three of its best and brightest on Cape Kennedy's launch pad. That was before the fire.

Friday, January 27 saw one of the many dress rehearsals for the long anticipated Apollo 1 mission set for February 21. This rehearsal, known as a "plugs out" test, assessed the spacecraft's ability to operate exclusively on internal power. Situated on Pad 34 at Cape Kennedy, a 225-foot tall Saturn 1B launch vehicle topped by an Apollo command module awaited the astronauts. At approximately 1:00 PM, Gus Grissom, Ed White, and

Roger Chaffee entered the capsule wearing their entire space suits with all life-support connections functioning. As part of the test, the capsule interior replicated real-world conditions to the greatest possible degree—to include filling the capsule with 100-percent pure oxygen at 16.7 pounds per square inch of pressure and completely sealing the three-layered hatch.[13]

Apollo 1 astronauts Gus Grissom, Ed White, and Roger Chaffee, killed in a launchpad fire on January 27, 1967. Courtesy NASA.

Throughout the afternoon, the test dragged on as communication equipment failed to function properly. At 6:20 PM, controllers paused the test in order to address additional issues. Then, suddenly, at 6:31 PM, controllers heard Gus Grissom exclaim—"Flame!"—followed by Roger Chaffee—"Fire in the cockpit!"—and then Chaffee again—"We're on fire! Get us out of here!" Then, less than 15 seconds from the first call of "fire," the capsule ruptured from overpressure, and flame burst from the previously-sealed hatch. Technicians outside the capsule were knocked to their feet as smoke and blast filled the room adjacent to the capsule. Several minutes later, at the first possible opportunity, workers pried open the hatch and peered into the capsule's incinerated interior. To no one's surprise, all three astronauts were dead, primarily asphyxiated by poisonous smoke and secondarily burned by the pure oxygen-fueled fire. The astronauts died quickly, only seconds after recognizing the threat. What began with a spark in the capsule's lower equipment bay quickly led to the first fatalities in an otherwise successful space program.[14]

Beyond the obvious need to investigate the tragedy, NASA, the federal government, and the entire Nation asked, "What's next?" The February 21 launch was postponed indefinitely. But what of Apollo? And, for that matter, the entire space program? While some wondered out loud if the race to the moon should go on, Congressman George P. Miller, Chairman of the House Science and Astronautics Committee, voiced the majority opinion: "This is a tragedy; nevertheless, it is one of the hazards that take place. Remember, every new aircraft has cost the lives of test pilots, and the pilots know it. I am certain that if Grissom, White, and Chaffee could come back, they would be the first to urge that the program go on." In fact, Gus Grissom expressed the same sentiment not long before the Apollo 1 fire: "If we die, we want people to accept it. We are in a risky business, and we hope that if anything happens to us it will not delay the program. The conquest of space is worth the risk of life."[15]

THE SAINTS GO MARCHING IN AND MARCHING ON

March and April marked two key milestones in the master plan for reaching Brevard County for Jesus: the occupation of Unit 1 on March 19 and the groundbreaking for Unit 2 on April 30 with concurrent dedication of Unit 1 on the same day. Both events demonstrated just how committed pastor and people were to the strategic vision set before them. Moreover, these events brought First Baptist Church closer to maximizing its unique and historic ministry opportunity.

March 19 was "Growth Day" as hundreds of children and their teachers began utilizing the newly-finished Children's Building, and a total of ten new Sunday School departments were created. *The Thrust* trumpeted the event as "MOVING DAY!" for nurseries, beginners, primaries, and intermediates. Adrian announced the long-anticipated relocation of classes by offering this observation and challenge: "It looks like the saints will 'go marching in' as we move into our beautiful new building....Yet space without the Spirit is not enough. Oh that we might pray for Him to fill the house with His blessed presence this Sunday!"[16]

Then, at a church business meeting on Wednesday, March 29, members voted to award the construction contract for Unit 2 at a projected cost of $655,396. This unit would feature numerous buildings and improvements, including 15 Sunday School departments, a four-lane bowling alley and snack bar, a gymnasium, and additional space for skating, ceramics, weight lifting, a sauna, game room, library, music suite, commercial kitchen, and dining for upward of 600 people. Additionally, a sanctuary remodeling would include an overflow area allowing for seating up to 1,350 people in total.[17]

Finally, on Sunday, April 30 at 10:45 AM, members gathered between the Sunday School hour and 11:00 AM service to dedicate the Children's Building and break ground for the Family Activities Building. In addition to a building dedication and ground-breaking, April witnessed an average of 463 evangelistic contacts per week, a Sunday School enrollment of 2,262, an average attendance of 1,038 per Sunday, and a new attendance record of 1,184 on April 19.[18] The saints, indeed, were marching on.

THE JAI-ALAI LIE, REVISITED

In April and May, the Jai Alai issue came around once again as a county-wide referendum on the matter approached. At issue was the construction of a $1.5 million Jai Alai fronton north of Eau Gallie which would be, according to Adrian, one of the few places in the world where "the windows clean the people."[19] Proponents and opponents voiced their views across Brevard ahead of the May 2 vote. In no uncertain terms, Adrian steeled the congregation for the days ahead:

> OUR CHURCH TO GO TO WAR! The battle is on. The gambling crowd is planning to bring legalized gambling into Brevard County. We will resist with all our might. ...There are people in our community who absolutely despise Christians for the stand they have taken. Then there are others who love us. In fact, if you mention the name Adrian Rogers or the First Baptist Church of Merritt Island, either duck or pucker because they'll kiss you or hit you. And I think, in a sense, that's the way it ought to be—the line ought to be drawn.[20]

In addition to exhorting the congregation, Adrian addressed the issue in the community as well. On April 19, at the Wednesday meeting of the Cocoa Beach Noon Rotary Club, he participated in a debate with Martin Segal of the Florida Racing Commission. Segal told attendees that fronton betting would be tightly controlled by its internal police force and by the state racing commission and that Jai Alai would increase county tax revenue. Moreover, he argued that legalized gambling would not bring "undesirables" into Brevard. In response, Adrian argued that money lost through gambling was far greater than anything gained—and that "the fronton people see only the money coming in and are not interested in the unfortunate people that fall prey to the problems directly linked to gambling."[21] Adrian, described by the press as the opposition's "most eloquent spokesman," also took to the airwaves on several local radio talk shows where he, according to the *Today* newspaper, "verbally slugged it out with Segal."[22]

On April 30, the Sunday immediately before the vote, Adrian brought a message entitled, "The World's Most Dangerous Game"—a verbal play on the Jai Alai promoters' label for their sport. While the broader message described the battle with sin in the heart, he shared in the sermon's introduction some thoughts about the pending vote. First, he encouraged the people to "stand tall, stand true, be courageous, do not be cowardly." Then, he wisely framed the issue in the broader conviction of Gospel compassion and priority:

> Remember, it is sin and not men that we are fighting. Remember that every person who is for Jai Alai and every person who is for gambling is a precious soul in the sight of our Savior. So while we take our stand and while we are courageous, at the same time we must be compassionate. We must not be bitter. If they win this election, we must not hate. If we win, we must not sneer and rub it in. My dear friend, the main thing is not to fight Jai Alai but to win men, women, boys, and girls to the Lord Jesus Christ.[23]

On the night of May 2, Adrian, Doyle Carlton, and a handful of other Brevard leaders opposed to the Jai Alai venue gathered for dinner and to await the results. Early the next morning, the news could announce, "Jai Alai Loses by a Whisker." In fact, of the 31,727 votes cast, 15,911 "no" ballots carried the night by only 95 votes—less than one-hundredth of a percentage point. In light of the tight race, Adrian noted, "If we had the same finances the pro forces had, it would not even have been close."[24] The degree of outcome notwithstanding, legalized gambling and the human fallout that would naturally follow had been blocked in Brevard.

OH COME, LET US SING TO THE LORD

As Summer approached, so too did the annual Senior High Choir Tour. As Jim Whitmire developed the Merritt Island music ministry, this tour became one of the highlights of the year for students and director alike. Scheduled for June 16-25, the 1967 tour included performances in Louisiana, Tennessee, Alabama, Georgia; and Florida.[25] These tours, as well as the entire scope of Jim Whitmire's ministry among students, transcended the music itself:

> At Merritt Island, I discovered that I genuinely loved working with young people. And I began loving the tours. I wanted the concerts to be incredible, but what was going on behind the scenes with the young people was really more important even than the concerts we did.[26]

First Baptist Church combined choirs in 1967. Note the sanctuary configuration as compared to the 1968 renovations (see page 138). Courtesy Joyce Rogers.

Jim's philosophy naturally generated influence and followership, and for years to come the students never forgot his impact. Angela Hunt remembered:

> I was a teenager during those years, and I have hundreds of memories from Merritt Island—most of which are affiliated in some way with Jim Whitmire and the music program. We didn't have a youth pastor in those days, but we had Jim Whitmire, and he functioned as a pastor in practically every area of our lives.[27]

Not surprisingly, as Steve Rogers recalled, "People who were younger at First Baptist Church in those days are just as fiercely loyal to Jim Whitmire today as they are to Adrian Rogers."[28]

Beyond the student choir, the Merritt Island music ministry continued to grow exponentially. Choirs for adults, students, and children, as well as handbells—the list went on and on. One key layman remembered, "Jim Whitmire was the greatest minister of music I've ever seen, and he doesn't always get the credit he deserves for the Merritt Island successes."[29]

NELSON RUTLEDGE

As First Baptist Church eagerly anticipated the completion of its Family Activities Building, Adrian called a man to provide key and dynamic leadership over the many ministries it would support. The candidate, Nelson Rutledge, needed no introduction to the congregation, as he had played an integral role in the church as Sunday School Teacher, Deacon, and Committee Chair since joining in 1963. Nelson had also accompanied Adrian when he took a team to see the activities facility at Pompano Beach in late 1964. In fact, God used that trip to spark an interest in his heart for a Gospel-centered activities ministry. Subsequently, Adrian mentored Nelson through the prayerful process of transitioning from his job with General Electric at the Cape to full-time Gospel service at First Baptist Church.[30]

When Nelson began his ministry as part of the church staff on August 7, Adrian welcomed him enthusiastically:

> God has been so good in sending us Nelson and Flo Rutledge and their lovely family. Nelson is a grand addition to our staff. I believe he has a rare mixture of qualities that will make him the most effective Minister of Christian Activities in our Convention. Nelson Rutledge is first of all a Christian. He's a businessman, he's an athlete, he's a soul-

> winner and a Bible scholar. We're grateful to our Heavenly Father for His goodness in supplying our needs in this realm.[31]

As time would reveal, not only would Nelson Rutledge provide outstanding leadership over the Family Activities Building, but he would also be a key witness in the lives of many at Merritt Island and Brevard County.

MATERIAL MODESTY AND GOSPEL MINISTRY

Throughout their marriage, Adrian and Joyce displayed a material modesty that prevented personal and public distractions from their Gospel ministry, and the Merritt Island years included numerous examples.

For instance, the construction of a new pastorium illustrated this humble conviction. When the Rogers family arrived in 1964, the church pastorium at 975 North Tropical Trail left much to be desired. During construction of the new home, Adrian diplomatically described the need: "How grateful we are that a new pastorium is being built....A pastor's home is more than a house. It will contain facilities for entertaining [as] we have longed to do but have not been able."[32] Steve Rogers, looking back, was more pointed in his assessment: "We had a small house in Fort Pierce, but it was newer. It had three small bedrooms, one bath, a small Florida room, and a carport. I liked that house. Then we moved to Merritt Island, and the pastorium was terrible."[33] As part of the campus expansion and bond program, church leaders agreed that the Rogers needed a new home. As a result, Doyle Carlton donated land adjacent to his property, and the architect responsible for the campus expansion also drafted plans for a new pastorium to be financed as part of the bond program. When the builder presented a cost of $60,000 for the home as designed, Joyce insisted to Gene Baird, Pastorium Committee Chairman, that the plans be modified because "we are not going to live in a house that costs more than $50,000." Steve Rogers recalled, "My parents did not want to be seen as above the people."[34] The final product was a very comfortable pastorium at 465 Melody Lane that featured a unique atrium in the center of the home. To mark his fourth anniversary as pastor, the Rogers hosted an open house for the congregation on August 14, and Adrian thanked the congregation shortly thereafter: "The pastorium 'open house' was just marvelous. You have been so kind and thoughtful. The house is beyond description and is far more than we could ever deserve!"[35]

Another example of Adrian's material modesty came when the church renovated the front half of the Jobe building for office space. As the men of the church designed and conducted modifications, they wanted to install wall-to-wall carpet. But as Jim Whitmire remembered, "Adrian didn't want it in his office or in our offices. He said, 'I just can't spend the people's tithe on that.'" So the men went and worked out the numbers, then came back to Adrian and pointed out that a tile floor required additional upkeep and costs and that wall-to-wall carpet was cheaper over time. Once he saw that, Adrian agreed to carpeting the offices. Again, Jim Whitmire commented on Adrian's outlook: "With Adrian, there was always an integrity in the finances, so that when you gave your money, you knew it was going toward the Gospel ministry of the church. He wanted to be so far above board when it came to finances."[36]

Adrian applied the same principle of material modesty to the car that he drove. When he came to Merritt Island, he owned a 1960 Volkswagen—nothing fancy, just a dependable vehicle. But after several years as pastor, as Steve Rogers recalled, "Doyle Carlton got tired of seeing my dad drive that Volkswagen, so he offered to buy him a new car."[37] Adrian described the conversation this way:

> One time, Doyle Carlton, who became one of my best friends in the whole world, said, "Pastor, I want to buy you a brand-new car." And I didn't argue with him. So he bought me an Oldsmobile. And I said to him, "Doyle, I really appreciate this. But I don't receive it from you; I receive it from the Lord *through* you. But I want to tell you something

before I take the keys to this car. First of all, if I ever find you in any kind of sin, I'll preach to you. And furthermore, if God ever calls me away from this church, I'm taking this car with me!"[38]

Official Pastoral Picture, 1967. Courtesy Joyce Rogers.

The truth was that Adrian always defaulted to a modest vehicle. At Merritt Island, he agreed to drive an Oldsmobile, rather than a more expensive car that he could have easily driven. In later years, he would still choose a Ford or Mercury over a Lincoln or Cadillac. That was who he was—materially modest—"ostentation was not where he was."[39]

ANIS SHORROSH COMES TO MERRITT ISLAND

In late August and early September, Jordanian evangelist Anis Shorrosh led a week of dynamic revival services at First Baptist Church. Born in Nazareth and raised in Jordan, his father was killed when he was a small boy, leaving his family "practically penniless." In spite of meager opportunities as a teenager, God nevertheless provided a job at the Baptist Hospital in Ajloun, Jordan. Additional opportunities came when he moved to the United States and attended Mississippi College and ultimately New Orleans Baptist Theological Seminary. Having completed his theological education, Anis returned to the Middle East with his wife and small children to lead a church in Jordan from 1959 to 1966.[40]

From August 27 to September 3, Anis challenged the First Baptist Church to follow Jesus unconditionally. In addition, given that the "Six Day War" between Israel and its Arab neighbors had taken place only three months earlier, he provided the congregation with keen insights into events in the Middle East. His reflections on the swift and smashing Israeli victory in light of eschatological prophecies were warmly received.[41]

In the days following the revival services, Adrian celebrated God's goodness: "We can only praise God! Since revival comes from His gracious hand, then to Him alone must our thanks be given. Only eternity will reveal all that was done through His servant, Anis Shorrosh. We have had other meetings when we have had more additions, but never greater blessings."[42] Pastor and people alike looked forward to having Anis visit once again. In fact, less one year later, he would return for a multi-week stay.

DIALOGUE CAPE KENNEDY

On numerous occasions, Adrian demonstrated a willingness to step outside Southern Baptist lines in order to embrace fellow inerrantists and promote trans-denominational evangelism. In early September, collaboration of this sort with good friend Peter Lord, Jess Moody, Pastor of First Baptist Church of West Palm Beach, and Ed French, Pastor of Haverhill Baptist Church of West Palm Beach resulted in a two-day conference in Cocoa Beach named "Dialogue Cape Kennedy." The theme was "a study of the new evangelical ecumenical movement," with a focus on uniting Christians for the purpose of evangelism without forming new structures and denominational groups. Unlike previous ecumenical movements that blurred denominational lines and often promoted Protestant liberalism, Dialogue Cape Kennedy proposed a "mutual pooling of our resources for worldwide evangelism."[43]

Keynote speakers rallied more than 100 attendees to join forces in sharing Jesus across America. Sherwood Wirt, Editor of Billy Graham's *Decision* magazine and a Presbyterian, highlighted "the crying need" for a Billy Graham type of ecumenical evangelistic cooperation across America: "Mr. Graham is able to reach only three or four major cities a year. The nation can never be changed at that rate."[44] Jess Moody presented a comprehensive, multi-year plan whereby 100,000 evangelical churches, regardless of denomination, would ultimately participate in a month-long, nationwide evangelistic crusade at a time yet to be determined either in 1972 or 1973. During the month-long emphasis, Moody called for one million prayer meetings per day, with each church hosting ten each. With so many churches on board, organizers would set a goal of winning one million people to Christ during the month-long crusade.[45]

Baptist organizers thought it critical to stress that evangelistic cooperation would not dilute Baptist distinctives or identity. Professor Kenneth L. Chafin of the Southern Baptist Theological Seminary agreed that "Southern Baptists are intensely interested in working with other groups to do evangelism," but warned that Baptists would not favor "evangelical ecumenicity on an organized, structured basis." In response, Ed French reminded attendees that Dialogue Cape Kennedy "was an informally created meeting that elected no officers, formed no groups, and only sought the Spirit's leadership"—but also that "history won't forget Dialogue Cape Kennedy."[46]

FALL 1967: GROWTH, UNITY, AND INFLUENCE

As Summer gave way to Fall, momentum continued to build at First Baptist Church. On Sunday, October 15, over 1,200 packed the campus—a new attendance record—"with no push, no drive" or special emphasis otherwise:

> POWER, BLESSING, JOY!!! How marvelous were the services Sunday. There is nothing sweeter than being a member of a church when the glory is on it. Prayers are answered, tears flow, and fellowship flourishes. Thank you, Jesus, thank you so much![47]

With construction on the Family Activities Building well underway and sanctuary renovations commencing in early November, the congregation began meeting for Sunday services in the newly-constructed gymnasium on November 12. The congregation previously met on Sunday mornings across two services, 8:00 AM and 11:00 AM. But for nearly six months, until sanctuary renovations were complete, the church family met in the gym for one consolidated service at 11:00 AM. In spite of these changes, momentum continued unabated. In fact, on November 19, First Baptist Church once again experienced record Sunday morning attendance with 1,215 on campus.[48]

The new gymnasium not only provided temporary space for worship, but it also facilitated a heightened sense of unity as the entire congregation gathered for one service each week. In the midst of amazing growth, numerous members recalled that these services brought the church together in a way that no other program could. Gene and Norma Baird even mentioned this season as one of the most memorable in the history of First Baptist Church.[49]

Meanwhile, Adrian's influence among Florida Baptists continued to increase. When pastors from across the state met on November 13 at the First Baptist Church of Sarasota for the 1967 Florida Baptist Convention Pastor's Conference, they elected Adrian Vice President. Then, at the Convention's

Annual Meeting held the same week, President Edgar R. Cooper appointed Adrian, among others, to the Committee on Nominations.[50] While his priority always remained the pastorate, numerous leaders clearly saw Adrian as a rising influencer among Florida Baptists.

Over 1,000 worshippers packed the gymnasium each week from November 1967 to April 1968 as the sanctuary underwent renovations. Courtesy Joyce Rogers.

FAMILIES IN DESPERATE NEED OF THE GOSPEL

In the 1960s, in spite of numerous advantages, Brevard families often struggled to thrive. On the one hand, levels of education and income frequently exceeded state and national norms. In Brevard, nearly one-fourth of all residents possessed a college degree, which was six times the national average. Moreover, the Florida Development Commission's promotional video entitled "Florida: Moon Port USA" claimed that

Brevard enjoyed a higher concentration of PhDs than anywhere else in the United States. Financially, engineers and their families enjoyed salaries "from $8,000 to the moon, with most families owning a boat and at least two cars."[51]

However, all was not well among Brevard families. Divorce rates were more than double the national average while out-of-wedlock births occurred at almost five times the national rate. Plagued by what local counselors described as "the engineer syndrome," families often endured hectic schedules where a husband and father worked 14-hour days and lived by the mantra, "Oversmoke, overeat, overdrink, overworry, and undersleep."[52] One psychiatrist noted, "These are perfectionist males who are usually intolerant of the feelings of those around them." In addition, the allures of Cocoa Beach nightlife—or, what Adrian frequently called "Sodom on the Banana" [River]—sometimes made it difficult for stressed-out missile men to differentiate between their wives and the large pool of single girls and divorcees drawn to NASA's secretarial ranks. Indeed, infidelity trends far outpaced other areas in Florida and beyond. On top of that, the transient nature of engineer and contractor life prevented most from developing meaningful relationships: nearly twenty percent of Brevard residents had been there less than one year, and less than five percent expected to stay more than five years.[53]

Given these numerous challenges, Adrian frequently reminded the congregation that Brevard families desperately needed the Gospel. And as 1967 came to a close, he repeatedly forecasted the potential of the soon-to-be completed Family Activities Building:

> Satan's attack on Adam was body, soul, and spirit; Satan's attack on Jesus was body, soul, and spirit; and Satan's attack on us is body, soul, and spirit. This is the reason why we at the First Baptist Church of Merritt Island are trying to have a three-fold ministry—this is the reason why we will have our Family Activities Building—because we know that Satan is attacking the whole man, and we're trying to minister to the whole man.[54]

As Adrian and the church prepared with great expectation for the new year, even they did not fully realize what God had in store. In many ways, as Adrian's primary vision became reality in 1968, the church reached a zenith that not even Adrian could have predicted. And the best was yet to come.

8

GEARED TO THE TIMES, ANCHORED TO THE ROCK (1968)

Although the first of six successful lunar landings did not occur until July 1969—with the final mission taking place in December 1972—the Apollo Program, in many ways, reached its peak in 1968 in terms of federal funding, personnel employed, infrastructure expansion, and spacecraft development. Similarly, while First Baptist Church enjoyed a solid trajectory up to and even immediately after Adrian's departure in 1972, the year 1968 holds a particularly noteworthy place in his Merritt Island pastorate. From the completion of the Family Activities Building and sanctuary renovation to the launch of several new and innovative ministries to testimonies of amazing spiritual transformation, 1968 shines especially brightly in the story of the Moon Port Pastor. In fact, a few days after the dawning of the new year, Adrian forecasted as much: "1968—THE GREATEST YEAR EVER! It should be; it can be; and by the grace of God, it will be....1968 will have its difficulties, but every smart crow knows that where there is a scarecrow, there's good corn around. Satan will not scare us away!"[1]

GOD'S MERRITT ISLAND BRANCH OFFICE

By 1968, growing cultural upheaval included, among other things, the popularization of the "God is dead" movement. Philosophers since at least the time of Nietzsche have debated the concept. But when the April 8, 1966 cover of *Time* famously put the question "Is God dead?" before the masses, the idea brazenly moved from the ivory towers to the American highways and byways. As with many other sentiments of the era, the "death of God" divided Americans sharply along ideological lines. Adrian's answer to the question left no doubt as to where he stood:

> God isn't dead—he isn't even sick! I know God is not dead for three reasons. In the first place, you have to know someone sufficiently enough to identify the corpse, and these who say that he's dead don't even know him. In the second place, they always notify the next of kin, but nobody's told me and I'm his child. In the third place, it wouldn't bother me even if he did 'die'—he'd just go to Heaven and start all over![2]

Beyond what Adrian shared sermonically, God's powerful movement on his congregation provided all the evidence many in Merritt Island needed regarding the supposed death of God. For example, a January 15 editorial in the *Today* newspaper offered First Baptist Church as a strong counterpoint to the "death" of God and the social ills of the day:

> Words like "hippies" and phrases such as "God is dead" scream for attention and get it; the loose morals get looser; and drugs are as common as buttered popcorn. But those who prate "God is dead" would do well to check His branch office on Merritt Island where the First Baptist Church is one of the fastest-growing congregations of any denomination in our land and saw more members baptized last year than in any of the 1,400 Baptist churches in Florida.[3]

Indeed, God was very much alive, and he clearly set First Baptist Church as a shining city on a hill. As we shall see, throughout 1968, an increasing number of people outside of Brevard would learn just how bright that light was.

EASTER 1968: SATAN DEFEATED AGAIN!

As winter gave way to spring, all eyes at First Baptist Church cast an optimistic gaze toward Easter, April 14. After worshipping in the gymnasium for nearly six months, the congregation would gather in its newly renovated and expanded sanctuary. As part of the growing expectation, Adrian set a four-week attendance challenge before the congregation: 1,250 on March 24; 1,350 on March 31; 1450 on April 7; and 1,550 on April 14. With 1,201 on campus on March 17, the following Sundays looked promising.[4]

As part of the pre-Easter emphasis, Adrian also planned a special treat for the congregation: Bill Bright, founder of Campus Crusade for Christ and author of *The Four Spiritual Laws*, would preach on Palm Sunday, April 7. As a young college graduate in the late 1940s, Bill Bright had shown great entrepreneurial promise. But in the early 1950s, feeling strongly led of the Lord, he abandoned his growing commercial enterprise to pursue full-time evangelism and Gospel ministry. What began at that time on the campus of the University of California at Los Angeles eventually became one of the largest international Christian ministries in history. With a shared passion for evangelism, Bill and Adrian became close friends as did their wives, Vonette and Joyce. Adrian recalled that Bill Bright "stretched my vision perhaps more than any man. Every time I thought I was thinking big, I would meet with Bill Bright and came away feeling like a pigmy. His eyes would glow as he talked about fulfilling the Great Commission in our generation."[5]

Just days before celebrating the Resurrection in the newly renovated sanctuary, Adrian called the people to maximize their Gospel opportunities: "Let's make Easter the best ever. A great opportunity is ours to lay a harvest of golden grain (souls) at the feet of our Savior. Many lost people will be in the services. Plan to be at your best. Look for visitors. Make them welcome. Give them the best seats. Pray for spiritual power. We could see scores saved!"[6]

Adrian preaches on Easter Sunday in the newly renovated sanctuary. Courtesy Joyce Rogers.

When Easter Sunday attendees found their seats in the two services at 8:00 AM and 11:00 AM, sanctuary improvements did not disappoint. A carpeted, cascading arc of steps leading up to the platform replaced the railing that had stretched the entire width of the sanctuary. New vertical wood paneling surrounded the platform with a matching pulpit at the center. An overflow seating area, located between the sanctuary and the recently constructed atrium added space for well over two hundred. More seating at the back of the sanctuary replaced the street-side entrance and former classroom space. All told, with the overflow area filled, the renovations provided space for upwards of 1,350 worshippers. Easter was a time for members to celebrate both the Resurrection as well as a new era in the life of their church. Additionally, Easter Sunday saw over fifteen hundred in attendance, twenty-two additions to the church, and twelve professions of faith. A banner headline in *The Thrust* summed up the sentiment of the day: "Satan Defeated Again!"[7]

FAMILY ACTIVITIES BUILDING DEDICATION WEEK

Adrian labeled May 5-12 "Dedication Week" as the church officially thanked God for the completion of the Family Activities Building and sanctuary renovations. While much Gospel work remained, Dedication Week saw the completion of every major piece of the vision God laid on Adrian's heart in 1965. In the months and years to come, the fruits of the completed vision would become evident to all.

One of the key highlights of Dedication Week was the grand opening of the Family Activities Building which included a myriad of opportunities for families to enjoy. A glance at the 1968 Activities Program Guide gives evidence that Nelson Rutledge, the Minister of Christian Activities, went above and beyond in creating—and managing—a mind-boggling activities schedule throughout the week. Church members and their guests could choose from volleyball leagues, bowling leagues, and basketball leagues. Throughout the week, patrons could enjoy roller skating, crafts and ceramics, individual bowling, a game room, weight-lifting, gymnasium sports, sauna, and the SNAC RAC, a fully-stocked and operated snack bar and kitchen.[8]

Friday and Saturday nights were set aside especially for family recreation with childcare available for children three and under. While promoting the Family Activities Building, Adrian emphasized the key benefit of families playing together:

> We're not calling this a 'youth' building or a 'recreational' building, we're calling it a 'family activities building.' We've often heard it said that 'the family that prays together, stays together.' Well, the family that plays together will stay together, too. R. Lofton Hudson, the Christian counselor, has said that of the 3,000 cases of marriage and family problems that he has studied, upwards of 90 percent had no form of family recreation. Now, they might have had recreation with Poppa going bowling and Mama playing bridge and Junior going to the football game and Sister going to the dance—but they didn't have family recreation together.[9]

1968 campus completed to include Unit 1 and Unit 2 of the 1965 vision. Original 1950 sanctuary stood where Atrium connects with the 1960 sanctuary; remnants of the 1952 educational wing, which were incorporated into Atrium, can be seen on the backside of Atrium. Courtesy Joyce Rogers (text added).

Patrons were expected to dress appropriately—"pedal-pushers, culottes, skirts, or slacks" for women and "blue jeans, slacks, warm-ups, and sweatpants" for men. Bermuda shorts were allowed only during exercise classes and competitive sports (which did not include bowling or skating). Additionally, smoking and card playing were prohibited.[10]

As a result of the broad programming—and in spite of what anyone might have thought of the dress policies—the Family Activities Building was an immediate hit. Such success was due in large part to the immense need for family-friendly venues, as Lyvonne Burleson recalled:

> In those days, there were very few acceptable leisure opportunities for Merritt Island families. The one public bowling alley allowed smoking and drinking; there was the Barn theater and the adjacent drive-in theater. Otherwise, a trip to the beach or fishing were about the only options for family entertainment. Skating, bowling, basketball and volleyball leagues, exercise classes, saunas, planned activities for all age groups as well as family nights met the needs of the Church family and their guests in a Christian environment.[11]

Those who came to the Family Activities Building—and there were many—heard the Gospel in various ways. For example, Nelson Rutledge enlisted a group of ladies he named "Inquirettes" who volunteered when the building was open. These ladies, dressed in brown linen outfits, met with guests, answered questions about activities and schedules, and remained sensitive at all times to opportunities for sharing the Gospel with attendees.[12]

The local news media also took note of the new Family Activities Building. *The Brevard Sentinel* mentioned that "Church Offers Family Program" and quoted Adrian's now-familiar talking points:

> We are in the center of the space capital of the world—where men are trying to get to the heavens—we wantto bring heaven to the hearts of men. We have a space-age church with a space-age mission....We believe that not only should families worship together—they should play together.[13]

Meanwhile, the *Today* newspaper announced, "Baptist Rec Complex Opens," and highlighted that "no one is admitted without an activities card, which you get when you become a member of the church." Non-members could also enjoy the facilities if accompanied by a member.

Cost for skate rental? Twenty-five cents. Cost to bowl a game? Seventy-five cents.[14]

THE DIFFERENCE CHRIST CAN MAKE IN A WOMAN'S WORLD

During Dedication Week, a new and innovative women's ministry emerged at First Baptist Church. Its inaugural event, a women's evangelistic luncheon with the theme "The Difference Christ Can Make in a Woman's World," took place on Thursday, May 9 in the newly dedicated Atrium. Much to everyone's delight, no less than 600 women from across Brevard County packed the new facility to hear guest speaker Barbara Ball.

How did this powerful event come to be? Joyce Rogers had an ongoing burden for women on Merritt Island, and God gave her a vision that would prove exceptionally successful: "At Merritt Island, we had a Women's Missionary Union (WMU). But even though the church was booming, and we had about 1,200 in Sunday School at the time, our women's group couldn't get more than about 10 women to come out each month."[15] So Joyce began to pray about what God might do in and through the women of First Baptist Church. Then, in early 1968, Adrian and Joyce attended a Campus Crusade retreat for pastors and wives led by Bill and Vonnette Bright. Joyce was especially inspired by Vonnette's message as well as Barbara Ball, a speaker who shared creative ideas for reaching women: "When I heard those speakers, my heart just burned within me."[16]

Based on this visionary conviction, Joyce and other key ladies at First Baptist Church planned the women's luncheon to coincide with the opening of the Family Activities Building:

> We invited the First Baptist women and told them to bring their neighbors and their friends. And I'll never forget that day when I stood at the door, remembering that we had only about 10 women show up for our previous meetings—and 600 women came that day. They all

walked in and shook my hand saying, 'This is my neighbor' and 'This is my friend' and 'This is my neighbor' and 'This is my friend.' And on that day 52 ladies checked response cards that they had prayed silently to receive Christ![17]

As we shall see, this luncheon was the first of several key events for women that Joyce and other ladies would host during the Merritt Island years.

R. G. LEE LAUNCHES PASTOR-LED REVIVAL WEEK

The day after the women's luncheon, the *Orlando Sentinel* reported, "This Sunday, Dr. R. G. Lee, three-time president of the Southern Baptist Convention and world-renown preacher, will be guest speaker at First Baptist Church of Merritt Island." The paper went on to report that Adrian would lead nightly revival services throughout the week to follow in connection with special events for all ages: a breakfast for high school students on Monday morning, a breakfast for college and career young adults on Tuesday morning, a dinner for junior high students on Thursday night, and a dinner for senior high students on Saturday. Lastly, Sunday, May 19, would be "Old Fashioned Day."[18]

Adrian expected big things from this week of revival: "Pentecost at any cost! Let us pray for revival in sin-soaked Brevard. It will be Pentecost or plenty lost. God is not willing that there should be any lost. Endeavor to lead at least one soul to make a public profession of faith before our revival closes on May 19!"[19] Much was planned for Revival Week, but even Adrian could not imagine what God would do when it was all said and done.

R. G. Lee, pastor emeritus of Bellevue Baptist Church in Memphis, launched Revival Week with his world-famous message, "Pay Day Someday." Over the course of his ministry, Lee delivered the message over 1,200 times in churches and other venues across America. Adrian

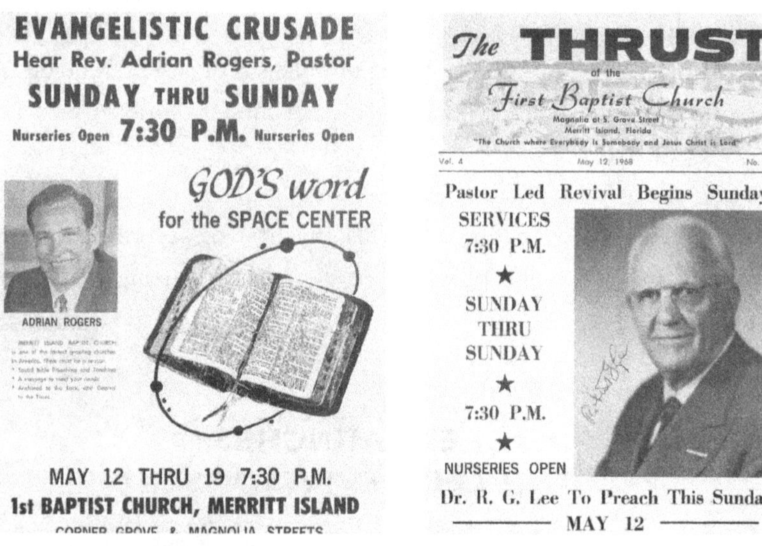

Flyer for May 1968 pastor-led revival services and front page of *The Thrust* that R. G. Lee autographed. Courtesy Lyvonne Burleson and Joyce Rogers.

greatly admired the Baptist elder statesman and described him thus in *The Evening Tribune*: "We are really fortunate to have Dr. Lee coming to Central Brevard. He is a very famous Christian. To be elected president of the Southern Baptist Convention once is an honor, but to be elected three times is like being elected President of the United States three times."[20]

Throughout Revival Week, Adrian held forth and brought stirring messages on a variety of topics: "The End of the World—How Much Time Do We Have?" on Monday night and "The Dirtiest Deed Ever Done—Is Brevard Crucifying Jesus Afresh?" on Tuesday night. On Wednesday night, Adrian talked about "The Path to Personal Power" after Paul Anderson, the "strongest man in the world," shared his testimony and demonstrated his strength by, among other things, driving a nail through a two-inch thick board with his bare hand and effortlessly lifting a table with nine high school boys sitting on it. On Thursday night, treasure hunter Bob Johnson recounted how he had salvaged over six million dollars' worth of sunken treasure off the Florida coast in 1967, then Adrian challenged attendees to "Discover Your Treasure." On Friday night, Adrian highlighted "The

1960s—Decade of Demons," then on Saturday he brought a simple Gospel message entitled, "How to Be Saved and Know It."[21]

On Sunday, May 19, Adrian wrapped up Revival Week and introduced "Old Fashioned Day," a theme that had proven successful in Fort Pierce. The theme was "Old Time Religion," and Adrian highlighted the relevance of the timeless Gospel for the space age. Many attendees wore attire circa 1875-1925, antique cars and horse-drawn wagons made their way to the church, and over 1,400 enjoyed "dinner on the grounds" in the air-conditioned gymnasium.[22]

R. G. Lee with Adrian in Cocoa, Florida. Courtesy Joyce Rogers.

GEORGE KORDA: TROPHY OF GRACE

Revival Week witnessed numerous victories, but the crusade's greatest miracle—and perhaps the most amazing work of spiritual transformation during all of Adrian's Merritt Island years—occurred when an angry, teenage atheist boldly confessed Jesus as Savior and Lord. His name was George Korda, and he came to faith in Jesus at the culmination of Revival Week.

George and his family had relocated to Brevard County from California in 1962 when he was nine years old, ultimately settling on Merritt Island one year later. George's father worked with the space program, and the family enjoyed "mild affluence," but life at home was "troubled and explosive." When George was fourteen years old, his father was incarcerated, and the family fell into poverty: "My mother, sister, and I were on our own, moving from one apartment to the next as evictions became common." As a result, George became "angry and bitter, furious at the world." Ayn Rand's *Atlas Shrugged* became an influential voice in his life, and an older, atheistic friend began to introduce George to a worldview without God. Although George's father was a non-practicing Catholic and his mother had a Jewish background, George eventually became a self-proclaimed atheist.[23]

In early May 1968, feeling emboldened by his convictions, George sent a manifesto-like letter to the editor of the *Today* newspaper which appeared on Monday, May 6:

> To have survived on this planet as long as he has, man has had to overcome many of his superstitious fears. The main superstition that man has left unconquered has held him back from progress of the most essential kind. Its very foundation should expose it as false. This superstition is what proves that man has still not progressed past the stone age. The superstition is religion, the believing in a God. If someone can read the Bible and believe it, then he is a fool. If he can read it and question it, see where it is ridiculous, reject many or all of its stories, then there is hope for this human race, yet. In ancient times men sacrificed living humans to their gods. Most people now look on this as a barbaric practice, which it was. Man is still just as stupid. He is still sacrificing his life to his God. Now we go once a week to pray to a nonexistent Deity not to condemn us to a nonexistent Hell. I feel

> secure in the knowledge that I am in complete control of my life. I do not need to hang on to something as foolish as a God. I am a person and therefore I will live out my life as I feel, without fear of damnation. When the rest of the world recognizes this, our world will finally be populated by men and not sheep.[24]

George recalled, "That letter generated a lot of reaction, much anger, and also some concern. Regardless, I loved the attention. It got me noticed."[25] Indeed, two high school students from First Baptist Church, Randy Sprayberry and Stanley Matlow, noticed George and began speaking with him about God. Motivated by Adrian's challenge to win someone to Jesus during the revival, they also invited him to the special services.[26]

Describing himself as "moderately interested," George walked into the sanctuary on Friday evening, May 17. Impressed to see a packed house, he took a seat in the new overflow area. While Adrian brought the message, "The 1960s—Decade of Demons" and the congregation replied with "YES" and "AMEN," George sat bewildered: "These are adults. They're actually taking this stuff seriously?!" Agitated outwardly by what he heard and saw, George caught the attention of Nelson Rutledge, who was seated a few rows behind him.

After the service, Nelson approached George and asked his name. When he replied, "George Korda," Nelson inquired, "Did your father write that letter to the newspaper?" George proudly claimed authorship, and Nelson, maintaining composure, said that God at least appreciated his honesty. As the two continued the conversation in Nelson's office, he began probing George's beliefs and shared "The Four Spiritual Laws" with him. When Nelson explained Law #3—"Jesus Christ is God's only provision for our sin; through Him alone, we can know God personally and experience God's love and plan"—something happened in George's heart:

> I was a little shaken, and I didn't want to admit it. I thought to myself, "I understand this, but I don't want to understand this." I didn't want to believe it, but I believed that it was believable. I pushed back and

> said, "I don't believe this stuff," to which Mr. Rutledge replied, "What if you're wrong?" I responded arrogantly, "I guess I'll burn for it."[27]

George returned the next night, "a very conflicted young man," and dropped a note to Adrian in the offering plate: "Dear Mr. Rogers, Yesterday I was here to see your Friday night revival. I wrote on a visitor's card a terrible thing. I said I was here to learn how to fight your church."[28] The hint of remorse in George's words gave evidence that God was working on his heart. Then, Adrian's message that evening, "How to Be Saved and Know It," seemed custom-tailored for George. In fact, God spoke powerfully to George through the simple message, and when Adrian gave the invitation to accept Christ, George went forward and made a profession of faith. Adrian told George, "I want to talk to you after the service," so they went to his office for a long conversation. At one point, George told Adrian, "I'm so amazed," to which Adrian replied, "About what?" George said, "Until now, I was so sure there was no God, and now I can't even remember the arguments."[29]

Immediate fruit followed George's conversion. On Sunday, George shared his testimony with his mother and then visited his father, telling him that he had accepted Jesus. At the evening service that night, Adrian baptized George, and he shared his testimony with the congregation, saying that "Atheism only filled my heart with hate, but trusting Christ filled me with love." By Monday, George had already memorized four Bible verses, and on Tuesday he went to school carrying a new Bible and Bill Bright's book, *The Uniqueness of Jesus*. He shared his testimony with students and teachers alike and received "some ridicule and much encouragement."[30]

As the days went by, Joyce made notes in her journal about George's spiritual growth: "This is only the beginning of the wonderful love story of George Korda and Jesus Christ. Jesus has been pursuing George for a long time and had His messengers along the way. George didn't have a chance. He couldn't escape the wonderful love of God."[31]

In June, George wrote another letter to the editor of the *Today* newspaper, but this one was the polar opposite of his atheistic manifesto:

> Since my letter was printed in *Today* several weeks ago, there have been many answers by many people. The vast majority of these letters were in the negative to my position. Only now have I begun to understand the point they were trying to get across to me. On a recent Sunday I was baptized. The day before I had dedicated the rest of my natural life to Christ. It's hard to explain what prompted me to do this, but when I sat there in the First Baptist Church of Merritt Island and listened to Pastor Adrian Rogers telling me that if I opened up my heart, Jesus Christ would come in and take over my life, I tried it and it happened. Friday of that week I went to the revival of the church. The sermon I heard that night cracked me up. I joked about it, laughed, and once walked out of the church. Saturday I was converted. I was told that when I asked Christ into my heart, I would be reborn. By the feeling that went through me after I had been converted, I know that it was no joke. The thing I called a ridiculous superstition and crutch has made me a different person, a much cleaner and more decent person. I would like to thank all those who prayed for me while I was lost. Your prayers have been answered. God bless you all.[32]

In the weeks and months to come, George would lead his 13-year-old sister to Jesus, and another woman from First Baptist Church would eventually lead his mother to faith in Christ. In addition, George became fully invested in the senior high choir. When he first heard of the group, he thought, "What a bunch of losers." But six months after he joined, "The choir had become the most important thing in my life." George eventually graduated high school and joined the Army. Looking back, he described his years at First Baptist Church as an "extraordinary time—the best time of my life."[33]

SUMMER 1968: BUSY AND BLESSED

Summer 1968 proved busy and blessed. Jim Whitmire led the inaugural senior high choir tour to Niagara Falls, New York with stops in Georgia, Tennessee, Kentucky, Virginia, North Carolina, South Carolina, Pennsylvania, Ohio, and Florida. No less than 43 students and four adult chaperones shared the Gospel in song over the course of two weeks.[34]

Back in Merritt Island, in order to maximize the new space at First Baptist Church, Vacation Bible School spanned two separate weeks and saw 816 children enrolled the first week and 1,057 enrolled the second. Adrian encouraged First Baptist parents with small children to avoid taking vacation during Vacation Bible School, resulting in no less than 200 church members volunteering. Meanwhile, at Mount Zion Baptist Church—the African American congregation with which First Baptist traditionally partnered each summer—150 children attended Vacation Bible School and 25 First Baptist members assisted.[35]

Adrian and Joyce experienced a unique summer in 1968: instead of traveling to the Southern Baptist Convention, they traveled to Europe and the Holy Land for two weeks. During the Rogers' absence, Evangelist Anis Shorrosh, who had led revival services at First Baptist Church the year prior, filled the pulpit while his family "borrowed" the new pastorium. Upon his return, Adrian brought a message entitled "Israel and Prophecy" and shared insights from his trip. *The Evening Tribune* reported Adrian's observations: "We were particularly interested in the areas related to Jesus' life. The part of Jerusalem held by the Arabs until the 1967 war looked much the same as it did 2,000 years ago when Christ walked the streets."[36]

Throughout the summer, the recent campus additions continued to bring new dimensions of growth to Merritt Island. In July, "Family Night Dinners" became a weekly occurrence on Wednesday nights with over 400 diners routinely filling the Atrium. Fridays continued to be "family night" in the Family Activities Building, and Saturdays saw the building "crawling with teenagers and children."[37]

Sunday morning attendance continued to blossom across the summer to the point that *The Evening Tribune* reported, "Baptists Overflow New Church." Pastor and people celebrated the growth, but to the media Adrian especially reflected on the depth that accompanied the numbers: "I marvel at the fact that here in the middle of the space community, so many people are dedicated so deeply to God. Instead of tending to stray away from God because of the great amount of activity in the area, the residents seem more interested in maintaining close fellowship with the Lord."[38] To the congregation, Adrian rejoiced over the increasing depth of fellowship and growing momentum:

> Already our church family is so much closer. Our fellowship is deepening. We are already harvesting souls from this newly cultivated field, and I believe this harvest will multiply. I believe our program to be the finest of its kind in the Convention....This summer is astounding. Our auditorium is overflowing with people. Tears of conviction continue to flow. We had some twenty additions last Sunday. The music was heavenly. If this is the summer slump, I can hardly wait until the fall![39]

The fellowship among members was, in fact, remarkably deep, especially for a church with well over 1,000 attendees. Gene and Norma Baird recalled that "many members knew the names of many other members because we all utilized the Family Activities Building at the same time—it truly became the crossroads of our church."[40]

BROADER EXPOSURE, GREATER INFLUENCE, AND THE DEEPER LIFE

As summer gave way to fall, the *All Florida TV Weekly*, a supplement carried by 26 newspapers across the entire state, included a feature on First Baptist Church entitled, "The Bread of Life, Family Style."[41] The four-page article offered glowing descriptions of the various activities available to members and their guests as well as references to numerous First Baptist superlatives: first among the 1,400 Florida Baptist congregations and fifth among the 34,000 Southern Baptist congregations in baptisms; Sunday School enrollment of nearly 3,200; and a multi-generational music program with nearly 700 participants. Throughout the article, however, Adrian repeatedly emphasized the church's Gospel priority:

> We are presenting God's Word for the Space Center. The message is the same. Only the method is different. We realize a church building is only a tool. It must never be an end to itself. Our buildings are a "spiritual launching pad," and our desire is to minister to the people of this dynamic area with the all-sufficient message of Jesus.[42]

In the days after the article appeared, the church received numerous letters from Pensacola to Miami and everywhere in between expressing congratulations and affirmation of its visionary ministries. Adrian shared one letter in particular with the congregation from Mrs. Leora Daly of Ormond Beach:

> Honorable Sir, The *All Florida TV Weekly* just came to hand—about your church. And having read the inspiring article, I am impelled to write and tell you how wonderful I think your ideas are—the manifold uses of your church building for this day and time when the family life is so far away from the blessed home life and teaching in days gone by. I am one of the old citizens retired from active business life in Florida for almost 50 years. My days are now filled with reading news, national and international, which is mostly dreadful. So it gave me a lift up to read of your grand new adventure in the church world. "Things have changed since Martha was a girl," and this church change I think is wonderful.[43]

About the same time, Adrian received an especially encouraging letter from R. G. Lee:

> Dear Servant of Jesus, So glad and grateful am I for God's great use of you in your great church—one of the greatest I have ever had fellowship with. Your seven hundred and forty additions to the church this last associational year made me think of some blessed years I once had at Bellevue....To know that I preached the first message from your new pulpit is a matter of joy ever rich and abiding to me.[44]

In early November, the First Baptist ladies once again filled the Atrium with a creative, disciple-making event. On November 9, Vonette Bright, wife of Bill Bright, spoke to some 500 ladies and their daughters on the topic "Women—Fearful or Forceful?" Vonette, a treasured partner to her husband at Campus Crusade for Christ, was led to the Lord in 1947 by Henrietta Mears, the matriarch of twentieth-century evangelicalism. At the mother-daughter brunch, she challenged women to take a "forceful" stand for Christ:

Joyce and Vonette Bright after she spoke about "Women—Fearful or Forceful" at the mother-daughter brunch. Courtesy Joyce Rogers.

> I believe women can help in changing the world. Women hold the key to what our next generation is going to be. In our homes, what we make our families. One woman had the "nerve"—or "courage"—to face the Supreme Court of this land and take prayer out of the schools. Where were you? Where was I? I believe it's time for Christian women to band together. We must be forceful, not fearful, as we face the shining horizon ahead.[45]

The following week, on November 12-14, Florida Baptists gathered in Daytona Beach for their annual Convention meeting. First Baptist Church of Merritt Island took center stage as Doyle Carlton was elected president of the Florida Baptist Convention and Adrian was elected President of the Florida Baptist Pastor's Conference. Upon their return to Merritt Island, the church celebrated their key leaders:

> We of the First Baptist Church feel that God has really blessed us. First, in giving us a pastor who loves Jesus and is dedicated to the task of reaching people for Him. Second, for giving us Doyle Carlton, a fine Christian gentleman, who has a great love for Jesus and a burden for people on his heart. Congratulations! We're proud of you and pledge to you our FULL SUPPORT![46]

Early December saw First Baptist Church welcome one of Southern Baptist's most prominent missionaries, Miss Bertha Smith, for a week-long "Deeper Life Conference" with special emphasis on foreign missions. "Miss Bertha," as she was affectionately known across the Southern Baptist Convention, had served on the mission field in China and later Taiwan from 1917 until she reached the mandatory retirement age of 70 in 1958. During her service overseas, she participated in the Shantung Revival which swept across portions of China in the late 1920s and early 1930s. Upon returning to the United States, she embarked on a vigorous schedule of Bible conferences across the country, focusing on missions and the Spirit-filled life.[47]

Showing no sign of diminished strength at age 80, she maintained a busy schedule during her week at First Baptist Church. Each morning at 10:00 AM, she led sessions during which, Adrian anticipated, "our ladies will be blessed and challenged as never before" about the Spirit-filled life. Then, at 7:30 PM each evening, she spoke to the entire congregation. Although labeled "The Deeper Life Conference," Adrian encouraged the people to "come as to a revival meeting."[48] Five years after visiting Merritt Island, Miss Bertha would write *How the Spirit Filled My Life*. She would also play an instrumental role in Adrian's election as President of the Southern Baptist Convention in 1979.[49]

FROM THE EARTH TO THE MOON

As First Baptist Church made major strides in 1968, the Apollo Program also moved forward in significant ways. Following the Apollo 1 tragedy, the entire Apollo command module underwent redesign at a cost of $75 million. Although flights were delayed, spacecraft improvements ensured more positive results once missions resumed. In late 1967 and into 1968, four unmanned missions had validated the new systems. Then, on October 11, 1968, Apollo 7—the first manned flight—blasted into orbit atop a Saturn 1B rocket. During the 11-day mission, the three-man crew tested all command module systems while orbiting the earth 163 times. NASA planners anticipated that Apollo 8 would likewise orbit the earth in December to further assess all systems, especially the lunar module.

However, NASA had learned in late September that the Soviet Union had sent an unmanned spacecraft to lunar orbit, and planners feared that the Russians would soon send men to orbit the moon. Facing the possibility of such an unacceptable defeat, NASA opted to send Apollo 8 to lunar orbit in late December. The mission would not attempt a landing; rather, it would demonstrate the full capabilities of the massive Saturn V launch vehicle as well as the translunar mission.

Thus, on Saturday, December 21, as the thunderous Saturn V shockwave swept across Merritt Island, Adrian and Joyce herded Steve, Gayle, David, and Janice into the backyard to watch the colossal rocket lift astronauts Frank Borman, Michael Collins, and William Anders into the sky. Steve recalled, "My parents never lost the awe and wonder of the space program. As we rushed out to watch the launch, the ground shook."[50] Personally, Adrian always enjoyed the spiritual application of the countdown to launch:

> Whenever we get to launch time, I get to thinking about the second coming of Jesus. I can't help it. There's just something about the launching of a missile and the second coming of Jesus Christ that go hand-in-hand in my heart. ...These missiles are man's puny firecrackers compared to Jesus. Never forget that it's not who's going up but who's coming down that will change the history of this world.[51]

Along those same lines, The Evening Tribune reported that Adrian's Sunday sermon would mention "the irony of three astronauts leaving Earth for the moon over the Christmas holidays and the fact that Christ descended from the heavens."[52]

At the close of 1968, Apollo 8 brought a ray of light to a nation bombarded by riots, assassinations, violence, social upheaval, and carnage in Vietnam. Not only did the astronauts capture the first-ever images of Earth from that distance—no one would ever forget the stunning "Earthrise" photo—but they also famously read from Genesis during their Christmas Eve broadcast. Atheists cried foul, but Adrian was thrilled. Not long after splashdown on December 27, Frank Borman noted, "We got millions of telegrams after we landed, but the one I remember most was, 'Congratulations to the crew of Apollo 8. You saved 1968.'"[53]

9

POINTING MEN BEYOND THE STARS (1969)

As 1969 unfolded at First Baptist Church, the essential pieces of the Merritt Island puzzle were firmly in place. In less than four and a half years, the physical campus had experienced a breathtaking transformation. But more importantly, the congregation had solidly established its evangelistic culture under Adrian's dynamic preaching and innovative leadership. Gospel momentum and a state of almost perpetual revival had become normal. While NASA and the Nation, riding high on the success of the Apollo 8 mission, could anticipate a lunar landing later in the year, First Baptist members, enjoying a weekly attendance average of nearly 1,300 men, women, boys, and girls on campus in January and February, could anticipate reaching greater heights for God's glory in 1969. Adrian rejoiced with his people on February 3: "Sunday was another great day! We had over 1,300 in the main Sunday School. The Spirit of God is moving, and our church is getting sweeter and sweeter. How I love this church. What a privilege to be a member of First Baptist Church Merritt Island!"[1]

THE CRUSADE OF THE AMERICAS

During the 1965 Baptist World Alliance annual Congress held in Miami, Florida, Pastor Rubens Lopes of Sao Paulo, Brazil proposed a hemisphere-wide evangelistic campaign for 1969 to be called "the Crusade of the Americas." The following year, nearly one hundred leaders from numerous Baptist denominations and 25 countries gathered in Cali, Columbia to discuss the details of the Crusade, which would be "a vast cooperative Baptist evangelistic campaign to encompass North, Central, and South America in 1969" under the theme of "Christ the Only Hope." Southern Baptist leaders in attendance—to include Herschel Hobbs, Baker James Cauthen, and C. E. Autrey—enthusiastically supported the concept. Subsequently, efforts were made across the SBC to achieve maximum evangelistic synergy ahead of the Crusade, to include encouraging all SBC congregations to plan for local revival meetings in the Spring of 1969.[2]

Florida Baptists wholeheartedly embraced the Crusade of the Americas. Not only did they adopt the "Christ the Only Hope" theme for their 1968 annual meeting, but the *Florida Baptist Witness* repeatedly kept the Crusade in front of its readers, such as this reference in November 1968:

> We are much encouraged by the interest in and concern for the Crusade of the Americas being expressed in the Associations across Florida. There seems to be a kind of divinely stirred restlessness in the hearts of many pastors and other leaders in what God, through the Crusade, can bring to pass. Nevertheless, one of the great tragedies to be observed all around us is a lack of concern for lost people or a sense of responsibility to reach them with the Gospel. ...If I should find that I don't feel the concern I should for lost sinners, that I am hesitant or negligent about witnessing to those who need my witness, then I must allow the Holy Spirit who indwells me to infill and overflow me. Let us then let the Crusade of the Americas become an intensely personal and moving thing.[3]

Crusade of the Americas was envisioned as "a vast cooperative Baptist evangelistic campaign to encompass North, Central, and South America in 1969." *Crusade of the Americas: 1968, 1969, 1970 Guidebook* (Raleigh: Baptist State Convention, 1967), 1.

For its part in the Crusade of the Americas, First Baptist Church of Merritt Island scheduled a week-long crusade for March 10-15 to be led by Don Manuel, Pastor of Allapattah Baptist Church in Miami. Although Adrian needed no prodding to prioritize evangelism, he eagerly looked forward to these services in particular:

> The Crusade of the Americas is coming—one of the greatest cooperative efforts of evangelism in Christian history is at the threshold. This could be the answer to the prayers of thousands of saints around the world for revival. Don Manuel will be our evangelist. He and I have prayed and are planning for a Pentecost. I have a feeling in my bones that we will have our greatest meeting.[4]

On the eve of the Crusade, Adrian called the congregation to make intentional and specific preparation with a "Crusade Checklist":

1. CALENDAR CLEARED. The Crusade will take precedence over all routine meetings. Any church activity in conflict with the Crusade should be canceled.
2. SUNDAY SCHOOL TEACHERS. Plan to be in every service, personally contact every class member and prospect to attend, and lead at least one lost person to Christ during the Crusade.
3. CHOIR MEMBERS. Be present and ready to sing for every service. No one can overestimate the importance of Spirit-filled music in a revival.
4. DEACONS. Meet in the Pastor's study every night before the service at 7:00 PM for prayer and instruction. All Deacons should set the example by their attendance, soul-winning, and prayer. Each deacon should take for their goal to lead one soul to Christ during the Crusade.
5. EVERY MEMBER. This is the one series of meetings that demands the best from all of us. It is not enough to say, "I will come one night." You are needed every night to sing, pray, witness, and show concern. I am asking you to attend every night at the cost of personal sacrifice.
6. CONFESSION of sin, prayer, concern, and faithfulness from all will bring an awakening that will shake Merritt Island.[5]

Throughout the week of services, while Don Manuel challenged the congregation and led the lost to Christ, Jerry Spenser and Gloria Roe provided stirring music. Ultimately, dozens made professions of faith in Jesus while others united with First Baptist Church as members.[6]

THE POWER TO WITNESS

Following an electric Easter Sunday on April 6 that saw 17 professions of faith and six other additions to the church, Adrian focused the congregation's attention on personal evangelism training and the power that God gives

His people to share Jesus: "You shall receive power when the Holy Spirit has come upon you; and you shall be witnesses to Me in Jerusalem, and in all Judea and Samaria, and to the end of the earth" (Acts 1:8). The week of May 5-11 focused on L-I-F-E: "Lay Institute For Evangelism"—another Bill Bright brainchild. Each night featured personal evangelism training on campus followed by on-the-job training through visitation in the community for adults as well as students in grades 7-12.[7]

But as Adrian often emphasized, witnessing for Christ apart from the power of the Holy Spirit in and through the Believer is fruitless. So, in addition to practical LIFE training, Adrian kept the Spirit-filled life in front of the people. For example, the two-page interior of *The Thrust* published on May 11 featured Bill Bright's diagram of the differences between the Lost Man, Carnal Man, and the Spiritual Man.[8] Taken from material that would become central to Bright's booklet *How You Can Be Filled With the Holy Spirit* in his "Transferable Concepts" series, the diagram illustrated the same basic yet profound concepts found in Ian Thomas' *The Saving Life of Christ* which had impacted Adrian's life nearly 10 years earlier. Grounded both in 1 Corinthians 2:14-3:2 as well as the Old Testament Egypt-Wildness-Canaan paradigm, Adrian frequently challenged the people to witness out of an overflow of the Spirit-filled life. In fact, he often prefaced sermons about the Egypt-Wilderness-Canaan paradigm by saying something along these lines: "I want you to learn something that perhaps you've never heard before—but I know you've heard it if you've been a member of this church for very long."[9]

Regarding the Spirit-filled life, Adrian made it a point to share the words of historic Christians on the matter from one of Bill Bright's books in his message about "The Lost Axe Head":

> A book from Campus Crusade includes quotes from Christians in the past about the Spirit-filled life. For example, Andrew Murray said, "Men ought to seek with their whole hearts to be filled with the Spirit of God. Without being filled with the Spirit, it is utterly impossible to ever live or work as God desires." And Norman G. Harrison said, "The

Spirit-filled life is the only life, the life that permits his fullness in a sustained overflow, that can please God." Then notice what J. Edwin Owen has said: "The great purpose in the filling of the Holy Spirit is power for service. The best, most used Christians known to me are those who have testified to a deeper experience of the filling of the Holy Spirit. And Henrietta Mears said, "I believe it is impossible for any Christian to be effective in life or service unless he is filled with the Holy Spirit, who is God's only provision for power. Lastly, Oswald J. Smith said, "Read the biographies of God's men and you will discover each one sought and obtained the enduement of power from on high. One sermon preached in the anointing is worth a thousand preached in the energy of the flesh."[10]

Adrian then ended his list of quotations by saying,

I desire to pastor a church where the members know something of the Spirit-filled life. Now the devil would love to get us sidetracked with some kind of fanaticism, but we won't do that. However, when all the dust has settled, there still remains the command of the Lord to "be filled with the Spirit." And the command is to every one of us—not just to the song leader and not just to the pastor, but to every one of us!"[11]

Training and sending Spirit-filled witnesses produced God-honoring results as Adrian observed following the Lay Institute:

I'm excited! Our church is at a higher point than I've ever seen it. Your spirit is a benediction to my soul. The Lay Institute was all that I could hope for. Wasn't it great to get on the offensive and invade Satan's territory? Well over 100 people professed faith in Christ through your witness. Glory![12]

What stood behind these collective results? Individual, Spirit-filled church members going two-by-two into homes across Merritt Island throughout the week, intentionally sharing the Gospel and inviting people to trust Christ:

> Soul-winning is our main job! Let's keep the "go" in Gospel. This past Lord's Day, a lovely lady presented herself at the front of the church during the invitation and said, "I was saved in my home Tuesday morning when two ladies from the church came and told me about Jesus. Now I want to make it public and be baptized. Thank you, Carolyn and Lee. This is how it ought to be.[13]

"ONE GIANT LEAP FOR MANKIND"

As the reality of the American flag on the moon's surface came within reach, Adrian prayed about how to leverage the momentous event for God's glory. How should First Baptist Church make the best use of its God-given facilities? How could its members best mobilize to connect with those coming to Brevard for the historic Apollo 11 launch? For Adrian, evangelism would be the priority, and he said as much in response to the Apollo 10 mission in May. As the command module orbited the moon on May 22 and the lunar module descended to a mere 14 kilometers above the surface of the moon before reuniting with the command module, he wrote, "I don't mind telling you that Apollo 10 made the 'goosebumps' want to come upon me, but pointing men beyond the stars is still the most exciting thing. There is no thrill like introducing a soul to Jesus."[14]

Early July saw scores of space spectators descend upon Brevard in anticipation of the Apollo 11 launch on July 16. The local chamber of commerce predicted upwards of 1,000,000 visitors to the area.[15] Indeed, by launch day America had seemingly invaded Brevard. Planes, trains, and automobiles brought people from all walks of life to witness history in the making. Motels were jammed full, campers and make-shift sleeper trucks made use of every square inch of open real estate, and restaurants could hardly keep food and beverages in stock.

In preparation for this groundswell of humanity, Adrian cast his vision for the ministry that would take place:

> The moon launch is at hand. This will be a special opportunity to witness. We will have a special fellowship at the church on Tuesday night before the launch. Many of you will have visitors to bring to the church. We will conclude with prayer for Apollo 11. Then after the launch on Wednesday [morning], we will have open house at the church and special services during prayer meeting. I will preach on "What the Bible Says About Man Going to the Moon."[16]

As advertised, launch-week activities at First Baptist Church catered to members and guests alike, all in the name of Jesus. On Tuesday evening, a special "Moon Island Pre-Departure Rally" at 7:30 PM featured a band, watermelon, and prayer. Copies of a special "Apollo 11" edition of *The Thrust* were made available also. The front cover featured Campus Crusade's "Four Spiritual Laws" as well as a warm pastoral introduction: "Pointing Men BEYOND the Stars is our goal. Our task is greater in significance than all of the amazing goals of NASA. Our task is not to help man to reach the moon but to point him to the One who hung it there." Meanwhile, the interior pictured Tom Clayton, Jim Whitmire, and Nelson Rutledge along with descriptions of their respective ministries. In addition, a large, fold-out section featured an illustrated map of Brevard County with key points of interest noted and First Baptist Church prominently highlighted at the center of it all.[17] On Wednesday, following the 9:32 AM launch, the campus was open all day to members, their guests, and tourists with activities and refreshments available.

Family night supper at 5:30 PM served "Moon Chips," then the evening service at 6:30 PM featured special prayer for the astronauts as well as Adrian's message about the Bible and the moon mission.[18]

Then on Sunday, July 21—just hours prior to Neil Armstrong's first steps on the moon—Adrian brought a message from Psalm 8 entitled,

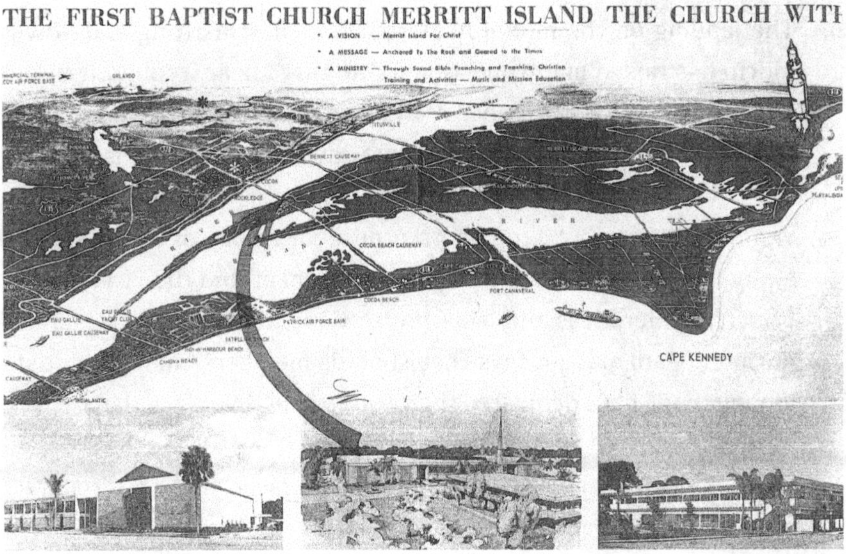

A special "Apollo 11" edition of *The Thrust* featured a fold-out map of Brevard County with First Baptist Church at the center of it all. Courtesy Lyvonne Burleson.

"When I Consider the Heavens." In the message, he noted that the moon is commanded to give God glory in Psalm 148:3—"Praise ye Him, sun and moon." Then he reminded the congregation, "When you see these things take place on television today and tonight and you hear the commentators talk about the moon, give God glory!" Furthermore, he compared the significance of the Apollo mission in human terms to the immensity of the universe and the greatness of God: "We talk about man going to the moon, but when we talk about going to the moon, we haven't really gone anywhere. In terms of the entire universe and the greatness of God, going to the moon is kind of a frog jump."[19] For Adrian, the grandeur of the decade-in-the-making moon landing paled in comparison to the glory and majesty of God.

In the days following the Apollo 11 mission, numerous Christian leaders reflected on the meaning of the moon mission, not least of whom was Billy Graham. In a July 26 article written for UPI and distributed across America, the world's most well-known evangelist suggested that the recent scientific feats were a "tribute to God" and highlighted, among things, God's work among the space scientists on Merritt Island:

> The landing on the moon by astronaut Neil Armstrong and Edwin Aldrin has raised many questions. One that I hear frequently asked is if space exploits in general and this landing in particular have any theological implications? I must say that any moon landing or any other human achievement in the universe can only be, in my view, another tribute to the greatness and glory of our creator.... Many men of science agree. Scores of them attend the First Baptist Church of Merritt Island, adjacent to Cape Kennedy. The Reverend Adrian Rogers, pastor, says that 71 of his members, many scientists among them, have dedicated their lives to full time Christian work.[20]

Billy Graham's article represented the most widely circulated description of First Baptist Church and what God was doing on Merritt Island during Adrian's years as pastor. But there would be much more to tell in the years to come.

"LET THE WHOLE WORLD KNOW"

In July, Jim Whitmire continued to raise the bar for the annual choir tour. Traveling as far West as Colorado with stops also in Georgia, Alabama, Mississippi, Arkansas, Louisiana, Oklahoma, Texas, and New Mexico, some 50 students and adult leaders brought a broad array of musical presentations to churches from the Space Coast to the Rocky Mountains. George Korda, who once considered choir members "a bunch of losers," not only joined the choir but became a featured soloist on the tour:

> Before the 1969 choir tour, after Jim Whitmire had tried about a dozen different choir members for a solo in "Who's On the Lord's Side," I went to him and asked if I could give it a try. He looked at me with a quizzical expression and asked, "Do you really want to?" It sounded much like, "Are you serious?" I hadn't been in the choir long, so I said, "Yes, I am." When the moment came in the song, he

pointed at me. When the solo finished, the choir cheered, probably from relief that they thought no one else would be asked to attempt it. Dr. Whitmire asked me to stay after rehearsal. He handed me the music for a satirical version of the Rigoletto Quartet and taught me the lead tenor part. Within a few months, the choir became the most important thing I was doing in my life.[21]

Jim Whitmire recalled, "The 1969 tour was something of a 'forced march' with performances each night and long drives between each location. But the kids did great!" One especially noteworthy memory for tour members was watching the Apollo 11 moonwalk from hotel rooms in Lafayette, Louisiana.[22]

The choir returned from the tour and conducted its home concert at First Baptist Church on July 27. A few days later, choir members

1969 Choir Tour photograph that became the album cover for "Let the Whole World Know." George Korda is seventh from left. Courtesy Jim Whitmire.

recorded "Let the Whole World Know," a music album featuring songs and performances from the tour. This and other choir tour records were a hit during Jim Whitmire's tenure at First Baptist Church.

CELEBRATING SIGNIFICANT MILESTONES

August and September brought recognition of significant milestones for First Baptist Church. In August, the church celebrated the beginning of Adrian's sixth year as pastor. Only Heaven could have engineered what transpired over the five years since his first Sunday in August 1964. By God's grace and for His glory, while those five years represented only 25 percent of the entire history of the church, they saw 74 percent of all additions and 82 percent of all baptisms.[23] The details were staggering: 3,458 total additions to the church, 1,185 baptisms, and membership grew from 1,133 to nearly 2,800. Moreover, the church led the Florida Baptist Convention in baptisms in 1967 and 1968, and Adrian baptized no less than 255 people from January to August 1969. Meanwhile, the church budget had grown in five years from $75,000 to $348,000.[24] To celebrate his anniversary, the Rogers family accompanied close friend Peter Lord—pastor of Park Avenue Baptist Church in Titusville—and his family on vacation to Jamaica, the country of Peter's birth.

September marked First Baptist's twentieth anniversary, and Adrian determined to make the entire month count for Jesus. The 30-day celebration included a historical panorama in the Atrium depicting the church's first twenty years, Wednesday evenings filled with slides, movies, and skits, and Homecoming Day on September 21 that included dinner on the grounds and recognition of long-time and charter members. Numerous local newspapers described the anniversary in various ways. *The Evening Tribune* reported "Island Baptists Record 20 Years" and noted membership had risen from the original 19 charter members to 2,784 twenty years later. An article entitled "Church for the Whole Man" in the Today paper highlighted innovations such as the Family Activities

The First Baptist Church 20th Anniversary graphic highlighted the church's connection to the 1969 Apollo-centric Zeitgeist that swept the Nation. Courtesy Lyvonne Burleson.

Building and the renovated sanctuary including "auditorium spotlights and a complete lighting system for religious plays as well as a sound and light booth." Meanwhile, the *Orlando Sentinel* reported that "Merritt Island Baptists Observe 20th Anniversary" with mention that "big things are happening this month in the mushrooming congregation."[25]

Then, during the week of September 22-28, Evangelist Hyman Appelman conducted a revival crusade at First Baptist Church. Appelman, born in Russia in 1902, emigrated to America with his Jewish family in 1914 and settled in Chicago.

He earned his law degree in 1921 and became a successful trial lawyer. But in 1924, during a visit to Kansas City, he wandered into a YMCA and read a Gideon Bible he found in his hotel room. After several months of Holy Spirit conviction, he received Jesus Christ as Savior and Lord. Following his conversion, he received theological training at Southwestern Baptist Theological Seminary then began a dynamic itinerate evangelism ministry that would eventually take him around the world multiple times. At the height of his evangelistic ministry, an estimated average of 7,000 people per year made professions of faith in Christ at his meetings.[26] Billy Graham wrote of his ministry:

> Hyman Appelman is one of the greatest and most powerful preachers of the Gospel I have ever heard. I used to listen to him preach night after night and made notes on his sermons. Some of my own knowledge and inspiration concerning mass evangelism came from his ministry. Thousands of names are written in the Lamb's Book of Life because Hyman Appelman passed their way.[27]

Adrian enthusiastically anticipated the Appelman crusade, and he prepared his congregation accordingly in his message "Blueprint for Victory":

> I'll tell you why most churches don't see revival—they're not broken. We sit in churches with no tears, no confession, no getting right with God, and we think God is going to bless us anyway. But he's not going to do it until there's brokenness. That's why we've set aside Saturday, September 13 for a day of fasting and prayer, a day of brokenness before God. ...I believe Hyman Appelman is one of God's greatest servants in the world, and he is coming to lead us in this revival. But he's not going to have a revival in his suitcase when he gets here. Jesus could do no mighty works in his own hometown because of their unbelief. Our prayer must be, "O God, bend me, break me, mold me; make me into the person you want me to be."[28]

Likewise, in *The Thrust*, Adrian spurred his people to prepare for the coming revival with a testimony from Hyman Appelman:

> In the past 35 years of active evangelistic ministry, Hyman Appelman has spoken at least 25,000 times, for he rarely misses even one day in the year preaching. Often he will speak two or three or more times a day. Listen to his heart: "My only interest in life is to preach the Gospel of Jesus Christ to more and more and yet more people. I am never satisfied. I have never reached the place where I have felt I could sit down and take life easy. I love to preach and see people come to Jesus Christ."[29]

As Homecoming Sunday and Revival Week came, Sunday attendance swelled to over 1,600 on both September 21 and September 28, and dozens made professions of faith in Jesus as Savior and Lord.

UNIVERSITY OF CHRISTIAN EDUCATION

In October, First Baptist Church departed from the traditional Sunday evening "Training Union" model common among Southern Baptist churches, opting rather for a home-grown innovation called "University of Christian Education" (UCE). Conducted on Sundays at 6:00-7:15 PM prior to the evening service at 7:30 PM, a broad array of classes offered for all ages were grouped in give departments: Bible, Doctrine and Polity, Christian Life, Missionary Education, and Special Ministries. Adrian taught "Principles of Prophecy" while Joyce taught "Introduction to the Bible." Tom Clayton led the "New Member Orientation" with emphasis upon salvation, assurance, Baptist doctrine, the Spirit-filled life, and witnessing. In addition, numerous lay leaders taught a variety of other classes: a study on the Book of John, a class on creation and evolution, classes on presenting Christ through drama and using puppets to make the Bible real, a class on Christ as the cure for Communism, a class on dealing with the devil—along with many others. Classes were open to members and visitors alike at no cost.[30]

Word began to spread about this new and creative opportunity. The *Orlando Sentinel* reported, "First Baptist Offers Christian Education for

All Ages," while the *Evening Tribune* announced, "Island Church Opens Christian University." Both articles included Tom Clayton's statement of purpose for the program: "We want to help people address the needs and problems that come up TODAY."[31] Promotion of UCE, both internally and externally, aided in building momentum. By early November, enrollment already topped 700 with over 500 attending on any given Sunday.[32] Beyond central Florida, others took note. Bill Cochran recalled, "University of Christian Education was a major success, and many churches across the Southern Baptist Convention were watching what we were doing."[33]

FOR GALS ONLY

In early November, Joyce Rogers' passionate desire to reach women manifested itself once again in a unique overnight women's retreat, "For Gals Only." Earlier in the year, Joyce had heard of an upcoming women's conference in Ontario called 'Winning Women in Canada." Led by Jill Renich, the grand-daughter of R. A. Torrey, upwards of two thousand women were expected to attend the conference. She could hardly contain her excitement about the event. So she spoke with Merritt Island members Lyvonne Burleson and Ruth Wotring as well as her dear friend Johnnie Lord from Park Avenue Baptist Church in Titusville (wife of Peter Lord) and Park Avenue member June Andrews about traveling to Canada to attend the conference. The five ladies flew to Detroit, then drove a rental car across the border to the event. Joyce recalled:

> It was a dream come true! There were 2,000 women present. The emphasis was on women meeting the everyday needs of women, all rooted in a strong belief in God's Word and a love for missions. Jill Renich and her planning committee met with us before we left Canada, and I was so excited about our possibilities. On the way home, we talked about how we could start a women's retreat in our churches. We decided that each of our churches would sponsor a

retreat on alternating years, inviting ladies from both churches and the surrounding areas.[34]

From that germ of inspiration, the ladies planned the first retreat for November 8-9 at First Baptist Church with Jill Renich as guest speaker and Gloria Roe as worship leader. The *Orlando Sentinel*, in an article entitled "Retreat for 'Gals' Held at Church," reported that "a full schedule of worship, study, recreation, fun, fellowship, and singing is planned."[35]

Hundreds of ladies and their teenage daughters brought cots and sleeping bags to the overnight event. To accommodate the young ladies registered for the retreat but concerned about missing the Merritt Island Mustangs football game, a "Victory Celebration" was planned at the retreat for Friday night at 10:30 PM. After the ministry-packed weekend, Joyce assessed its merits: "The event was an overwhelming success. Several hundred women attended, needs were met, and lives were changed. We knew then that women will respond if programs were planned that were relevant and challenging."[36]

"A CONVENTION IN TENSION"

Florida Baptists gathered November 10-13 at Central Baptist Church in Miami for their 1969 Pastor's Conference and Annual Meeting. With Doyle Carlton as Convention President and Adrian as President of the Pastor's Conference, First Baptist Church of Merritt Island had a significant presence. Ahead of traveling to Miami, Adrian described the stakes to his people: "This will be an important Convention. There are grave dangers of a deadly drifting away from the great principles that have made us Southern Baptists. Unless we have the courage to stand, we will go the way of other denominations into liberalism and insipidness."[37]

Adrian called the Pastor's Conference to order on Monday morning, November 10 with the theme, "The Seventies: Decade For Decision." As President, he had selected conference speakers he knew from experience to be powerful preachers of God's Word: Ian Thomas spoke three times, Anis Shorrosh twice, and Arthur Blessett—a California evangelist to the "Now Generation" and hippies of Los Angeles—also spoke twice. In addition, Adrian brought a message entitled, "We Can Have Revival Now." He also selected Gloria Roe and Jeff Stiles, with whom he had served at Parkview Baptist Church in Fort Pierce, to lead music. Noticeably absent was the Stetson University Glee Club. Rather, Adrian asked The Palm Beach Atlantic College Chorale to provide special songs and Jess Moody—Palm Beach Atlantic President—to deliver a brief message following the songs.[38]

When the Annual Meeting began on Tuesday morning, Doyle Carlton was unfortunately not available to call the 1,000-plus messengers to order as he had undergone emergency surgery the weekend prior and was hospitalized in Orlando. So, when the time came for his President's Address, Adrian read Doyle's prepared message entitled, "The World and the Church." Described by the *Miami Herald* as a "fire and brimstone attack on radical youth, liberal educators, and the U.S. Supreme Court," Doyle warned of the rising menaces of Communism infecting college campuses, the New Morality plaguing the next generation, and Atheism with its tyranny of the minority over the rest of the nation.[39] He also directly addressed the issue of Christian higher education:

> I believe that the Church, the Body of Christ, should be the final authority in the administration of a Baptist Christian college or seminary. Now hear me out! This should be done through Baptist-elected trustees who select a predominantly Baptist faculty of professors who give witness to their faith in Jesus Christ, that He is the virgin-born Son of God; and who openly declare their conviction that the Bible is the inspired, all-sufficient Word of God.[40]

Under any other circumstances, the reading of a President's Address by someone other than the President might have been somewhat awkward. But given the deep like-mindedness that Adrian and Doyle shared, Adrian might well have been preaching one of his own sermons. For that matter, much of Doyle's content would have been familiar to anyone accustomed to Adrian's preaching as Doyle clearly drew from his pastor's sermons.

Doyle's admonition regarding Baptist colleges and seminaries was not an abstract statement. Given the ongoing tension between Stetson University and many Florida Baptists over theological accountability and relaxed on-campus morality, Doyle was weighing in on a matter at the forefront of everyone's minds. In fact, the same issue that Adrian addressed at the 1966 Annual Meeting with his motion to discontinue Stetson University's funding was again in the spotlight when Don Manuel, Pastor of Allapattah Baptist Church in Miami (and Merritt Island's Crusade of the Americas speaker earlier that year) brought a motion almost identical to Adrian's 1966 resolution. After nearly three hours of "hot debate," his resolution failed. But whereas Adrian's 1966 motion failed by a 60-to-40 margin, this motion failed by a mere five votes—382 to 377.[41] Apart from reading Doyle's address, Adrian shared his own opinion on the matter: "I could never vote support for a school that hurts my Christian conscience. The theology [of Stetson] is not what I feel is compatible with the Bible or morality—not when young ladies can come into the men's dorm and visit."[42] W. G. Stracener, Florida Baptist Witness Editor, summarized the post-Convention sentiments of many when he wrote, "The vote on the matter sounds like an unmistakable warning to [the University] that if the situation and certain disturbing practices are not soon cleared up, there is small likelihood that budget support will be approved by the next Convention."[43]

"SOARING INTO THE SEVENTIES WITH THE SAVIOR"

December brought numerous opportunities to celebrate the coming of Jesus as newborn King, most notably the presentation of Handel's "Messiah" on Sunday night, December 14. The combined 120 voices of the Adult and Youth Choirs along with a 25-piece orchestra resonated throughout the sanctuary filled to capacity. Adrian reflected: "I don't think we could have gotten many more people into the auditorium with a crowbar. The music was glorious, and the choir and orchestra gave their best. At my guess, there were at least 1,300-1,400 present." In addition, Nelson Rutledge led a massive "Christmas Party for the Needy," Adrian and the Tour Choir presented a Christmas program entitled "The Real Meaning of Christmas" for Sears employees, and Sunday School classes brought "mountains of food" for the needy in the community.[44]

December also provided an opportunity for Adrian to reflect on the past and offer a challenge about the future. Much had taken place since he arrived as pastor. And as the church stood in the doorway to the 1970s, much more awaited:

> My dear people, our past is exciting—our future is glorious. So much has happened in the past five years. We have developed into a great, multi-ministry, soul-winning church. We have sold over one million dollars in bonds, constructed fabulous facilities, launched our wonderful activities program, started the University of Christian Education, and watched our Sunday School and Music Ministry soar! For the past three years, we have led the Florida Baptist Convention in baptisms. Our past has been exciting. Our future is here! Our biggest challenge is before us. We are just now getting the decks cleared for action. While I am very grateful for what God has done for us in the past, I am not at all satisfied with our church as it is now. We are on the outer fringes of real spiritual maturity. Our visitation program is but the ghost of what it should be, could be, and what it will be. Our giving could easily be increased by one-third and our Sunday School could average 1,500 soon. These are not idle dreams, and I confess that I confidently expect to see this and much more. Are you with me? We are not showing off. We are not in competition with any other church. We just want to do the best job we can for our Lord. We are not afraid to try new methods and not above keeping time-honored, well-worn ones that work. How I love this church and all of you. It is

> such a joy to think of "soaring into the Seventies with the Savior" in fellowship with all of you.[45]

Only God could know what the next decade would hold in store for the Moon Port Pastor and the First Baptist Church of Merritt Island. But the people at least knew that their pastor's commitment had not diminished since he first said to them, "If God is in our plans, we must plan big!"

10

CHALLENGES AT THE CAPE, PERSISTENCE IN THE CHURCH (1970-1971)

As the 1970s dawned on Brevard County, the previous decade's phenomenal growth shifted as the novelty of Apollo 11 gave way to budgetary realities and manpower cutbacks. In short, Brevard could no longer claim the title of fastest-growing county in America. Meanwhile, Adrian doubled down on the fundamentals that God had called First Baptist Church to be and do—namely, Spirit-filled, dynamic preaching coupled with innovative ministry, intentional soul-winning, and a big vision for reaching people across Brevard. As a result, notwithstanding the challenges, the church maintained a special degree of Gospel momentum well into the new decade.

CUTBACKS AT THE CAPE

President Kennedy's go-for-broke goal of beating the Russians to the moon by the end of 1969 generated massive national enthusiasm and a laser focus on winning the space race. In hindsight, given the many other national challenges in the late 1960s—such as significant social upheaval, the Vietnam War, and widespread violence—without such a lofty objective and ambitious timeline America might never have reached the moon. But the one-dimensional strategy also brought with it unintended consequences:

> Kennedy's challenge called for NASA to proceed directly to the most difficult goal that seemed achievable in 1961, but it doomed whatever followed to be anticlimactic. The public was encouraged to view the Apollo landing as the grand climax of the space program—a geopolitical horse race—and not as a dramatic means to the greater end of developing a far-ranging capability.[1]

Specifically, how did this impact the space program? Among other things, funding was at stake. In February 1970, NASA requested a budget of $3.3 billion, down $500 million from the previous year. By mid-1970, the space program budget had fallen to a level not seen since 1965. Additionally, NASA leaders eliminated two of the remaining planned Apollo missions.

In Brevard, NASA budgets directly impacted employment numbers. Space program manpower had peaked in 1968 with some 26,000 workers employed at the Cape, which was 40 percent of Brevard's entire workforce. But by 1970, that number had fallen to 18,500. (In 1974, that number was less than 10,000.) Furthermore, annual contractor turnover had reached 25 percent, thus increasing Brevard's transient professional population.[2]

Not surprisingly, First Baptist Church felt a pinch in terms of people and resources. With fewer space program families moving to the area and an increase in transfers, Adrian lamented:

> In the cutbacks at the Cape, we have lost many of our best workers. How hard it has been to turn them loose....We have also lost many of our most faithful givers and multiplied hundreds of dollars each week....We have seen hundreds of the best families on earth move away due to these cutbacks. Some of these workers held key positions in our church. It has been like losing a right hand.[3]

However, Adrian never wavered in his commitment to winning Merritt Island and Brevard County for Christ. In fact, he saw an open door in the midst of challenges and assured the congregation, "We're just getting started!"

REVIVAL, RESURRECTION, AND RUDIMENTS

Evangelist Eddie Martin returned to First Baptist Church for a week of revival services on February 1-8: "These are days of great opportunity! May this week of fervent Bible preaching be a great blessing to you, your family, and your friends. Attend every service and find out for yourself why they call Eddie Martin 'One of America's finest preachers.'"[4] Adrian also challenged the congregation with a creative twist. All members living north of Highway 520 were from the "North" and those living south of Highway 520 were from the "South," and members received points for attending (one point), bringing a visitor (two points), and bringing a visitor from across the "Mason-Dixon Line" (three points). Services on February 8 capped the revival with over 1,400 in attendance. All told, the church saw 105 professions of faith, 58 baptisms, and 20 new members joining by transfer of membership letter.[5] Then, as the church gathered on Easter Sunday, March 29, to celebrate the Resurrection, over 2,500 gathered for services, 19 made professions of faith in Christ, and 10 joined by transfer of membership letter.[6]

As Spring gave way to Summer, cutbacks at the Cape and conversions on the campus ultimately resulted in a zero-sum change at First Baptist Church. Adrian described the reality in this way: "We have had to redouble our efforts. In statistics, we've had to run hard to stand still." In fact, the church was baptizing more new Christians than it ever had in its history. But while the church had maintained its numerical advantage, the culture of the congregation had shifted somewhat with many of the new members yet to be discipled in the rudiments of the Christian faith—to include the spiritual discipline of stewardship. Indeed, many of the most faithful givers had relocated due to cutbacks at the Cape. Yet, as Adrian reminded the people, "We have won others to take their places, but these new Christians need to be trained in giving. Our buildings and programs are a venture in faith. It will take the best from all of us to make it work. Start to tithe this week!"[7] Thus, a noticeable uptick in practical messaging about giving began to appear in *The Thrust*, such as these principles:

There are five unanswerable reasons why every Christian ought to tithe:

1. Honesty says we ought to tithe. The tithe is the Lord's. If we spend it on ourselves, we're stealing money that does not belong to us.
2. Gratitude says we ought to tithe. If God loved us enough to send His Son to die for us, ten cents out of every dollar is not too much to give.
3. Love says we ought to tithe. If we love our Lord, then we are going to keep His commandments. We don't mind lavishing gifts upon those we love.
4. Obedience says we ought to tithe. God says to. If there were no other reasons, this would be enough. We claim to be people of the Book; then we must obey that book if we want to God's power in our lives.
5. Faith says that we ought to tithe. God has promised that if we bring the tithe, He will bless us.[8]

Given that the church had just approved an annual budget of $400,000—by far the largest in its history—faithful stewardship was a must: "If everyone tithed, we would OVERGIVE this budget in 6 months!"[9]

A VOICE BEYOND THE SUNSHINE STATE

Looking back across the full scope of Adrian's life and ministry, it is hard to imagine a time when his voice was not well known across the Southern Baptist Convention. But that was, in fact, the case for most of his Merritt Island years. For example, in 1967 C. E. Autrey, Director of Evangelism for the Southern Baptist Home Mission Board (precursor to the North American Mission Board), lobbied to have Adrian deliver keynote messages at Ridgecrest and Glorieta Baptist Assemblies during Home Missions

In January 1971, the "Moon Port Pastor" preached at the Arizona Baptist State Evangelism Conference. *The Baptist Beacon* (January 7, 1971), 1.

Week. Unfortunately, his efforts were hindered by Adrian's perceived lack of notoriety:

> Dear Brother Rogers, I remember very distinctly your message at the Evangelistic Conference in Orlando [January 1967]. I appreciated it so much that I have been saying encouraging and recommending words about you ever since. The truth is I brought your name before our committee to be the preacher at Ridgecrest and Glorieta during Home Missions Week and tried to get them to select you, but they debated against it due to the fact that they said your name was not well enough known.[10]

Three years later, having led First Baptist Church to amazing, God-sized victories over and over, no one could argue that his name was "not well enough known."

As a result, Adrian began to receive invitations from across the SBC to conduct revival services and speak at state conventions and evangelism conferences. For example, in March 1970 he was the featured preacher at the First Southern Baptist Church of Phoenix, Arizona for a week of revival meetings. Then, in January 1971 he preached at the Arizona Baptist Evangelism Conference in Tucson where he was billed as the "Moon Port Pastor." During what state leaders projected as "the most unusual and exciting Evangelism Conference," Adrian challenged listeners to GO: "The spirit of the Gospel is to GO. Regardless of who we are—preacher, deacon, layman, teacher—we have one common command, and that command is to GO." In March 1971, promoted once again as the "Moon Port Pastor," he conducted revival services for Emmanuel Baptist Church in Alexandria, Louisiana. Later, in November 1971, he spoke three times at the Ohio Baptist State Convention Annual Meeting. In January 1972, he brought three messages at the Kentucky Baptist Evangelism Conference: "The Power of His Resurrection," "Christ Will Return," and "Developing an Evangelistic Church." The Kentucky Baptist paper, *The Western Recorder*, devoted an entire page to describing Adrian's message about church evangelism. The paper, which was hardly sympathetic to his theological stance, described the message as the "dogmatic preaching of an ultra-conservative, highly successful, soul-winning pastor-evangelist in the R. G. Lee oratorical style."[11] (One can only assume that Adrian received the description as a compliment!) Looking back, Joyce Rogers recalled that it was through these types of speaking engagements that God began to elevate Adrian to high levels of influence and leadership in the Southern Baptist Convention.[12]

THE BROADMAN COMMENTARY: SHOWDOWN IN DENVER

The rift between conservative and liberal Southern Baptists rose to the national forefront as the 1970 Southern Baptist Convention Annual Meeting in Denver drew near. While Southern Baptists had traditionally embraced a high view of the Scripture as infallible and wholly inspired, encroaching liberalism—the likes of which Adrian had encountered at Stetson—had gained an increasing foothold in the twentieth century.

Rumblings had echoed across the previous decade, not least because of the 1961 release of Ralph Elliott's book, *The Message of Genesis.* Printed by Broadman Press, the publishing wing of the Southern Baptist Convention, the volume showcased numerous historical-critical assumptions and conclusions that the majority of Southern Baptists found incompatible with the plain message of the Bible. Many Southern Baptists were particularly annoyed that the author was a professor at Midwestern Baptist Theological Seminary whose salary was paid by Southern Baptist congregations. As a result, at the 1962 Annual Meeting in San Francisco, Southern Baptists roundly criticized the book and called for greater theological accountability. Subsequently, Southern Baptists called for a revision to the 1925 *Baptist Faith and Message.* Conservatives had made their voices known, but the prevailing mood among Convention leaders was to favor peace and unity at all costs. For those who, like Adrian Rogers, preferred to be "divided by truth rather than united in error," the battle was far from over. In fact, it was just beginning.[13]

In 1969, Broadman Press released the *Genesis-Exodus* volume of the Broadman Bible Commentary series. Written by G. Henton Davies, a British Baptist, the commentary on Genesis contained many of the same historical-critical assumptions and conclusions found nearly 10 years earlier in *The Message of Genesis*. Published by Broadman Press and endorsed by the Southern Baptist Sunday School Board (precursor to LifeWay Christian Resources), many Baptists bought and read the work. Along with numerous other conservative pastors and leaders, Adrian immediately identified its defects and moved to warn his congregation about the book, especially after a member told him that she had already bought the commentary, assuming that "anything that our Sunday School Board recommended was bound to be alright." In his message, "Five Fundamentals," he shared his concerns:

> The Bible is miracle, not myth. Yet we have some in our Southern Baptist Convention who do not believe this. You will read in your Sunday School quarterly an advertisement for a new commentary, the Broadman Bible Commentary. Don't waste your money buying it. It breaks my heart to say it, but it is untrustworthy. Consider what it says about Genesis 22, which is one of the sweetest chapters in all of the Bible. If there was ever a passage in the Old Testament that pictures the Gospel, it is Genesis 22—it's a picture of the substitutionary death of the Lord Jesus Christ. Well, let me quote our Southern Baptist commentary: "Did Abraham's conviction correspond to a real divine request? Did God in fact make such a demand upon Abraham? There are those who would accept the command literally. Our answer, however, is no." Well, wait a minute friends, because we have a problem. This reminds us of the serpent in Genesis 2: "Did God say?" But that's exactly what the author of the commentary is saying. ...My friends, that is nothing but pure, old-fashioned, unvarnished, liberal heresy—that's all it is. And I believe the time has come to fight sin where we find it,

> even in the Southern Baptist Convention. It's easy to sit around and talk about what is happening to these other denominations. But if we as Southern Baptists don't wake up, we're going to go down the same road that these other denominations have gone down because we're ashamed to take a stand for that which is right and against that which is wrong. We believe that the Bible is the inspired, inerrant, infallible Word of God.[14]

As the 1970 Annual Meeting drew near and battle lines were drawn, Adrian called the First Baptist Church to pray and act in his message entitled "Revival":

> You'd better pray for the Southern Baptist Convention that's meeting in Denver because the latest Southern Baptist commentary is a disgrace to Almighty God. It's published by the Broadman Press. But I'm telling you that sin is sin in the Southern Baptist Convention just as sin is sin anyplace else. The same sin that led the Methodists down the wrong trail and led the Presbyterians down the wrong trail and wrecked once-great denominations is trying to wreck the Southern Baptist Convention—and God help us if we don't stand up against it and say that the Bible is the inspired Word of God.[15]

When Messengers gathered in Denver, they debated extensively over the commentary. Gwin Turner, Pastor of First Baptist Church of Mar Vista, California, made a motion that publication of the *Genesis-Exodus* commentary cease immediately and be re-written from a more conservative perspective: "It is one thing to interpret the Bible. It is something else to directly contradict its clear statements. This kind of approach to the Bible is completely out of character with this Convention's statement of faith."[16] Messengers overwhelmingly agreed with the motion, voting 5,394 in favor and 2,170 against.[17] Regarding the commentary's re-writing, Adrian was quoted in numerous papers: "Let's not waste money writing something which will not be swallowed by Bible Believers."[18]

PRESSING FORWARD FOR JESUS

In spite of cutbacks at the Cape and other challenges, Adrian led First Baptist Church to press forward in 1970-1971 with reaching Merritt Island and Brevard County of Jesus. The *Today* newspaper, in an article entitled, "There's No Magic Formula for Building a Church," highlighted Adrian's ministry philosophy: "Although Reverend Adrian Rogers confesses to no 'magic formula' at the First Baptist Church of Merritt Island, he seems to have a magic wand somewhere." Adrian, however, was quick to point out that the secret was not in the state-of-the-art Family Activities Building, the 1,300-seat sanctuary, or any creative programs. Instead, "The Spirit of God has worked, not I....Jesus Christ said, 'I will build my church. It's not our church, it's his church. The Lord builds the church. It's God's work—it's supernatural, and no human being can do it."[19]

In fact, the Spirit of God worked through intentional and proactive Great Commission ministry, and Adrian's relentless emphasis upon soul-winning never subsided. In his August 2, 1970 "Pastor's Paragraphs," he reminded the people of "four ways to encourage yourself to continue soul-winning":

1. Set aside one day a week to visit. If you cannot take an entire day, give the entire evening. Let nothing interfere with this time.
2. Have a visiting partner each month. Have it understood that the two of you will visit on a certain day each week. If you are tempted to skip visitation, the fact of his depending on you to go with him will produce an added effort on your part.
3. Set a goal to win at least one soul to Christ each week. The joy of winning souls each week will become an addiction and keep you going back. If you fail to win one for the week, do not become discouraged but seek to win two the next week.
4. Write four facts in the back of your Bible and read them constantly:
    (1) God wants me to go and will bless me. (Matthew 28:19, "Go ye therefore...")

(2) God will empower me as I go. (Acts 1:8, "But ye shall receive power...")

(3) The Holy Spirit will convict them as I give them the Gospel. (John 16:8, "And when He is come, He will convict the world of sin and of righteousness and of judgment")

(4) Some soul is at stake, and I can change the course of his destiny. (James 5:20, "Let him know, that he that converteth a sinner from the error of his way shall save a soul from death, and shall hide a multitude of sins")[20]

In addition to these practical principles, First Baptist Church also hosted "Faith Promise Week" in September 1970. Intended to "supercharge our people with a desire to win souls," Adrian focused on the already-scheduled Sunday and Wednesday services on September 20, 23, and 27. Homer Lindsay, Jr., among others, brought special messages in these services highlighting the need to witness and the power to witness.[21]

These exhortations—and many others like them—were not abstract messages to the congregation. Instead, Adrian provided concrete opportunities to accompany the motivation. In September, that opportunity came in the form of a new visitation initiative called "God's Invasion Army." Weekly visitation had always been a part of the church calendar since Adrian came as pastor, but God's Invasion Army creatively provided new visitation opportunities for ladies on Tuesday mornings and the entire congregation on Tuesday nights. On September 6, *The Thrust* announced in a large-font banner, "WANTED! 1,200 PROSPECTS NOW! Church to launch intensified outreach and witnessing campaign." Adrian described the initiative in simple terms: "God's Invasion Army will be a new kind of visitation program. We will declare war on Satan and his forces and make an all-out effort to bring captives bound in the golden chains of the Gospel to lay at Jesus' blessed feet."[22] On October 11, Adrian could report, "Merritt Island was invaded by 204 commandos for Christ last Tuesday. They were part of the Invasion Army who have declared their intent to sabotage Satan's Kingdom of Darkness and liberate souls.

It was a taste of New Testament Christianity as we went to turn the world upside down for Christ."[23] By Spring 1971, *The Thrust* announced, "God's Invasion Army on the Move! 186 decisions for Christ during the past 5 weeks! 376 won in 20 weeks! Don't You Want to Be a Soul-Winner?"[24] By the end of the 1970-1971 church year, a staggering 342 soul-winners in God's Invasion Army had led 3,335 men, women, boys, and girls to Jesus.[25]

In January 1971, First Baptist Church adopted another creative method for bringing Jesus to people and people to Jesus. For some time, Adrian had admired the emerging bus ministries at several large and growing churches regardless of denomination:

> There are churches in America doing a fantastic job—some of them are Independent Baptist churches—going out in buses, winning people to Jesus Christ, and baptizing more people in churches than have been baptized in Christendom since the days of the Apostles, and I say I want some of whatever it is they're doing.[26]

Adrian was a firm believer in the bus ministry concept, not because of the busses but because of the potential to win souls for Jesus:

> As far as I can see with my mental ability and spiritual insight, bringing kids on buses to Sunday School is the most economical dollar spent that I know of to get souls won to Jesus in this day and this age. Now, that may change, and if that changes then we'll change. But if you know a better way right now, then you tell me. And if your way is a good way and not something ridiculous, then we'll lay aside this and do that.[27]

Initial results from the new bus ministry were encouraging. On January 10, the church saw 115 children arrive in buses as over 1,300 of all ages worshipped on campus with 12 professions of faith and over a dozen new members joining.[28] At the height of the bus ministry during Adrian's pastorate, six buses named Snoopy, Charlie Brown, Linus, Road Runner, Hot Dog, and Smokey brought hundreds of children to First Baptist

Church each Sunday where they heard the saving Gospel and frequently responded with faith.[29]

Meanwhile, Adrian also maximized Vacation Bible School (VBS) and the opportunities that it created. Whereas most churches at that time held VBS in the mornings, in 1969 and every year following during Adrian's Merritt Island ministry, First Baptist Church conducted its annual VBS in the evenings—but with a twist. While the children engaged in Bible lessons, games, and other activities nightly from 7:00-8:30 PM, Adrian personally led sessions for parents with marriage and family discipleship themes. For example, during VBS in 1970, he brought these messages: "A Man's Place in the Home," "Homes Under the Blood," "The Miracle of Marriage," "The Bible and Sex," "Courtship," "How to Argue Successfully," and "How to Win Your Family to Jesus Christ." On Friday night of that week, he explained in the adult session the "why" behind the strategy:

> This is Vacation Bible School, only we're doing something different. Rather than having Vacation Bible School in the daytime as we've normally had it, we've had it this week in the evening. Why? Because we here at the First Baptist Church of Merritt Island have tried to put an emphasis on the entire family. This is why we feel that, in a sense, even Vacation Bible School is a failure if the parents are sending their children to Vacation Bible School rather than bringing them. Vacation Bible School should be a family affair.[30]

Throughout the 1970 VBS week, average attendance for all ages hovered near 860 each night, and the church saw a number of professions of faith and additions to the congregation.[31]

ACCOLADES FOR GOD'S MEN

During Adrian's Merritt Island years, God assembled a noteworthy team of ministers at First Baptist Church, and he was the first to acknowledge that the phenomenal Merritt Island successes simply could not have happened without the Spirit-filled synergy between these men of God. From the pulpit, in *The Thrust*, and through other means, Adrian often took time to recognize their talents and contributions as well as his sincere affection for them.

Jim Whitmire, of course, was already a staff member when Adrian arrived, and he quickly came to love and appreciate Jim's leadership and abilities. Of special note, on Jim's eighth anniversary at First Baptist Church, Adrian devoted his "Pastor's Paragraphs" to recognizing Jim and his wife Linda:

> Jim Whitmire was serving this church as combination minister of music, education, and youth when I came to be the pastor 6 1/2 years ago. I was really impressed by the young man with the bright eyes and the big smile, but little did I dream just how much I would grow to love and admire him. How can we ever measure the effects of his ministry accurately? His life has literally touched scores of thousands with Heaven's harmony here and across the nation. Our choir program is second to none that I know of in Florida and perhaps in the entire Convention....
>
> Our choirs recently have come back from the state music festival with "rave notices." Yet, while the music is high-quality, it is Christ-centered and Spirit-filled. Yes, the choirs can do the "heavy stuff" and do it well, but Jim is more interested in reaching souls and blessing hearts than impressing other ministers of music or the "Nashville brass." He is a soul-winner, a counselor, and when called upon—a good preacher. I don't know what we would ever do without him. Perish the thought....
>
> And, of course, behind every great man is a great woman. Linda has had to share Jim with so many of us, and we have asked her to put up with a lot as we have often made unreasonable demands on his time, yet she has been the other half of a dedicated team. We as a church love and appreciate all the Whitmires. God bless you, Jim. May

> the next eight years be the greatest ever for you. We'll all do our part to make it so.[32]

By all accounts, Adrian Rogers and Jim Whitmire had a special bond together in Gospel service at Merritt Island[34]. George Korda recalled, "Adrian Rogers and Jim Whitmire made for an inspired combination. They had an enthusiasm and exuberance of spirit with 100 ideas coming out of their heads at any given time."[33] David Rogers, who was a small boy during those years, thought of them as "Batman and Robin" at Merritt Island.[34] But that bond transcended the 1960s and early 1970s, as Adrian called Jim to Bellevue just a few years after leaving for Memphis. All told, they served 38 years together.

Tom Clayton was Adrian's first addition to the staff after he arrived as pastor, and he proved to be an exceptionally able leader of the burgeoning Sunday School at First Baptist Church. Accordingly, Adrian took time in his "Pastor's Paragraphs" to highlight Tom's leadership and ministry:

> Give honor to whom honor is due! These words are written in grateful appreciation for the ministry of Brother Thomas Clayton, our minister of education. He works like a beaver, is bold as a lion, sympathetic as an angel, and has a smile that would melt the heart of the meanest Scrooge. Over his past five years of service, less than ten educational directors in the world have seen the accomplishments this man has seen in a five-year period. Under his ministry, we have come from a run-of-the-mill Sunday School to a multi-ministering, well-organized Sunday School with an organization studied by many other churches. The thing I like about Tom is that he is not afraid to try something new, no matter how different, yet he is not stampeded into following every fad that comes along. Working under the handicap of the recent loss of scores of well-trained leaders, he has led our educational program through a difficult time. Now we are getting set for a bold advance in Bible teaching. The best is yet to be. Along with the fact that Brother Clayton is all the aforementioned

> things, he is my friend. I am grateful to love and be loved by men like Tom, Nelson, and Jim. God is so good! Happy anniversary, Tom![35]

Adrian loved Tom and later called him to Bellevue. Joyce likewise had a deep affection for Tom and his wife, Dot: "I loved Tom like a brother, and Dot was one my all-time favorite friends."[36]

Nelson Rutledge, a space industry worker and First Baptist Deacon whom Adrian had specially selected to oversee the Family Activities Building and related ministries became as invaluable as Jim Whitmire and Tom Clayton. Accordingly, Adrian made use of opportunities to highlight his efforts:

> How could we ever express our love and gratitude to Nelson and Flo Rutledge for what they have done and what they mean to us? His

First Baptist Church Pastor, Ministers, and their Wives in 1970. Courtesy Lyvonne Burleson.

> ministry has been fantastically fruitful—he is the best in the business, to my knowledge. He has been a dear friend to me as well as a faithful staff member. Praise God for what the Rutledges have meant, do mean, and we trust will mean to First Baptist Church of Merritt Island. We love the Rutledges so much—they are the greatest![37]

As a mark of his affirmation of these men, Adrian took an innovative step not common at that time: he ordained Jim Whitmire, Tom Clayton, and Nelson Rutledge. Jim Whitmire recalled, "In those days, most churches weren't ordaining ministers of music, ministers of education, and ministers of activities, so that was an innovative step." In taking that step, Adrian had a two-fold motive. First, he had a spiritual motive in that he sought to strongly affirm his co-laborers as "God-called ministers who should be ordained." Second, as Jim Whitmire recalled, he had a practical motive: he needed others to assist with the many weddings and funerals taking place in the growing congregation, and a team of ordained ministers would be more than capable in that area.[38]

In addition to the full-time staff ministers, in 1971 Adrian brought James Godley, a retired pastor, on the staff as "Pastor's Assistant." His roles and responsibilities included counseling, hospital visitation, soul-winning, and follow-up. Adrian described him as "effective in a most amazing way with a contagious spirit." Lyvonne Burleson remembered him as an "energetic, enthusiastic servant who loved the Lord, our church, and its members."[39]

CONTINUED MUSICAL DISCIPLE MAKING

Throughout his years at Merritt Island, in addition to leading numerous adult, children's, and handbell choirs, Jim Whitmire consistently cultivated ministry influence with students through his music leadership. By 1970, the High School Choir sang each week at the 8:00 AM Sunday service and also the Sunday evening services:

They sang at 8:00 AM, which meant they had to be there at 7:00 AM, which meant they had to be up at 6:00 AM. With Saturday late-night television shows keeping them up, there were weeks I wondered if I'd have a choir on Sunday morning at 8:00 AM. They didn't have to come, but I trusted the Lord, and they came.[40]

The "Revelationaries," the highly popular young men's quartet featured Norman Jones, George Richards, George Korda, and Bob Taylor. Courtesy Jim Whitmire.

By 1970, among other student ensembles, Jim Whitmire had created a male quartet comprised of Norman Jones, George Richards, George Korda, and Bob Taylor. As a counterpoint to the revolutionaries of the day calling for violence, anarchy, and social upheaval, the group was named "The Revelationaries." The group was extremely popular both on tour performances and in Central Florida churches. Jim recalled, "Those four guys were characters who were always up to something, but they were also probably the best quartet I ever had in my ministry."[41]

Additionally, the annual High School Choir tours he led beginning in 1968 traveled to upwards of 30 states and featured new talent, new music, and new destinations each year. Not surprisingly, many of the students said participating in the choir was the "most important" thing in their lives at that time. The 1970 tour included 47 students and 13 concert stops in Florida, South Carolina, Kentucky, Virginia, West Virginia, Georgia, Alabama, Pennsylvania, Tennessee, Maryland, and New York—to include ministry among Harlem's Puerto Rican population. The record album "The Way of Gladness" followed the 1970 tour. The 1971 tour included 53 students with multiple concerts up and down the east coast. This tour focused primarily on missional work in Kingston, New York supporting the endeavors of missionary Don Crum. Following that tour, the choir recorded another album entitled "Amen."[42]

A BUZZ IN THE FALL OF 1971

Key events in the Fall of 1971 created a buzz on the Merritt Island campus and beyond. Old Fashioned Day made a second appearance on September 5, 1971, three years after its inaugural occurrence. Adrian explained:

> Why Old-Fashioned Day? It will be lots of good spiritual fun, and I believe it's part of the heritage of the children of the Lord to have a good time—I really do—it's one of our birthrights. But this is not the main reason. The day will be part of an object lesson. In this day of jets and missiles, the Gospel is the same—"Jesus Christ is the same yesterday, today, and forever."...There is need in the modern age for old-time religion. The three old-fashioned problems—sin, sorrow, and death—haven't changed with all that man has invented. There is no answer except the old-time Gospel.[43]

Adrian and Joyce at Old-Fashioned Day. Courtesy Joyce Rogers.

Over 1,400 enjoyed old-fashioned worship services complete with oil lamps, a 100-year-old pump organ playing the hymns of yesteryear, specials from the recent choir tour sung by the Revelationaries, and Adrian's dynamic message about "The Old Time Religion." Attendees were encouraged not only to wear period attire dating from 1875 to 1925, but also to bring historical items and, if possible, travel to church in some form of old-fashioned conveyance. Fortunately, a special parking area was arranged complete a with hitching post as at least one person rode a horse to church, and another arrived by mule-drawn buggy. Prizes were awarded for the most unique historical items, to include a side saddle, a 125-year-old teddy bear, and a Bible from the year 1815.[44]

The following month, *The Thrust* announced, "We're Out of Space Again!" as continued Sunday School growth required creative solutions for starting 13 new departments. So, on October 3, First Baptist Church introduced a second Sunday School hour which allowed classes to run concurrently with two worship services. Whereas the church had previously conducted services at 8:00 AM and 11:00 AM with Sunday School at 9:30 AM, the new schedule featured simultaneous services and Sunday School hours at both 9:30 AM and 11:00 AM. Additionally, the new routine allowed for double the bus ministry routes, from 5 to 10.[45]

Labeled "Twin Sunday," Adrian encouraged everyone to invite a "twin" to attend church on October 3, with prayerful expectation of 2,000 in attendance. And to sweeten the day, Adrian provided a creative opportunity for all to remember in the form of a 2,000- person "human cross." Thus, on "Twin Sunday," as the 9:30 AM worship service and

"Twin Sunday," October 3, 1971, saw 2,000 people form a "human cross" on the First Baptist Church campus. Courtesy Lyvonne Burleson.

Sunday School dismissed, over 2,000 people scurried out to Magnolia Avenue where they found a 200-foot-long outline of a cross on the street. After everyone had squeezed into the outline, a photographer perched atop a crane snapped a picture that would, in many ways, define Adrian Rogers' Merritt Island years: the priority of the Cross; thousands of lives changed by the power of God, united in one accord; and the visionary, space-age campus that facilitated a broad array of ministries in Jesus' name. In retrospect, more than a few of those in attendance remembered October 3, 1971, as "the greatest day in the life of our church."[46]

11

TOWARD A HIGHER ORBIT (1972)

When a spacecraft circles the earth, the ship sometimes moves to a higher orbit to fulfill mission objectives. Such a maneuver requires additional energy and thrust, which results in a greater orbital altitude relative to the earth's surface. The higher altitude, among other things, provides a new perspective on the earth below and the stars above.

For Adrian Rogers, 1972 was the year that God moved him to a higher orbit to fulfill broader purposes. Adrian personally did not anticipate this move and said as much to a newspaper reporter in May of that year: "Go someplace else? No sir, I don't think so. In fact, I'd like to go to heaven right from here." Similarly, he announced from the pulpit, "I was Florida born and Florida bred, and when I die I'll be Florida dead—I *hope!*"[1] Yet, hindsight shows a noticeable change in the tone and tenor of Adrian's ministry beginning as early as 1970 as First Baptist Church reached the fulfillment of his creative campus vision. At the same time, Adrian was becoming more aware—and more involved—in strategic-level needs in the Southern Baptist Convention. Nevertheless, with no intention of departing Merritt Island, Adrian boldly anticipated that 1972 would be an amazing year for First Baptist Church:

> Beloved, these are exciting days in which to live. The line is being drawn. God's people seem to be growing brighter as the world is growing darker. Never before have I seen so many Spirit-filled Christians, and never before have I seen so much apostasy and sin all at the same time. Something is about to happen.[2]

"THE BIGGEST THING EVER TO HIT THE ISLAND"

January 1972 saw what would simply be known thereafter as the "Freddie Gage Crusade." Freddie Gage, a former drug addict turned evangelist from Houston, Texas led a dynamic street ministry to "victims of drug abuse, hippies, motorcycle gangs, and other restless youth" named "Pulpit in the Shadows." Brevard County, with its persistent social tensions, drug problems, and upheaval among students, seemed a prime place for Freddie's message.

Adrian went above and beyond to promote the week-long crusade, to include unprecedented coverage for five weeksin his "Pastor's Paragraphs." In those columns, he painted a stark picture of the problem as well as an optimistic projection of the Gospel solution that Freddie Gage would bring to Brevard:

> The drug problem has been a prominent item in all the news media this year. Batteries of experts line up, waiting their turn to wring their hands and express concern over youth involvement with drugs. Yet, although all the experts agree that there's a problem, not many offer a solution that works. One man that understands the problem and has a solution is Freddie Gage. His weapon against drugs is Christianity. Gage's way of helping these kids works. His ministry helps hundreds get off and stay off drugs through Christ....
>
> Young people, listen to Freddie Gage, the turned-on preacher. Since the dramatic moment when he accepted Christ, Freddie Gage's

> dream was to start a ministry in the streets to reach restless youths and victims of drug abuse. His dream has become a reality in "Pulpit in the Shadows" in Houston, Texas where there is something happening for God every minute. Known among the young people as "Freddie's Place" with the purpose of bringing Christianity to rebellious youth and convert their hatred of the establishment to a new way of life through Christ. Freddie Gage firmly believes that the only answer for young people is a personal encounter with Jesus Christ....
>
> Thousands are finding solace and hope through his ministry. Living proof of his effectiveness are six young men, formally drug users with police records, who are now working for Christ as evangelists. Young people relate to Freddie Gage because he knows how to communicate with them in a meaningful way. He talks their language. Freddie has lived and worked among them....
>
> Kids, he really tells it like it is. This could be the biggest thing ever to hit the island. Hundreds could be saved. Let's trust Jesus for a miracle.[3]

In addition to building momentum through *The Thrust*, the church also conducted a special youth rally on Sunday morning, December 12 at 11:00 AM in the gymnasium. As a result, by the time the crusade began on Sunday, January 9, young and old alike were ripe for revival.[4]

The crusade began meeting in the church sanctuary, but by Wednesday night capacity crowds required that all further meetings be moved to the Merritt Island High School "Mustang" Stadium where over 3,000 assembled to hear Freddie Gage. The *Orlando Sentinel* announced "Gage, One-Time Drug Addict, Electrifies Audience." Similarly, the *Today* newspaper featured the article "Gage: Flashy Preacher on New Trip," describing—in somewhat cynical terms—the preacher as such: "This guy in black pants, CLEAN white boots, wearing this incredible technicolor SNAKY-looking jacket... was sing-songing the damnations of hell and how you are sure to get there in one drug trip or another." As for the audience: "It was a smorgasbord of people and attitudes, kids with shoes and without; with bras and without; fresh-scrubbed and scruffy; tight-lipped grandmothers and freckled 5-year-old kids."[5]

Each night dozens and dozens came forward to receive Christ, and post-service evangelistic counseling extended into late-night hours. Years later, Freddie Gage recalled:

> Adrian would stay up past midnight in the foyer of the church, weeping with teenage hippies, druggies, and young street prostitutes as they prayed to receive Christ. I met very few people like him with such a great passion for Jesus and the souls of lost people. What an impression he made on me![6]

On Saturday afternoon, January 15, at the Kiwanis Island Park, Adrian conducted a mass-baptism service for a multitude of people who made professions of faith that week. Meanwhile, just before the January 16 edition of *The Thrust* was mailed out, all copies received a last-minute, red rubber stamp on the front: "URGENT: All Sunday Services Moved to Merritt Island Mustang Stadium. PRAISE GOD!"[7]

In the days immediately following the Freddie Gage Crusade, *The Thrust* announced: "MAN! WHATTA MEETIN! God Did a Wonderful Thing on Merritt Island Last Week!" The spiritual tally included 432 professions of faith, 15 new church members, and 99 other commitments. Additionally, a total of 3,658 attended the two Sunday morning services at Mustang Stadium. In his "Pastor's Paragraphs," Adrian stated simply: "The week that was! How do you explain it? You don't! You just experience it and say, 'Hallelujah!'"[8]

A God-sized revival called for God-sized follow-up. First and foremost, Adrian led God's Invasion Army to make follow-up contacts. The *Orlando Sentinel* featured an article entitled "Invasion Army Stirred Deep Christian Feelings" and quoted Adrian and Tom Clayton about the plan:

> It will take a mass effort to reap the benefits and minister to the hundreds of people who made decisions for Christ at the recent

evangelistic crusade of Freddie Gage. ...Five names of those who made decisions have been given to each member of the Invasion Army for contact before the next Sunday.[9]

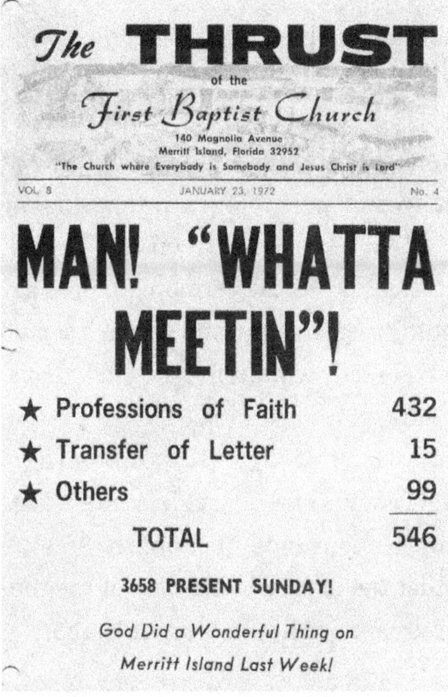

The THRUST

of the

First Baptist Church

140 Magnolia Avenue
Merritt Island, Florida 32952
"The Church where Everybody is Somebody and Jesus Christ is Lord"

VOL. 8 JANUARY 23, 1972 No. 4

MAN! "WHATTA MEETIN"!

★ Professions of Faith	432
★ Transfer of Letter	15
★ Others	99
TOTAL	546

3658 PRESENT SUNDAY!

God Did a Wonderful Thing on Merritt Island Last Week!

The Thrust announces the fruit of the Freddie Gage Crusade. Courtesy Lyvonne Burleson.

Additionally, First Baptist Church offered six weeks of Sunday morning youth rallies at the 11:00 AM hour in the gymnasium. Centered on Bill Bright's booklet *Your New Life in Christ*, each rally focused on one aspect of growing as a new Believer.[10] As the rallies kicked off on January 23, Adrian announced in the sanctuary:

> God is doing great things in our church. Down in our gymnasium, which we've turned into another auditorium, we have over 500 young people—I'm talking about teenagers—in a youth rally. For the

> next five Sunday mornings, we'll have these Jesus rallies as a follow-up on the Freddie Gage Crusade.[11]

Of the many teenagers impacted by the crusade, one 18-year-old young man wrote a letter to the *Today* newspaper with this testimony:

> The Freddie Gage Crusade was not a gimmick or a joke. I know because I was part of it. I arrived at the stadium at 7:00 PM and there were already well over a thousand people in the stands. At 7:30, the Revelationaries were the first ones to appear before the crowd of approximately 3,500 people. We then had prayer and the crusade was off and running. ...After the sermon, Freddie gave an invitation for people to accept Christ, and you should have seen the people coming. It was unusual and really wonderful. After all, that's what it's all about. This is God at work.[12]

Ultimately, the Freddie Gage Crusade made a lasting impact on the lives of hundreds, if not thousands, of people in Brevard County. Lyvonne Burleson recalled that the crusade was "one of the most dynamic things ever to occur at First Baptist Church Merritt Island."[13]

MAJOR THOMAS, COLONEL IRWIN, AND DOCTOR ROGERS

As winter became spring, Adrian's strategy to disciple those won during the Freddie Gage Crusade continued to unfold as world-famous author and Bible teacher, Major Ian Thomas, presented a week of messages in late March. As early as December 19 of the previous year, Adrian had cast his vision:

> I believe when Freddie Gage is here, we are going to see literally hundreds and hundreds of teenagers saved; and then all of us are

going to be sweetened and blessed and deepened and helped by the ministry of Ian Thomas....I think this series of meetings in conjunction with our regular worship services Sunday by Sunday has been put together by the Holy Spirit to strengthen His body at Merritt Island.[14]

A newly-installed church sign included the motto "Pointing Men Beyond the Stars" and announced Astronaut James Irwin as guest speaker. Courtesy Lyvonne Burleson.

Not surprisingly, Adrian placed a major emphasis upon Ian Thomas' visit, not least because of the impact that Thomas' writings on the Spirit-filled life and the victorious Christian life had on Adrian nearly ten years prior:

> Major Ian Thomas is a man you will not want to miss. The Holy Spirit has endowed him in a special way to teach the victorious life....He is a best-selling author. His book, *The Saving Life of Christ*, is one of the most influential books in my own personal life. I recommend it

> over and over to others. By all means, attend the Bible Conference here at the church. It can transform your life. So many of the Lord's people are living on a lower plane than they ought. They are traveling second-class to Heaven. It's time to stop enduring religion and start enjoying victory.[15]

Indeed, as Ian Thomas spoke daily at both 10:00 AM and 7:30 PM, many accepted his challenge to see that "the Christian life is the life of the Lord Jesus Christ lived two thousand years ago, lived now by Him in you!" Adrian was thoroughly pleased with the discipleship momentum created by Ian Thomas' visit: "Beyond a doubt, the Spring Bible Conference was one of the most significant weeks we have ever known. Please, Lord, help us to remember what we have learned. Amen!"[16]

Two weeks after Ian Thomas departed, another notable speaker shared with the Merritt Island congregation. On Sunday, April 16, at a special evening service promoted as a "Spiritual Space Spectacular"—and only hours after the massive Apollo 16 Saturn V rocket thundered into the heavens from Cape Kennedy—Air Force Colonel and Astronaut Jim Irwin spoke about his adventures in space and his vibrant faith in Jesus. As the Lunar Module Pilot for the Apollo 15 mission, he had walked on the moon the previous year. Saved at age eleven during revival services at the First Baptist Church of New Port Richey, Florida, Jim went on to become an Air Force test pilot who narrowly escaped death in 1961 while flying an experimental jet that crashed at Edwards Air Force Base. Miraculously, he left the hospital after two months and eventually returned to flight status, ultimately joining the astronaut corps in 1966.[17]

During his Merritt Island message, Jim described the Saturn V launch as "the most exciting ride a person could ever go on—the thrill, the joy, the superlative exhilaration of leaving the Earth." As for his time on the lunar surface, "We could feel God's presence all around us in the quiet stillness and beauty. The days I spent on the moon were very exciting, not because I was there but because God was there." In fact, as he surveyed the massive Montes Apenninus during one of his moonwalks, he quoted Psalm 121 over his intercom: "I will lift up mine eyes unto the hills, from whence cometh my help. My help comes from the Lord, which made heaven and earth."[18]

After returning to Earth, the Astronauts made three goodwill tours, one of which took them behind the Iron Curtain. On that trip, Jim and his wife, Mary, took some extra baggage along: 50 pounds of Bibles given to them by their home church in Houston, the Nassau Bay Baptist Church. Irwin recalled:

> We found out that people all over the world were so hungry for God's Word. We had a chance to witness, share with other Christians, and give every one of those Bibles to individuals or churches. People everywhere I went said they had prayed for me while I was on the moon, and, yes, we felt the power of those prayers.[19]

Reflecting on his journey to the moon and his faith in Jesus, Jim ultimately concluded that "the most important moment of my life was when I committed my life to Christ, which even exceeds lifting off on Apollo 15. Nothing can compare to a personal relationship with Jesus Christ."[20]

On May 14, Adrian delivered the commencement address at Trinity College in Dunedin, Florida—the same school Billy Graham attended 35 years earlier. His address, a message about the Prophet Elisha from 2 Kings 13, was entitled, "The Man of God." In his message, he wondered aloud what was written on Elisha's tombstone: "It didn't say, 'Elisha, Man of Genius,' and it didn't say, 'Elisha, Man of Eloquence,' and it didn't say, 'Elisha, Man of Influence.' But it said this: 'Elisha, Man of God.' Can you think of anything better than to be called a 'Man of God'? I tell you, this is the greatest thing you could call a person. I'd rather be called a 'Man of God' than anything else." Following his message, the school conferred upon Adrian an honorary Doctor of Divinity degree in recognition of his exemplary leadership and preaching.[21]

"REV ROGERS AND HIS ISLAND IN THE SUN"

In April, a reporter from the Today newspaper called Adrian and said, "I'm going to do an investigative story about you. You can cooperate with me, or you don't have to. I'm going to write the story either way." The reporter, a known atheist with a disdain for Christians and Baptist preachers—and one Baptist preacher in particular—was adamant in his purpose. In short, "He was against everything that we were for, and he was for everything we were against." In response, two thoughts crossed Adrian's mind. First, he knew he had nothing to hide, and any resistance to the reporter might imply otherwise. Second, God specifically gave him Isaiah 54:17 as assurance that he had nothing to fear: "'No weapon formed against you shall prosper, and every tongue which rises against you in judgment you shall condemn. This is the heritage of the servants of the Lord, and their righteousness is from Me,' says the Lord." As a result, he invited the reporter to attend services, follow him while he carried out his daily duties, and even offered to allow the reporter to observe some of his counseling sessions—"My life is an open book."[22]

In late April and early May, the reporter took every opportunity to observe Adrian in every way possible, all the while taking copious notes. One church member, who worked at the newspaper office, told Adrian, "Pastor, I know that reporter, and I know what he is writing about you. It's terrible. He's doing a hatchet job on you." Still, Adrian continued to claim the promise of Isaiah 54:17 "on my knees" and confidently went about his business.[23]

Throughout the process, God gave reminders that he would not let Adrian down. One Sunday when the reporter was in attendance, "God came into the service" and moved in a powerful way. Afterward, as Adrian stood at the main entrance greeting attendees, one of the deacons came to him and whispered in his ear, "Pastor, you'll never guess who's here today." Adrian said, "Who?" The deacon replied, "Johnny Unitas!" Adrian had no idea why the legendary Baltimore Colts quarterback was in attendance: "He had never been there before that day, and he never came again after that. He wasn't even Baptist; he was Roman Catholic." As much as Adrian wanted to get an autograph—to go "fanboy," as daughter Gayle recalled—he determined to greet the football legend just like anyone else and "play it straight." As Johnny Unitas approached, Adrian shook his hand and casually said, "Hi John, how are you? Good to have you with us today." After observing the exchange and snapping an informal picture, the reporter said to Adrian, "That was Johnny Unitas! What was he doing here?" Adrian replied nonchalantly, "Oh, he came to worship." The seemingly random episode left an impression on the newsman, but Adrian knew why it happened: "I thought it was really neat how the Lord dropped that little goodie in for me. He brought Johnny Unitas there so I could act so cavalier about it in front of the reporter."[24]

In early May, the reporter called Adrian with surprising news: "Well, I finished the piece and turned it in to the editor. He didn't like it. In fact, he

Adrian greets football legend Johnny Unitas after a Sunday service in May 1972. Courtesy Joyce Rogers.

fired me, and they're having someone else re-write the story!" Adrian was not surprised by the good news as he once again recalled Isaiah 54:17– "No weapon formed against you shall prosper."[25]

Adrian poses in the First Baptist Church Atrium for the article "Rev Rogers and His Island in the Sun." Courtesy Lyvonne Burleson.

The new, re-written article, entitled "Rev Rogers and His Island in the Sun," appeared in the *Today* Sunday Supplement on May 14 with a full-page picture of Adrian on the front cover and three pages of content inside. Among other things, the piece highlighted Adrian's call to the church:

> The First Baptist Church went looking for him in 1964 and attracted him with the "challenges." "It was a gut feeling, but I took the job

> because of the challenges. This place was on dead center at the time. There was some question about my "style"—the inference being I might be too loud, that my style would be too evangelistic. So I promised them: "If one person leaves, and I'm sure some will, I'll get ten people to take their place."[26]

The article also featured a variety of topics to include the busy Family Activities Building schedule each week, a typical day for Adrian, the strategic vision of the church, and Adrian's views on everything from Vietnam to abortion, from "women's lib" to the drug epidemic. Ultimately, the article mentioned the undeniable growth and influence the church had enjoyed since Adrian's arrival: "While one may find some argument with his fundamentalist Southern Baptist philosophy with its strict literal translation of the Bible—you cannot argue with success. And success shrouds the First Baptist Church of Merritt Island like icing on a cake." Adrian recalled, "God was so good! We got thousands of dollars' worth of free publicity from that piece."[27]

"NEW FACES" IN PHILADELPHIA

As the 1972 SBC Annual Meeting in Philadelphia approached, *Baptist Press* announced that "The Southern Baptist Convention Pastor's Conference will feature addresses in what John R. Bisagno, President of the Pastor's Conference, has described as a 'Sugar Stick Conference' with the theme 'New Faces.'" Bisagno, Pastor of Houston's First Baptist Church, had invited "several of Southern Baptists' outstanding new young men" each to bring "his best sermon...his favorite sugar stick." Listed among the "eight speakers who have not previously addressed the Pastors Conference" was the name Adrian Rogers—his first opportunity to preach at the national level. In addition to the 'new faces,' Bisagno also invited three Pastors Conference veterans, to include Adrian's hero, Robert G. Lee, and his friend and mentor from West Palm Beach, Jess Moody.[28]

In what might be called a "rendezvous with destiny," Adrian stepped to the podium in Philadelphia on Monday afternoon, June 5, and delivered his message, "Elisha, Man of God"—a shortened and slightly updated version of the message he brought at Trinity College one month earlier. The occasion was arguably a rendezvous with destiny for two reasons. First, for the next three decades following his first appearance on the national level, Adrian would become an immensely popular fixture at SBC Pastors Conferences and Annual Meetings. Second, unbeknownst to him, members of the Bellevue Baptist Church Pastor Search Committee were in attendance in Philadelphia that day, and they eagerly anticipated hearing from the man who was their top candidate for Bellevue's vacant pulpit.

Adrian electrified the audience as he highlighted the making of a man of God and shared some convictions about his own calling:

> God told Elijah to take his mantle and cast it upon Elisha. God told him to do that—God chose Elisha to be a man of God. And I want to tell you that no bishop can make a preacher, and no seminary can make a preacher, and no college can make a preacher—only God can make a preacher! And you may think I'm being cocky or arrogant, but I know that God has chosen me to be a man of God. I know that. I'm just as sure of my call to preach as I am of my salvation—I know that God has called me![29]

Similarly, he described the absolute necessity for God's power in the making and ministry of God's man:

> Elisha was divinely appointed, but he was also divinely anointed. He asked for a double portion of the Spirit that rested upon Elijah. And my friend, if I know anything about the urge of my heart and my soul, I want more than anything else for the power of God to rest upon my life. I'd rather die than preach without the anointing of the Holy Ghost. I mean that![30]

After the message, one of the Bellevue committee members, Orelle Ledbetter, wrote a single word at the top of his page of notes: "TREMENDOUS!"[31]

EXPLO 72

As the youth counter-culture in the late 1960s and early 1970s challenged almost every traditional dynamic of the establishment, a Jesus-filled counterpoint began to sweep across the Nation. Known by its participants as the Jesus Movement, it began among California hippies who turned from drugs—what Adrian called "synthetic salvation"—to Jesus Christ. By June 1971, some 300,000 ex-hippies on fire for Jesus had reportedly spread from coast to coast, and *Time* magazine featured an article about the "Jesus Revolution" along with a likeness of Jesus on the cover, looking akin to "the lead guitarist in a folk-funk band." In addition to hippies-turned-evangelists, tens of thousands of middle-class high school and college students also joined the Revolution. To be sure, the scope of this surge in young people embracing Jesus was perhaps the largest in United States history.[32]

Bill Bright saw enormous evangelistic potential in the Jesus Movement, and he envisioned an event that would feature "mass evangelism training in a huge football stadium" somewhere. So he appointed Paul Eshelman, the Campus Crusade Director at the University of Wisconsin, to develop the idea. The resulting plan, scheduled for June 12-17, 1972 in Dallas, Texas, was called Explo 72. Organizers anticipated upwards of 100,000 high school and college students as well as adults from across the Nation and around the world spending each day at evangelism training events spread across Dallas with mass rallies held in the Cotton Bowl each night. To cap things off, a massive one-day Christian music festival would be held on Saturday, June 17 with a projected attendance near 250,000.[33]

Given his relentless passion for personal evangelism as well as his friendship with Bill Bright, Adrian was not going to miss Explo 72. In fact,

Adrian eagerly watched the Jesus Movement unfolding with delight and was glad to go from observer to participant:

> We are seeing—praise God!—a great and wonderful mighty revival among young people. People ask me, "What do you think of the Jesus Movement?" I believe in it, and I believe, by and large, it is good and holy and wholesome, and I pray that it spreads.…I'd rather see kids carrying a big black Bible and saying 'Hallelujah' than smoking dope, practicing free love, popping pills, and shooting up with heroine.…In a few weeks, some of us will be going to Explo 72. They are expecting 100,000 young people to train to win souls. Can you imagine what Dallas will be like when 100,000 young people descend upon that city talking about how to share Jesus Christ?[34]

In May, the *Orlando Sentinel* reported in an article entitled, "Reverend Rogers to Lecture at 'Explo 72' Conference," that, "All roads will lead to Dallas when the largest gathering of college and high school students in history will converge for an international student congress on evangelism." Additionally, the Sentinel included this excerpt from Paul Eshelman's invitation to Adrian:

> In recent weeks God has been impressing us again with the need to be, above all else, holy, cleansed men of God. We would like for you to speak on the need for confession of sin, and the priority of a pure and holy life. Additionally, I believe that if we want to see revival take place in our world, it must begin with men and women of God who are enjoying His fullness.[35]

Specifically, Adrian would speak to more than 500 laymen at the Dallas Sheraton Hotel on Wednesday morning as part of the National Christian Leadership Conference meeting concurrently with Explo 72. Then, on Friday morning, he would speak to nearly 2,000 Explo attendees at the First Baptist Church of Dallas.[36]

Adrian was just one of many attendees representing Brevard County, as over 200 youth and adult counselors traveled to Dallas from Brevard. The largest Brevard contingent—over 110 loaded in three charter buses—was from Peter Lord's Park Avenue Baptist Church with a number of students from First Baptist Church of Merritt Island included.[37]

Explo 72 proved to be both a massive authentication of the Jesus Movement as well as, in many ways, its grand finale. For Bill Bright, it served as a key and unforgettable milestone on the road to worldwide evangelism as he told 85,000 attendees one evening: "If I could choose any time in all of human history to be alive, I'd choose right now."[38] Adrian summed up what he saw and heard in Dallas in this way: "Explo was fantastic! It was an experience that cannot be described in words. God is moving!"[39]

FROM MERRITT ISLAND TO MEMPHIS

In late July, Adrian and his family (minus Steve, who had stayed in Merritt Island) departed for vacation, riding in a motorhome up the East Coast with no fixed itinerary in mind. While stopped in Lynchburg, Virginia, they called Steve to check in, and he informed Adrian that a member of the Pastor Search Committee from Bellevue Baptist Church had called, asking to speak with Adrian. With no thought of leaving First Baptist Church for Bellevue—or any other opportunity, for that matter—Adrian returned the call only out of courtesy. When he did, he spoke with Roland Maddox, who told him that the committee would like to meet with him and was prepared to travel to his location. Adrian declined the offer, but he agreed to divert the vacation to Memphis and speak with the committee members there. Upon arrival, Adrian and Joyce spent almost three days in the first week of August with the committee, hearing their hearts for the kind of pastor that Bellevue needed and their research into Adrian's life and ministry. Among other things, knowing Adrian's heart for the state of the Southern Baptist Convention, they suggested that he could have a more significant position of influence to affect change if he was Bellevue's pastor. Upon their invitation, he agreed to return to Memphis to fill the pulpit two weeks later—but NOT as a pastoral candidate.[40]

Adrian returned from vacation energized and glad to be back in the Merritt Island pulpit on August 6. That evening, the Senior High Choir, fresh off the 1972 tour, performed their homecoming concert: "The church building was filled with great music, joyful hearts, and happy faces." As Adrian and Joyce walked out of the sanctuary that evening, they were met with a pleasant Florida breeze beneath a canopy of stars. Reflecting on all that First Baptist Church meant to him, Adrian said to Joyce, "I would be crazy if I ever left this place." But the matter of Bellevue nevertheless weighed on his heart as he and Joyce fasted and prayed about God's will.[41]

Adrian and Joyce returned to Memphis the next week, and he preached a message entitled "How to Please God" in the Sunday morning service. Although they assumed that he was merely filling the pulpit—and had informed the Merritt Island Deacons of that intent—the Pastor Search Committee fully intended to take a congregational vote following the service to call Adrian as Pastor. In fact, the Memphis Commercial Appeal newspaper announced as much one day earlier: "Bellevue Baptist to Hear Prospective Pastor Sunday." The article reported that, according to Al Childress, the Search Committee Chairman, "A biblically conservative pastor from Florida, Dr. Adrian Rogers, will be presented to members... for approval as its new pastor." The article also featured a photo of Adrian and Joyce on the front steps of the church.[42]

Following the sermon, Adrian and Joyce retired to the church office while committee members made individual recommendations to the congregation. After hearing from each member, the congregation voted unanimously to call Adrian as pastor. Soon after, Adrian and Joyce reappeared in the sanctuary, stunned that the congregation had voted. But Adrian knew God was at work and responded on the spot with a clarifying question to the entire congregation: "Is it my understanding that this church is asking me to be their pastor?" Al Childress responded, "Yes, Sir. One hundred percent." Moved by God's Spirit, Adrian then said, "To come to a church without preaching to it would be, to me, like marrying a girl without first kissing her. I wanted to feel your hearts, and I have this morning. You're marvelous people, and we want you to know that we feel it's God's will that we come, and we will."[43]

The next Wednesday evening at First Baptist Church, Adrian shared his resignation with a packed sanctuary and gave some details about how God had called him to Memphis:

> Dear people, the first mark of a good soldier is that he is obedient to his commander-in-chief. Since I am a soldier of Jesus Christ, and because I feel his clear leadership in my heart, I offer my resignation as Pastor of the First Baptist Church of Merritt Island to accept the pastorate of the Bellevue Baptist Church of Memphis, Tennessee. I trust you know my love for you all. To sever our relationship after eight Spirit-blessed years as your Shepherd is difficult beyond description. It seems impossible that Pastor and people could have loved each other more. You have been kind and good to us beyond (far beyond) that which is due. The accomplishments of these years speak for themselves. Glorious, unbelievable things have been done. For all of these, we give the Lamb of God the praise. He has been so good. There must be no panic and no fear. If we react wrongly, God may chasten us. If we trust him sweetly, he will surely bless us. And we will trust him![44]

Adrian's last Sunday as pastor was August 27, and *The Thrust* proclaimed it, "Adrian Rogers Day." Numbers alone could never summarize completely the work that God accomplished in his eight years as pastor, but the tally was nevertheless truly incredible:

Professions of Faith:	3,476
Transfer of membership:	2,922
Baptisms:	2,470
Total Additions:	6,615[45]

Truly, the numbers represent eight years of perpetual revival under Adrian's leadership and preaching. But beyond the metrics, the story of the Moon Port Pastor is one of God-engineered transformation that impacted lives far beyond Brevard County during one of American's most historic seasons.

PART IV

THE MEANS

12

A HIGH VIEW OF THE SCRIPTURE

On August 27, 1972, Adrian preached his final Sunday morning sermon as Pastor of the First Baptist Church. Naturally, he wanted to conclude his Merritt Island ministry with a message fitting for the occasion. So, as he introduced the sermon entitled, "The Book that Built a Church," he set the tone for a summation of his Merritt Island years:

> As I prepared this message, I thought of so many things today that I might speak to you about. I could have preached on Jesus or perhaps on the Holy Spirit or the need for evangelism or on the need for cooperation. So many thoughts flooded in on my mental doorstep. But I decided to see if I could say in one message something about the basis for what I've been trying to say for eight years. So I decided to remind you what we believe about the Bible and the inspiration of the Bible because it is the Bible that has built this church.[1]

As Adrian shared with the people the timeless truths about the Bible, he reminded them that "the Bible is supernatural in origin, infallible in authority, and inspired in totality from cover to cover."[2]

To be sure, the most fundamental and timeless principle that fueled Adrian's Merritt Island ministry was a high view of the Scripture as the inerrant and inspired Word of God. Listeners to his Merritt Island sermons would be hard-pressed to find a single message that did not somehow include this key theme. At the same time, listeners over time would begin to identify four ideas consistently occurring over and over in his Merritt Island preaching: (1) the nature of the Bible, (2) the Bible as priority for church health and growth, (3) warnings about compromising the Word of God, and (4) warnings about false prophets. In this chapter, we will share examples of each and offer contemporary applications for Pastors and Believers alike.

THE NATURE OF THE BIBLE

In a particular Merritt Island message entitled "False Prophets," Adrian recommended a comprehensive statement of faith for the congregation to consider and adopt. Not surprisingly, the very first part of the statement featured a high view of the Scripture:

> We believe in the Scriptures of the Old and New Testaments as verbally inspired by God and inerrant in the original writings. They are the supreme and final authority in faith and life.[3]

As we have seen, these convictions undergirded Adrian's life and ministry prior to and throughout his Merritt Island years—so much so that it would be easy to take the fact for granted. But he never hesitated to stir up his people "by way of reminder" (2 Peter 1:13) regarding the Bible's divine inspiration.

For example, in his message "The Book that Built a Church," Adrian highlighted four reasons for his unshakeable confidence that the Bible was truly the uniquely inspired Word of God. First, he mentioned the Bible's "wonderful unity" found among its 66 books written by approximately 40 men from all walks of life in three different languages over a span of more than 1,500 years. His conclusion? "When these 66 books come together, they don't make 66; they make one book that begins at Genesis and ends at Revelation, one perfect compilation of the will and wisdom of God. How was this possible? 'Holy men of God spake as they were moved by the Holy Ghost.'"[4] Additionally, Adrian pointed to the Bible's "fulfilled prophecy," which he described as "one of the greatest proofs of the inspiration of the Word of God." Considering things like Isaiah's prophecy about Cyrus "two hundred years before Cyrus came on the scene" (Isaiah 45:1) to the prophecies of the crucifixion found in Psalm 22 that sounded as if they were written "by a man standing with pen and paper at the foot of the cross," Adrian observed that "some of the things that God says in the Bible are so astoundingly accurate that they're almost raucous."[5] Furthermore, Adrian referenced what he called the Bible's "ever-living quality." In short, he argued that the Bible has always outlived its critics: "Emperors have decreed its extermination, atheists have railed against it, agnostics have smiled cynically upon it, modernists have moved heaven and earth to disprove its miracles, materialists have ignored it, and radicals have ranted against it, but the Bible lives on—they can't kill it!"[6] Lastly, Adrian highlighted the Bible's "life-changing ability," which he attributed to the power of God:

> My friend, if you were to take an atomic bomb and have it detonated between your lapels, there wouldn't be enough left of you to bury—you'd be gone—but it couldn't blow the sin out of your heart; you'd still be a sinner somewhere in eternity. But I've seen the Word of God go off in a man's heart and blow the sin out. It's the power of God unto salvation![7]

For Adrian, there was no question about the nature of the Bible. But that was just the beginning.

THE BIBLE AS PRIORITY FOR CHURCH HEALTH AND GROWTH

As the Merritt Island ministry became known throughout Florida and across the Southern Baptist Convention, more than a few pastors and theological educators wrote to Adrian, inquiring about the secrets of his success. Typically, he would write as he did to a New Orleans Baptist Theological Seminary professor: "I attribute our success to four words that start with the letter 'W'—and the first is WORD, the Word of God. There can be no fruitfulness and there can be no growth without the Word of God."[8] The key was to be found in John 15:7-8: "If you abide in Me, and My words abide in you, you will ask what you desire, and it shall be done for you. By this My Father is glorified, that you bear much fruit." For Adrian, there was an undeniable relationship between the phrases "if my words abide in you" and "you shall bear much fruit." What was the secret of fruitfulness and productivity in the Lord's vineyard? Jesus' words abiding in his people.

For the Merritt Island congregation, Adrian was absolutely convinced that First Baptist Church would never be greater than its belief in the Bible. Moreover, he argued:

> We must always say "Thus says the Lord God" without being afraid of people accusing us of being narrow-minded or dogmatic. If they want to accuse us of being narrow-minded, let them. And if some people say that we're so narrow-minded that they're not going to come back, don't get upset. For every person we lose, ten more will come and take their place.[9]

Moreover, Adrian's hallmark of his Merritt Island pulpit ministry was an unapologetic and uncompromising allegiance to the Word of God, and he acknowledged that without God's Word he had nothing to offer anyone:

> Do you want me to tell you why I have any power in the pulpit—if I have any power in the pulpit—it is because I preach the Book. Do you want to know what built the First Baptist Church of Merritt Island and will continue to build it? The Book! Therefore, we need to preach the Book, live the Book, share the Book, read the Book, and saturate our souls in the Book until we know the Christ of the Book!"[10]

WARNINGS ABOUT COMPROMISING THE WORD OF GOD

Adrian frequently warned his people about the dangers of compromising the non-negotiable truths of the Word of God—whether at the personal level, the congregational level, or the denominational level. For example, in his Merritt Island message entitled "It Costs to Serve Jesus," he issued a multifaceted warning at all levels:

> There are people who try to strike up a bargain with the devil: "Devil, if you leave me alone, I'll leave you alone. I'm not going to fight you, so please don't fight me." But you can't peacefully coexist with the devil any more than you can peacefully coexist with a roaring lion. If you meet a lion on the street, either he'll get you or you'll get him. There are preachers who are not willing to battle and have trimmed the message to keep their church—they compromise the Word of God. Parents not willing to battle and take a stand have let their teenagers get into all manner of sin—they've compromised and compromised and compromised. Our denomination has compromised: we're ashamed to take a stand for the whole Word of God, and so we have compromised. We want peace, and we don't want anything in the denomination to upset our peace, so we don't take a stand for the Word ofGod and we sit down at the conference table and we compromise.[11]

Adrian was a man who preferred to be "divided by truth rather than united in error," and he never failed to take a strong stand for that which was non-negotiable. His courage was never in question, and God used his example to challenge many.

WARNINGS ABOUT FALSE PROPHETS

Adrian frequently reminded his congregation about Jesus' warnings concerning false prophets: "Beware of false prophets, who come to you in sheep's clothing, but inwardly they are ravenous wolves. You will know them by their fruits....Not everyone who says to Me, 'Lord, Lord,' shall enter the kingdom of heaven" (Matthew 7:15-16,21). For Adrian, the bitterest fruit of all came from false prophets who "use the language of Christianity but who will die and go to hell, who are wolves in sheep's clothing, and who use their ministry not to lead people to Heaven and life everlasting but rather to lead them to hell where they hear the Savior profess, 'Depart! I never knew you.'"[12] At the same time, Adrian was careful to differentiate between a false prophet and someone with different convictions on secondary matters: "I'm not talking about theological trifles; I'm not talking about whether there are seven or seven-and-a-half years in the tribulation. I'm talking about basic issues; I'm talking about things that make the difference between as to whether some soul will spend eternity in Heaven or eternity in hell."[13]

Adrian repeatedly presented a striking picture of these false prophets for his congregation. For example, he cited a National Council of Churches study of over 7,000 ministers across denominational lines that illustrated the dire theological situation. When asked if the bodily resurrection of Jesus Christ was historic in the same way that the death of Abraham Lincoln was historic, 28 percent of respondents said, "No." When asked if the virgin birth of Christ literally happened, 37 percent said, "No." When asked if they believed there would be a literal judgment after death, 65 percent said, "No." Furthermore, 36 percent expressed serious doubt that Jesus was the divine Son of God, 62 percent doubted that the miracles occurred as described in the Bible, and a staggering 33 percent expressed some degree of doubt in the existence of God.[14] For Adrian, the challenge was the disconnect between what false prophets say and what they really believe:

> False prophets use the 'language of Zion,' but they know that if the people who listened to them knew what they really believed in their hearts, the people would put them out of the pulpit. Therefore, they dare not say fully what they believe. This is the deceitfulness of modernism; this is the deceitfulness of liberalism...false prophets use double-talk and do not mean what they're saying.[15]

Adrian elaborated by describing how a false prophet might talk about the "resurrection' but would not mean 'resurrection' as found plainly in the Bible. "When you and I use the word 'resurrection,' we believe that Jesus Christ was in the grave, that God gave life to that dead body, and that Jesus' dead body came literally, physically, and visibly out of the grave—that's what we believe." On the other hand, "The false prophet will use the same word but with a different meaning."[16] Then he recounted a recent conversation with a Stetson University professor who had taught a course in Brevard County:

> I spoke to the man on the matter of theology. And I said to the man, "The thing that bothers me is that these liberals don't stand up and say, 'I don't believe in the virgin birth, I don't believe in the inspiration of the Bible, and I don't believe in the resurrection.' If they said that, then at least the people sitting there would know what they believe. The thing that bothers me is that they use one word but mean something else—it's theological double-talk. For example, they say 'resurrection,' but they don't mean 'resurrection.'"

> Then that man looked at me and said, "Well, you don't believe in a literal resurrection, do you?" So I said, "Yes, and if you really want to know what the resurrection is, I believe in the empty tomb of Jesus Christ—that's what I believe." So here was a man who was amazed that there is a preacher among these engineers and scientists who believes in a literal resurrection. And I daresay that he likely uses the word 'resurrection, resurrection, resurrection,' and those who hear him don't know the difference.[17]

But what about the inspiration of the Bible? Adrian discerned that while false prophets could and would speak of "inspiration," their nuanced definition allowed them to pick and choose what—in their minds—was inspired and what was not: "They believe the Bible is inspired in spots, and they are inspired to spot the spots."[18]

What motivated false prophets? In many cases, according to Adrian, they saw themselves as too educated, too smart, and too sophisticated for the God of the Bible—and believed that twentieth-century people would not swallow a simple, face-value reading of the Bible:

> They've gone through the doctrine of Heaven and tell us there's no gold there, they've gone through the doctrine of hell and told us there's no fire there, and they've gone through the doctrine of Christ and told us there's no God there. They've tried somehow to remodel Heaven, air-condition hell, explain away the devil, and make the Gospel palatable to the human mind and to this generation. They say, "We need a new and modern Gospel for a new and modern age."[19]

Adrian also saw false prophets as Satan's lieutenants, masquerading as ministers who, if possible, would deceive even the elect: "For such are false apostles, deceitful workers, transforming themselves into apostles of Christ. And no wonder! For Satan himself transforms himself into an angel of light. Therefore it is no great thing if his ministers also transform themselves into ministers of righteousness" (2 Corinthians 11:13-15). As a result, he offered this warning to the Merritt Island congregation:

> The Bible reminds us that when you look for Satan, never forget to look in the pulpit. Satan has his ministers, and they are hard to detect. Now, they don't come with long horns, cloven hooves, scaly red skin, and a pitchfork saying, "BOO, I'm a demon standing in the pulpit." They're very suave, very sophisticated, very educated, very erudite—and they transform themselves as an angel of light.[20]

While Adrian adamantly opposed false prophets, he also understood why they sought to undermine the Word of God:

> If I were Satan, I would do the same thing if I wanted to wound and cripple the church of God. Of course, there are many things that I would want to do: I would want to ruin a pastor's influence, I would want to have worldliness and sin in the church membership, I would get some slander out on a Christian worker, and I would make Christians lazy and so forth—but none of those things would be my main focal point of attack. If I were Satan, my main point of attack would be to destroy belief in God's Word and the integrity of the Scriptures.[21]

Some might have questioned Adrian's hard stance against false prophets—"He's an alarmist!"—but he never wavered. Why? He explained his method and motive in this way:

> All the writers in the Bible, commencing with Jesus and going on to the epistles and concluding with Jude and Revelation warn us of false prophets. So don't think that I'm simply crying, "Wolf, wolf!" when there is no wolf. And don't think that I'm simply an extremist. I would be unfair to you, and I would be unfair to my God if I did not warn you, because we are living in a day when the false prophet is having his heyday.[22]

CONTEMPORARY APPLICATIONS

Most readers of this work likely agree with Adrian's assessment of the Word of God, and they probably attend a church that also agrees. The danger for many, then, is taking these convictions for granted, failing adequately to instruct the next generation both about the inspiration of the Scripture and also about past battles with those whose disbelief has gutted mainline denominations and decimated prominent pulpits.

Indeed, each era in church history has seen orthodox priority on the Word of God pitted against some alternative "authority," whether it be tradition, reason, experience, or sentiment. The Protestant Reformation addressed the muddy relationship between the Bible and Roman Catholic tradition with a crystal-clear battle cry: Sola Scriptura! When higher-critical reason threatened to dismantle the Bible and dance upon its grave, scholars like J. Gresham Machen unmasked Liberalism for what it was, and Billy Graham gave millions of Christians the confidence to declare simply and humbly, "The Bible says." When post-modernity elevated experience and personal narrative above the Bible's timeless truth, men of God such as D. A. Carson and R. Albert Mohler demonstrated the fallacies of denying absolute truth as defined by Scripture.

But is the next generation aware of these past battles and equipped to recognize and overcome the present challenges? If previous generations wrestled with tradition, modernity, and experience, I would argue that the next generation finds itself at war with sentiment: "It's better to make a difference than to make a point," "We don't take positions; we have conversations," "We draw circles, not lines," and the ever-present "Follow your heart." We should be grateful, then, for Adrian's pace-setting example of prioritizing the question, "What does the Bible say?" But in today's culture, given its suspicion of anything found in the Bible, is that question still relevant? To be sure, twenty-first-century ministry requires a deeper and more thoughtful apologetic when teaching the Scripture, but the simplicity of presenting the plain sense of the entire Bible still resonates with those who have an ear to hear. The alternative, one in which we become "unhitched" from large portions of the Bible for the sake of apologetic relevance, is simply unacceptable for Believers and dishonest to a lost world. Regarding the sentiment of inclusion that has become culturally sacrosanct in the past two decades, church leaders and Jesus-following men and women would do well to remember Adrian's Merritt Island preference for being divided by truth rather than being united in error. Ultimately, Adrian's level of discernment regarding any compromise over theological essentials provides an excellent model for those who wish to remain true to "the faith which was once for all delivered to the saints." The need for discernment has never been greater.

13

THE SPIRIT-FILLED LIFE

While few readers will be surprised to hear that Adrian prioritized a high view of the Scripture, many may be unaware that at Merritt Island he highlighted the Spirit-filled life and the fulness of the Holy Spirit as often as he celebrated the inspiration of the Bible. But given his own profound experience with the Holy Spirit, his frequent preaching and teaching on the matter was merely the natural outworking of what he saw in the Scripture coupled with his own experience. As such, spiritual power is quite possibly the most profound and timeless principle behind his Merritt Island successes.

Adrian's over-arching concern when talking about the Holy Spirt was to find the Biblical balance between the less-then-Biblical extremes he observed in churches of all denominations:

> The devil wants to do two things concerning the Holy Spirit in the life of this church and every New Testament church. On the one hand, he wants us to be as they were in Acts 19:2, not even knowing so much as if there is a Holy Spirit. Or, on the other hand...he wants to take the doctrine of the Holy Spirit, warp and twist it, and get us out of function and out of whack someway and have us going off on a tangent. In other words, the devil has one of two things in mind for the church: either no fire or wildfire.[1]

Beyond his general quest for Biblical truth regarding the Holy Spirit, Adrian most frequently focused on the Spirit-filled life, both at the individual and congregational levels.

DEFINING THE SPIRIT-FILLED LIFE

Whenever Adrian spoke about the Holy Spirit, he did so with theological clarity. For example, he carefully differentiated between his perspective and that of Pentecostal and charismatic teaching, especially regarding the baptism of the Holy Spirit.[2] While Pentecostal and charismatic Christians teach that the baptism of the Holy Spirit takes place at some point in time after conversion (and accompanied by speaking in tongues), Adrian argued that the baptism of the Holy Spirit takes place at the moment of conversion: "For by one Spirit we were all baptized into one body—whether Jews or Greeks, whether slaves or free—and have all been made to drink into one Spirit" (1 Corinthians 12:13). At the same time, Adrian always mentioned that God commanded all Christians to be filled with the Spirit (Ephesians 5:18), which was meant to occur again and again after conversion. For him, this was squarely in keeping with the pattern displayed in the early church (Acts 4:8; 4:31; 13:9; 13:52).

To be sure, Adrian found it important to make theological distinctions as he saw them in the Bible. However, he was also careful to prevent the desire for theological information from quenching his deep thirst for a meaningful experience with God's Holy Spirit. In fact, he went so far as to say, "The Holy Spirit is sovereign, and his work is dynamic, creative, and demands a naivete on the part of God's servants."[3] Furthermore:

> I don't want to spend too much time on terminology, because, friend, you name it and I *want it*. It's possible that a person can have the wrong term and the right experience. It's also possible that a person can have his terms right but have no experience—and that would be a tragedy.

> Vance Havner said that people who argue too much about terms reminded him of beggars standing on the street corner arguing about the merits of different pocketbooks while all of them are broke.…We may have to admit that there are a lot of us who may not exactly know the terminology or the theology, but we know that there is a dimension missing in our lives—something that we haven't got but we desperately need, and it all starts with a thirst.[4]

How did Adrian define this filling of the Spirit? He said that "it simply means to be in a continual state of possession and control by the Spirit… [and] in a constate state of saying, 'Yes, Lord, what do you want me to do?'"[5] But the filling of the Spirit was more than a state of obedience. Ultimately, being filled with the Spirit meant God's power manifested in and through the Christian—an "enduement" of God's presence and his power. Self-effort was nothing and could produce nothing of eternal consequence. Rather, the Spirit-filled life, Adrian frequently taught, was the secret to holiness and the Christian life, just as Ian Thomas had influenced him to believe:

> Have you ever come to the place where you realized that all you can produce, at your best, is ashes? Did you ever come to the place where you presented yourself for what you are—*nothing*—to be filled with what He is—*everything*—and step out into every new day, conscious that the eternal I AM is all you need, for all His will!…The sad thing is that even a Christian may be so impressed with himself and with his own ability that even though he gives lip service to the fact, he may still see no personal relevance in the indwelling presence of Christ. It will smack to him of mysticism; he will consider such teaching to be exaggeratedly subjective and will pride himself on being a practical man of action rather than abiding in Christ.[6]

Adrian so strongly believed in the necessity of the Spirit-filled life and the futility of ministering in his own strength that he boldly said, "I would resign this church today if I had to stand up here and perform ministry in my own strength."[7]

How does one become filled with the Spirit? Adrian often shared the work of J. Oswald Sanders regarding the "how" of the Spirit-filled life in terms of seven words.[8] First, *acknowledge* your need for the Spirit's filling:

> Right now, you have all of God you want. The question is, 'Do you want more of God?' Even God cannot fill that which is already full, and some people are so stuffed full of themselves and the stagnant waters of self-love that they'll never be filled with the Holy Spirit. For many of us, our biggest need is to see our need.[9]

Second, *aspire* to be filled: "What is the great ambition of your life? Money, popularity, ease, early retirement? You'll find that you'll get what you desire the most. Jesus said, 'Blessed are they which do hunger and thirst after righteousness, for they shall be filled.'" Third, *abandon* your sin—not in order to be filled with the Spirit, "as if God will fill you once you live good enough." Rather, demonstrate to God through repentance that being filled with the Holy Spirit means more to you than the sins that you otherwise enjoy—"abandon your sin, get on your knees and search your heart, and confess every known sin, grudge, and attitude." Fourth, *abdicate* the throne. "Step down off the throne of your life; as Miss Bertha said when she was here, 'Take death to self.'" Fifth, *ask* to be filled: "If you then, being evil, know how to give good gifts to your children, how much more will your heavenly Father give the Holy Spirit to those who ask Him" (Luke 11:13)—"God wants you to be filled with the Holy Spirit; you don't have to talk him into it!" Sixth, *appropriate* the fullness. Claim it, receive it, and say, "Thank you, Lord." Seventh, *act* in faith. Believe God's Word, and "don't make the mistake of looking for a special feeling—we don't need a feeling, we need a filling."[10]

ILLUSTRATING THE SPIRIT-FILLED LIFE

Adrian's legendary ability to illustrate spiritual truths from the Bible, either directly or indirectly, figured heavily in his teaching about the Spirit-filled life. In particular, when reading the Old Testament, he saw 1 Corinthians 10:11 as a hermeneutical gateway: "Now all these things happened to them as examples, and they were written for our admonition, upon whom the ends of the ages have come." As a result, familiar Old Testament passages became practical instruction about the Spirit-filled life. For example, the "tragic story of King Saul" represented a Christian walking in the flesh rather than filled with the Spirit. And the lost axe head in 2 Kings 6:1-7 represented God's power through the fullness of the Holy Spirit that was loaned to the Christian by God, lost through spiritual carelessness, and located again through renewed submission to the Holy Spirit.[11]

Adrian's most commonly referenced Bible illustration for the Spirit-filled life, however, was found in Exodus 12-13, which he described as "one of the greatest spiritual truths in all of the Bible." Based largely upon Ian Thomas' teaching in *The Saving Life of Christ*, Adrian saw the story of Israel in Egypt, the Wilderness, and Canaan as a grand example of the three types of people described in 1 Corinthians 2:14-3:1—the natural man, the spiritual man, and the carnal man—a "picture of Christian experience."[12] The Egypt-Wilderness-Canaan paradigm was a common theme in his Merritt Island preaching, so much so that he prefaced his message "How to Live on the Mountaintop" by saying, "I want you to learn something that perhaps you've never heard before—but I know you've heard it if you've been a member of this church for very long."[13] Many of his messages featured this theme, but perhaps his sermon "Going Deeper" from Exodus 12-13 best represents the whole:

> There are basically three types of people in the world: there is the natural man, there is the carnal man, and there is the spiritual man. The natural man has never been saved, the carnal man has been saved

> but has not been Spirit-filled, and the spiritual man has been filled with the Holy Spirit. Everyone in this congregation is in one of those three categories.[14]

Adrian explained that the Hebrew experience in Egypt with its slavery and oppression represented the life of anyone before coming to Jesus for salvation. At the same time, any person to whom "the blood was applied" as it was in the first Passover was liberated from Egyptian bondage—"Christ, our Passover, is sacrificed for us" (1 Corinthians 5:7). Following that, God's people were commanded to observe the Passover annually *in the land of the Canaanites* (Exodus 13:5). And this is where Adrian addressed some misconceptions about "Canaan" in the Bible:

> Many times, we use Canaan as a picture of Heaven. People talk about "crossing over Jordan" and "on Jordan's stormy banks I stand and cast a wishful eye, to Canaan's fair and happy land where my possessions lie." We've got a lot of songs that don't have their theology exactly right. Canaan in the Bible is *not* a picture of Heaven. Canaan is a picture of the Spirit-filled life. There was war in Canaan; there's not going to be any war in Heaven. There was sin in Canaan; there's not going to be any sin in Heaven. There was death in Canaan; there's not going to be any death in Heaven.[15]

Adrian then pointed out that God intended for his people to leave Egypt and enter Canaan a short time thereafter. But because of their lack of faith and disobedience, they wandered in the Wilderness for forty years—that is, they limped along in a spirituallybarren place just as a Christian without the fulness of the Holy Spirit struggles with the life to which God has called him or her. That person, he would argue, has nothing to celebrate, just as God's people in the Wilderness had nothing to celebrate:

> Here's the teaching: you really don't have much to celebrate until you've been filled with the Spirit. Canaan stands for the Spirit-filled

> life—not Heaven one day, but Heaven right now; not victory in the sweet by and by, but victory in the nasty now and now. Canaan stands for Heaven in our hearts right now....
>
> Think about this picture. Here's a man living in the Wilderness who's decided to try and celebrate the Passover in the Wilderness. Then let's imagine that he's got a 13-year-old son with him in the Wilderness. His son has been in the Wilderness for 13 years. He's never been to Egypt, he's never been to Canaan, and he's never known any other food besides manna. He's heard sermons about Canaan, but that's all. And they're out there in the Wilderness—there are snakes crawling around; burning and blistering sand; stones and rocks all around; the son is sitting on a hot rock and the father is sitting on a cactus. As the father tries to celebrate the Passover in the Wilderness, the son says, "What does all of this mean?" The father says, "I'm celebrating what the Lord has done for us." Then the son says, "What *has* he done for us?" I can imagine the son might have also said, "If this is all he's done for us, don't you think it's about time we got back to Egypt?"[16]

For Adrian, the key takeaway from the Egypt-Wilderness-Canaan paradigm was that God calls every Christian to a deeper life of fullness and victory that cannot be attributed to anything other than the power of God: "What is it about your life that cannot be explained apart from the work of the Holy Spirit in you? Are you filled with the Holy Spirit? Is there something about you that people cannot explain except by saying, 'God is doing that!'"[17] The alternative was to be a "carnal Christian," living in his own strength, struggling to live the Christian life, and—in some cases—secretly wishing he wasn't a Christian at all. As a point of reference, Adrian quoted Billy Graham as saying, "Upwards of ninety percent of Christians are living defeated lives"—that is, the vast majority of Christians are living in the Wilderness rather than in Canaan.[18]

In addition to Bible passages that illustrate the Spirit-filled life, Adrian utilized meaningful stories and images to help his congregation understand the Spirit-filled life. For example, he shared this story from A. J. Gordon, the nineteenth-century Holiness-Baptist preacher:

> A. J. Gordon went to the World's Fair, and he said he looked across the field and saw a man dressed in a gaudy-colored kimono furiously pumping water from an old-fashioned pitcher pump. The man was working furiously, and the water was spewing out of the pump. Gordon thought, "I don't know who that man is, but I know one thing: he's really pumping water. I've got to see what makes him work so hard." Gordon said that when he got closer he found out that it wasn't a human being at all but rather a wooden dummy with a hinged arm strapped to the pump handle. He also saw that it wasn't an old-fashioned pitcher pump; it was an artesian well—and as the water came out of the ground it was driving the man. That man wasn't pumping water; the water was pumping him!... You know, sometimes we look at people whose lives seem to be blessed of God. They seem to be fruitful for God, and from them is issuing the sweet water life, and we say, "Oh, that must be a great man!" But probably, he's just a wooden man who's learned the secret of tapping into a fountain of living water.[19]

Adrian argued that every Christian has access to God's power in and through them, but many are ignorant that it is available and already theirs:

> We know there's a victorious life—a higher life—that's already ours, but many fail to appropriate it.…I heard about a woman who applied for welfare because she couldn't keep body and soul together. When the investigator from the welfare department came out to talk to this lady, he said to her, "Don't you have a husband or some children who can take care of you?" She said, "Yes, I have one son." "Where is he?" "He's out west somewhere working—he said he was going to try and make his fortune." The investigator said, "Doesn't he ever

> write you?" "Yes." "Don't you ever tell him about your need?" "Yes, I tell him in almost every letter." "Well, doesn't he ever send you anything?" "Well, he never sends me any money; all he sends is a letter and some little cards." "Do you have one of them?" She says, "Yes, I have many of them." Then she went back into that little hovel where she lived, and on the wall she had tacked many of the "cards"—they were money orders. She didn't know what to do with them, but she had almost decorated one whole wall with money orders from her son. They were hers all the time, yet she was starving and ready to go welfare. She didn't know how to possess her possessions; she didn't know how to appropriate what she already had.[20]

Adrian also used absurdity with a point to illustrate the life of a Christian unaware of the power he or she already possesses but hasn't employed:

> There are so many people who have received Christ as their personal Savior, whose Christianity—rather than being a joy and a happiness—has become a burden and drudge. They remind me of a man who buys a new automobile, and he's very proud of it. But he doesn't realize that it has a motor. And so he pushes it everywhere he goes—uphill and on level ground, and every once in a while he can coast going downhill. He's proud of his car, and he's always showing his friends his beautiful car with its fine paint job, beautiful upholstery, and everything else. But secretly he wishes he didn't have it. It's such a burden. But then one day, he discovers there's a motor in it—he wasn't meant to carry it, it was meant to carry him, and that made all the difference![21]

At the congregational level, Adrian shared a word of warning about becoming a church with programs but not power; a church attempting to do things for God rather than a church through which God's power flows and acts:

> Missionaries tell us that when they go overseas, they build a fire in the jungle, and the monkeys watch them. The monkeys see the missionary stack the wood, so the monkeys stack the wood. And the missionary puts the wood in order, and so the monkeys put the wood in order. The monkeys do everything that the missionary does, except the monkey doesn't know how to put the fire under the wood. And I've known a lot of churches like that. They're running around and around, imitating someone else's program. But there's no fire—there's no power.[22]

A SPIRIT-FILLED CHURCH

Speaking of the congregational level, Adrian left no one guessing about his desire for the Merritt Island church to be a Spirit-filled congregation:

> What is there about the First Baptist Church that cannot be explained by personality, by propaganda, by promotion, by paraphernalia, by organization, and all of these things? My dear friend, there ought to be another dimension in our church. There ought to be something unique. There ought to be something supernatural. When people come into this place, they ought to go away shaking their heads, saying, "I never saw it on that wise before!"[23]

When asking the question, "What kind of church does God want our church to be?" Adrian went to the Book of Acts and drew this conclusion:

> A great church, in God's estimation, will have great power—not great power in influence and not great power in money, but great supernatural power in the Holy Ghost of God. And my dear friend, if we don't have the power of the Holy Ghost of God, we're just playing church. Many churches are organized, and many churches are large, and many churches meet their budget, but they do not have the supernatural power of God that ought to characterize a great

> church....You know what Carl Bates said one time when I was in seminary—it frightened me to death. He said that if the Holy Spirit were to suddenly die (which is impossible), many churches would meet the next Sunday and carry on the program and never know the difference.[24]

Adrian also reminded the congregation that the fullness of the Holy Spirit was not intended for a select few but rather for the entire church:

> This is not just for Adrian Rogers and for Jim Whitmire. This is for every one of you: "The promise is unto you, and to your children, and to as many as the Lord our God shall call." It is for plain, vanilla Christians who come to church every Sunday and sit in the pew. God wants this entire congregation to be filled with the Holy Spirit![25]

Likewise, when talking about church leadership, Adrian prioritized the fullness of the Holy Spirit. For example, when selecting and ordaining deacons, he left no doubt about the number-one qualification as he saw it in the Bible:

> The main qualification for a deacon as we see in Acts 6 is that he's filled with the Holy Ghost. That's the main qualification, isn't it? Not that he's a great businessman, not that he is astute in the sciences of this world, and not that he has all the cosmopolitan polish of a well-met fellow; but that this man is filled with the Holy Ghost. A deacon, above all other things, ought to be a Spirit-filled man.[26]

SPIRIT-FILLED UNITY

While Adrian repeatedly emphasized the power of God and the role of the Holy Spirit in the life of First Baptist Church, he was mindful of potential distractions that could enter the church and bring disunity.

For example, his style of preaching, understandably, attracted some who sought to introduce tongues speaking in the church. While he appreciated their zeal, he ensured that the church was not drawn off on that or any other tangent related to the Holy Spirit: "Invariably when modern Pentecostalism hits a Baptist church, there comes a division, there comes a schism. It tortures the body of Christ, and the devil laughs because there's a little club that says, 'We have a gift, and everybody must exercise this gift.'"[27] Similarly, Adrian shared in *The Thrust* that "The Spirit-filled life is not a matter of visions, tongues, and ecstasies; but the very practical living of the Christian life. These other things may indeed be the devil's 'red herrings' drawn across our paths to detour us from real spiritual living and soul-winning power. May each of us settle for nothing less."[28]

Adrian argued that unity, not division, comes when a church embraces the Biblical power and person of the Holy Spirit:

> We as a church have a common life, and that life is the Holy Spirit. That's the reason why when people come into our services they say, "You know, I felt the presence of Jesus; I really felt at home in God's church." And I've really been amazed at this, especially when we first started because so many of us came and so many of us were saved—we didn't even know each other's names, and many of us still don't. And yet, you feel a part of something, don't you? There's a common bond, and I tell people that the glue that holds us together is the blessed, precious Holy Spirit of God.…We don't need to be wired together by organization, we don't need to be rusted together by tradition, and we don't need to be frozen together by formalism—we need to be melted together by the Holy Spirit.[29]

Adrian had reason to emphasize unity in the Holy Spirit (as well as theological clarity about the Holy Spirit), not least because of two movements beginning to appear in Brevard County at that time. First, an informal gathering of charismatic Christians began to assemble on the beaches on Sunday afternoons. In connection with the Jesus Movement, Christians began gathering for worship and fellowship with "guitars and flip flops"—and, in many cases, charismatic manifestations. Some students from First Baptist Church began to gravitate toward these gatherings, and others in the church began asking, "What should we do?" Jim Whitmire recalled:

> We had hippies from the Jesus Movement over at the beach who were getting into the "second blessing," and some of our young people were drifting that way on Sunday nights. And the parents were asking, "Pastor, our kids want to go to the beach. What do you think about that?"...Well, Adrian was sensitive to the need for Holy Spirit power, but he was also committed to Biblical clarity....So I remember when he preached the definitive sermon on the filling of the Holy Spirit, he nailed it down for our people once and for all. And that pretty much settled the issue for our people.[30]

The second reason for congregational unity and theological clarity was the growth of the Tabernacle Church in Brevard County (Melbourne) led by its pastor, Jamie Buckingham. Buckingham, a Baptist-turned-Pentecostal, saw the Tabernacle Church exceed 2,000 in membership in the late 1960s and early 1970s. He often chided Baptists about their excessive rigidity and resistance to the charismatic movement. Buckingham also heavily promoted the Full Gospel Business Men's Fellowship International (FGBMFI) in Brevard County, a charismatic "lay-oriented ministry that attracted business professionals who wanted a more vibrant spirituality" and played a "key role in the evolving identity of 'bapticostals'—Baptists who imbibed Pentecostal theology and practice."[31] For Adrian, the FGBMFI (and Pentecostal theology in general) wrongly made the Holy Spirit the prime focus of its gatherings, whereas he understood that the Holy Spirit's role was to testify about Jesus—"But when the Helper comes...the Spirit of truth...He will testify about me" (John 15:26):

> Let me say that the job of the Holy Spirit is to testify about Jesus—"He'll take the things of mine and show them unto you" (John 16:14). So you beware of any movement that has the Holy Spirit for a figurehead. That's one reason why I'm not a bit hepped-up on this Full Gospel Business Men's Fellowship and so forth. They miss the point.[32]

At the end of the day, Adrian resisted these and other tangents. As a result, by and large, the unity of the Spirit prevailed at First Baptist Church, and only a handful of people felt the need to worship elsewhere.

THEOLOGICAL CLARITY AND PENTECOSTAL SYMPATHIES

While Adrian never wavered from theological clarity about the Holy Spirit, he frequently voiced sympathies for those who made much of the Holy Spirit but differed with him on secondary theological issues. A casual observer might have even mistaken him for a charismatic Baptist who had embraced Pentecostal theology. In fact, Adrian occasionally heard questions from his Merritt Island members like this: "Brother Rogers, sometimes you preach like a person from another denomination. Have you got the 'second blessing'? Well, I say, 'No. I'm still enjoying the first one!'"[33]

Adrian openly admired his Pentecostal brothers and sisters, if not for their theological distinctives then certainly for their authentic zeal and genuine experience with the Holy Spirit:

> We need to get religion like the old-time Methodists, and we need to keep it like the Baptists. But I'll tell you what else we need to do: we need to enjoy it like the Pentecostals. We need to enjoy ourselves in Jesus Christ. If the Lord has saved us, "Let the redeemed of the

> Lord say so." Some churches that have cold, formal services are like the Church of the Holy Refrigerator where Jack Frost is the pastor.... The Assemblies of God is one of the fastest-growing denominations in America today because their people are not afraid to say "Amen." Their people are not afraid to express their joy....I'm not saying I'm ready to join the Assemblies of God, because I have some doctrinal differences with them. But they love Jesus, and they are not afraid to express their joy in the Lord.[34]

At the same time, he was not afraid to poke at his fellow Southern Baptists from time to time for their lack of Holy Spirit awareness and engagement, as he did when talking about the Egypt-Wilderness-Canaan paradigm:

> Moses pastored the First Baptist Church of the Wilderness....He must have been a Southern Baptist: he knew how to get them out, but he didn't know how to get them in. He got them out of Egypt—they were saved—but he couldn't get them into Canaan; he didn't know how to get them filled with the blessed Holy Spirit of God.[35]

On a related note, it is important to see that Adrian was not a "cessationist" in the classic sense. Rather, he was what today we might call a "cautious continuationist" (although he never used that terminology of himself):

> Every spiritual gift is a supernatural gift, and let me say that I believe in every gift mentioned in all of the Bible. I believe in all the Bible, and I believe in the supernatural. And the person who says that the supernatural has ended with the day of the Apostles, that burden of proof is on him. He cannot prove that. But to the contrary, I believe that as long as there's a God in Heaven, the Christian life is going to be a supernatural, miraculous life.[36]

ADRIAN ROGERS AND THE "DEEPER LIFE"

At Merritt Island, Adrian both admired his Pentecostal brothers and sisters in Christ while also distancing himself from their theological distinctives. At the same time, he maintained a much closer relationship with what can be called the "Deeper Life" movement within the Southern Baptist Convention. In the 1960s and 1970s, as Pentecostal and charismatic movements gained much ground across America, the Southern Baptist Convention was not entirely unaffected. While a very small minority of Southern Baptists eventually embraced key charismatic doctrines—James Robison, for example, and even Adrian's friend, Peter Lord—a somewhat-larger minority affirmed something akin to Keswick theology (pronounced KEZ-ik). Keswick is a small town in northwest England whose annual religious meetings in the late nineteenth and early twentieth centuries popularized the theological convictions that would become associated with the name. Although many early Keswick followers advocated a baptism of the Holy Spirit subsequent to conversion, other variations focused on a post-conversion fullness of the Spirit that must be revisited on a regular basis. This post-conversion fullness produced what proponents called the "deeper life" and the "Spirit-filled life."[37]

During his time at First Baptist Church, Adrian opened his pulpit to numerous proponents of "deeper life" Christianity—both from within and outside of the SBC—to include Bertha Smith (*How the Spirit Filled My Life*), Vance Havner (*Blood, Bread, and Fire: The Christian's Three-Fold Experience*), Bill Bright (*How to Be Filled With the Spirit*), and Ian Thomas (*The Saving Life of Christ*). Each of these speakers and others like them influenced Adrian's life and ministry, although he never used the term "Keswick" and only on rare occasions made reference to the "deeper life"—as he did when hosting the Bertha Smith "Deeper Life Conference" in December 1968. As we have already seen, his preferred terminology by far was the "Spirit-filled life." And his preaching repeatedly promoted an experience with the filling of the Holy Spirit subsequent to conversion, while clearly defining the experience apart from the baptism of the Holy Spirit at conversion. It is important to note also that Adrian frequently quoted other key voices associated with Keswick and deeper-life theology, to include A. J. Gordon, R. A. Torrey, F. B. Meyer, Andrew Murray, Ron Dunn, Manley Beasley, Stephen Olford, and even the holiness-fundamentalist Independent Baptist John R. Rice.

Not all Southern Baptists embraced—or were even aware of—this deeper life movement within the denomination. Joyce Rogers recalled, "In those days, not many in the Southern Baptist Convention were preaching about the Spirit-filled life."[38] Likewise, Steve Rogers noted, "Back then, the 'Deeper Life' movement in the Southern Baptist Convention wasn't high profile, because unless you heard these people speak or got their cassette tapes—there was no internet then—you would have never heard of them."[39] And Michael Catt recalled, "Many Southern Baptists didn't know what to do with Bertha Smith. You would not have found *How the Spirit Filled My Life* on the front shelves in a Baptist bookstore. Some churches wanted what she spoke about, but the majority did not."[40]

CONTEMPORARY APPLICATIONS

First and foremost, Adrian's confession about his own ignorance regarding the Holy Spirit in his early life and ministry should be highly instructive for every generation:

> Either when I was a young Christian I was deaf, or preachers did not preach the fullness of the Spirit. *I never heard it.* I was born again in a Southern Baptist Church, went to a Southern Baptist college, went to a Southern Baptist seminary, and yet I was out and preaching for about five years before I understood how to be filled with the Spirit—that God does not want me to do anything for him; rather, he wants to do something in and through me.[41]

By any measure, Adrian Rogers was a giant among Southern Baptists. And for a giant of his denominational stature to make such an admission is tremendous, indeed.

How many Southern Baptists today, if they were honest, would say the same thing? When personally I received Jesus as Savior in a Southern Baptist Church, not only did I not hear about the Spirit-filled life, I learned to be suspicious of anyone giving more than lip service to the Holy Spirit, lest I become entangled in Pentecostal theology. How sad that many Southern Baptists have missed out on the Biblically-based fullness of the Holy Spirit that gives power for living the Christian life and boldness in sharing the Gospel with a lost and dying world.

How many Southern Baptist pastors could honestly say that they are filled with the Holy Spirit? How many Southern Baptists are, as Adrian would say, "living defeated lives in the Wilderness" rather than enjoying in Canaan a prevailing victory over sin, an increasing Godly character, and an expanding witness for Jesus? While at Merritt Island, Adrian once lamented that in the previous year, upwards of 5,000 Southern Baptist churches did not baptize a single person: "What are they doing? They're certainly not filled with the Holy Spirit."[42] If denominational decline is any indication, I would argue that today's Southern Baptist Convention could use a good, stiff dose of the fullness of the Holy Spirit.

Beyond that, today's Southern Baptists would do well not only to hear Adrian's powerful preaching about the Spirit-filled life during the Merritt Island years, but they should also go upstream and hear the words of those who greatly influenced Adrian's theology and experience. Ian Thomas' *The Saving Life of Christ*, for example, is as timelessly relevant and powerful as it has ever been. Likewise, *How the Spirit Filled My Life* remains remarkably fresh as if "Miss Bertha" just returned from the Shantung Revival last week. And Bill Bright's numerous publications on the Spirit-filled life should be required reading for seminary students and faculty alike. The need has never been greater.

14

GOSPEL LEADERSHIP

"Was Adrian Rogers a better preacher or a better leader?" Ask anyone who served alongside the Moon Port Pastor in Merritt Island and, after a brief, thought-gathering pause, the response will likely be, "Both! He was an incredible preacher and an incredible leader." That answer might sound non-committal, but the truth is that Adrian led God's people just as powerfully as he preached God's Word. And if, as the old saying goes, "everything rises and falls on leadership," then much credit for First Baptist's phenomenal successes can be attributed to Adrian's leadership style. The *Cocoa Tribune* certainly agreed in an article entitled "Local Pastor is True Leader":

> Dynamic leadership has made the First Baptist Church of Merritt Island one of the largest churches in Central Brevard, and one of the fastest growing of its denomination in the United States.…We feel that most of the rapidly increasing membership is due to the effective leadership of the Rev. Adrian Rogers. It's gratifying to know that there in the midst of the space age community so many persons are

> dedicated to God. It's the dedicated and tireless efforts of a man such as the Rev. Adrian Rogers—an evangelist in the true sense of the word—that has turned many persons to Christianity.[1]

But what kind of leader was he? Leadership models abound across all organizations, and churches are no different: transactional leadership, transformational leadership, servant leadership, autocratic leadership, democratic leadership—the list goes on. Do any of these models best describe Adrian's style? Given the complex challenges and opportunities that Adrian faced at First Baptist Church, we would argue that none of the traditional categories adequately describe his leadership style. Instead, another model comes to mind—a model that comprehensively describes the many ways that he effectively led the congregation to God-sized, God-honoring heights. We would call that model "Gospel leadership."

What is Gospel leadership? Gospel leadership is powered by God, not man's effort. Gospel leadership exemplifies God's wisdom, not man's cleverness. Gospel leadership personifies Jesus' humility, not man's self-promotion. Gospel leadership provides a Godly example to those being asked to follow. And Gospel leadership is Kingdom-oriented—that is, it is concerned with more than one's own church, denomination, or tribe. As we shall see, Adrian Rogers was, above all other leadership models, a Gospel leader.

LEADERSHIP POWERED BY GOD

A Gospel leader has nothing to offer except to be a conduit for God's power in and through the leader. A Gospel leader may be exceptionally gifted, but he or she will not be distracted by his or her abilities. In fact, a Gospel leader will consider those strengths dead through absolute and total surrender to God's will and power. When preaching about Saul's blunder following his victory over the Amalekites (1 Samuel 15:1-

31), Adrian likened man-powered leadership to Saul's preservation of the best that God hated:

> Many times, as Christians, rather than dying to ourselves and putting the flesh to death, we take our old nature and we try to offer it to God as a sacrifice. We say, "Here, Lord, I'm going to give you my talents," and the flesh has been offered to God as a sacrifice in many churches. But God doesn't want it—he despises it. Many times, a man or woman will stand up to sing a song, but they're not singing in the Spirit—they're singing in the strength and the energy of the flesh. They're offering their abilities to God, but God says, "I don't want them. I want them utterly destroyed." All of us have this flesh, and the flesh wants to parade. The flesh says, "Get up and preach a good sermon so that everybody will think you're a good preacher." The flesh says, "Get up and sing a good solo so everybody will think you can really sing." And the devil says, "You've got a lot of talents. You don't need to die to yourself." Ladies and Gentlemen, this is one of the most sinister things the devil could do: trying to get you to offer your un-crucified flesh to God and trying to get you to take your talents and your abilities and attempt to do something for God. This may shock you, but I want you to listen to me: God doesn't want you to do anything for him. You can't do anything for him, and you might as well stop trying to do anything for him. Instead, God wants to do things himself *through you*. Come to the place where you say, "Lord, I am nothing. I can't do anything. I am nothing and Jesus is everything." Once that happens, then we'll use the same singing ability and preaching ability, but we'll do it with a new strength and a new power because it will no longer be us, but it will be Christ in us. That makes the difference.[2]

Adrian demonstrated in his own life that a Gospel leader dies to self and leads in the Spirit through God's strength. In fact, whoever and whatever Adrian might have been as a leader was merely a by-product of his total surrender to the power of God and the Spirit of God. His longtime friend, Joe Boatright, put it this way:

> First and foremost, Adrian was an extraordinary man of God, which made him not only a great preacher but also a great leader. And that's what gave him the ability to lead and produce other leaders. At Merritt Island, there was an incredible level of spiritual maturity among the other leaders because of Adrian's leadership.[3]

Similarly, daughter Gayle Rogers Foster noted that:

> My father had a deep conviction that the secret to leadership was not ultimately about applying different leadership principles, but rather it was about relying upon prayer and the Holy Spirit. When he came to Merritt Island, he didn't rely on a leadership formula. He had a God-given anointing."[4]

That anointing gave him an unusual amount of God's wisdom. Far beyond the basics of making sound decisions, a Gospel leader will possess insight that cannot be explained except that it came from God. For example, Joyce Rogers remembered her husband's leadership in this way: "Adrian had wisdom and discernment, and he always seemed to have more than everybody else. He seemed to always know what to do and what the right thing was to say."[5]

HUMILITY TO LEAD OTHERS WELL

Successful leaders, even those in full-time Gospel service, can easily become self-centered and full of themselves to the point that they miss the healthy leadership continuum between products and people, between results and relationships. Sadly, more than a few successful pastors have drifted into the delusion that their ministry—their "platform" or "brand"—is about them and not about God's glory and God's people.

Adrian Rogers expected results, but never at the expense of his genuine love for his people and the humility that God desires from his leaders. Joe Boatright mentioned what many others have observed: "Adrian had a way of communicating with people from all walks of life in a way that said, 'You are important to me.'"[6] Son David Rogers likewise spoke for many when he said, "My dad had a genuine warmth and sincerity, and whenever he was speaking with someone—no matter who they were—he made them feel like they were the most important person in the whole world to him at that moment."[7] Peter Lord added:

> Something special about Adrian was that he was always nice. Some of the other Southern Baptist leaders were mean—I mean really mean. He was always a gentleman, and no matter how low on the denominational totem pole you might be, he would be friends with you and recognize you. Some of those other guys would get up there, and you're nothing to them.[8]

Adrian's humility also allowed him to lead the Merritt Island people, many of whom had key and influential roles at the Cape. On the one hand, as their pastor, he was not intimidated by their stature with NASA or in the community. On the other hand, he often deferred to them on various matters, knowing in humility that he did not have all the answers and appreciating that God had brought people of their caliber to the church. Business meetings were never contentious, in many ways because Adrian had taken the time in advance to generate consensus and buy-in from the leaders. And on the rare occasion when Adrian brought an idea to key lay leaders, and they collectively agreed that the timing was not right, "he would back off," defer to their wisdom, and wait for a more prudent moment.[9]

As a leader, Adrian also understood the power of apology. Jim Whitmire came to appreciate this aspect of his leadership in a personal way:

> One of the things I loved about Adrian was that he could say, "I was wrong," and, "I'm sorry." I've talked to other ministers of music who were having problems in their church, and the statement they would make is, "If my pastor could just say he was wrong, or at least someday say, 'I'm sorry.'" But they were working with one of these guys that somehow put themselves on a pedestal.[10]

One example that happened at Merritt Island truly left an indelible impression on Jim's heart:

> On Sunday afternoons, I would sometimes keep the kids in youth choir rehearsal for a little longer than I was supposed to—we needed every moment of practice time because of all the songs they were singing in those days. So Adrian said at a staff meeting, "Jim, let those kids out on time so they can make it to Training Union." Well, they had practice from 4:00-5:00 PM, then they would eat a meal that the church provided, then they would go to Training Union. Many of them were in Adrian's class for new Christians. After that, they would get their robes on, because they sang each week in the Sunday evening service....
>
> Well, on one Sunday in particular, I let them out really early. But when it was time for Adrian's class, they didn't show up on time. He said to someone else in the room, "Where are those kids?!" And just about that time, I came walking around the corner. So he said to me, "Can I see you for just a minute?" So we walked into a side room, and he said, "I thought I told you to let those kids out early." He was really mad—madder than I'd ever seen him before or since. I said, "Oh pastor, normally I'm guilty as sin"—I didn't know whether to laugh or cry—"but I let them out early," and I was so glad that I did! "Sometimes they get out early, but then they leave campus to eat somewhere else." He was pretty upset, so he just turned around and walked out....
>
> Then about an hour or so later, I was in the choir room getting ready for the evening service, and Adrian came in and said, "I need

> to talk to you." I thought, "OK, this is it. I'm gone." I really knew I was fired. But he began tearing up and said, "I want you to forgive me for what I just did a while ago. I can't preach tonight knowing what I just did to you." I said, "I forgive you." And that taught me a lesson. You talk about his leadership. I thought, "If he needs to be that clean before he gets in the pulpit, and I'm up there with him, then I've got to be clean, too." That was a huge lesson for me. Plus, it was just a blessing that he would admit he was wrong. But he's done that all of his ministry. And in working together for 38 years, I saw him occasionally lose his temper, but there was always a quick apology. He kept a short list—and I think that's why people enjoyed working for him. He was real.[11]

While not directly related to the Merritt Island years, a testimony from Larry Nobles, former Vice President of Media at Love Worth Finding, about an incident that took place over 30 years after Jim Whitmire's account, affirms that Adrian maintained his humility throughout his ministry:

> We had recorded a long taping, then Dr. Rogers had to go, so he walked down the hallway to pick up his stuff before he walked out. Well, I forgot that I needed him to record another promo, so I ran down to where he was. What I should've said to him was, "Do you have a little more time to record a quick promo I forgot?" But I didn't say that. Instead, I said, "Dr. Rogers, what are you doing next?" Well, he looked at me, shook his head a bit, and said, "That's none of your business." Well, I was shocked by that, and my heart started to pound a little bit, because he was such a giant of a man. Then I said, "What I meant to say was, 'Do you have time to record a quick promo that I promised a guy I would get?'" He looked at me, he looked at his watch, then he said, "OK, but make it quick." So we went into the studio, recorded it, and came out laughing and smiling, saying, "Have a great day, goodbye." And he left. I went back to my office, and I was shaken a little bit. Well, two hours later, the phone rang, and it was Adrian. Now, I had worked there for 13 years, and he had never called me directly. He said, "Larry,

> this is Adrian," and I said, "Yes, Sir, what can I do for you?" He said, "I just want you to know that I am really, really sorry for the way I responded to you. That was not fair to you, and it just wasn't Christlike. I'm deeply sorry." And I said, "Oh, Dr. Rogers, that didn't bother me a bit"—but of course it did, and I didn't know what to say to him. And he said, "Well, I hope you'll forgive me." And I said, "Absolutely." So that's the kind of man who was such a giant in so many ways, that he was willing to call me back and ask for forgiveness for something that anyone else would have forgotten.[12]

As a defender of the faith once for all delivered to the saints, Adrian displayed a dogged zeal and energy few others could muster. However, one must avoid assuming that he was contentious while contending. In fact, the opposite was true, and at Merritt Island, Adrian encouraged others to exercise humility when taking a stand for the truth:

> Earnestly contend for the faith. But as you contend, don't become contentious. Take a stand but keep yourself sweet. So many people, wanting to stay true to the Bible and true to the faith, get a nasty, bitter spirit. We are to believe and behave. There are a lot of people who believe right but they don't behave right—they are overly narrow, bitter, and critical....It's possible to have a warm nose, sniffing out heresy, but a cold, loveless heart.[13]

A PACE-SETTING EXAMPLE

Gospel leaders influence others primarily through their example, and Adrian was an amazing pace-setting leader in that regard. Jim Whitmire and Nelson Rutledge acknowledged that while he rarely led formal mentoring of the staff or training of any kind, "to be with him was to be mentored...to be in his presence and to watch his example was powerful."[14] Joe Boatright likewise pointed to Adrian's example as a leader:

> Adrian communicated what he was and who he was to his staff, the deacons, and the Sunday School teachers through his example. He had high expectations of them all, and he communicated his expectations through his example, too.[15]

Adrian also possessed a stellar work ethic, as Jim Whitmire recalled: "He did more in a week than most pastors do in a month. He really, really worked hard." Even Adrian, in a moment of pulpit transparency, mentioned his Merritt Island workload, if only to highlight how Jesus gives strength to the weary:

> Sometimes I can get burdened down with the cares in the toil of the administration of this church, and you may not think it's a big job, but I'll tell you it's a big job. And I'm not feeling sorry for myself, but I'd match the hours I put in here on the job with the hours any man in this church puts in on the job. It's a job and there's a lot to it. Brother, when you're managing something that has 200 or more volunteer workers—I'm talking about our Sunday School staff, where we are spending a budget of over $200,000 a year and trying to reach people for Jesus Christ. There are many things that you don't know about, like when the telephone rings at all hours of the night, and when this problem and that problem happens. It's a lot to bear on your shoulders.[16]

As a counterpoint to his pace-setting workload, it is important to note how Adrian likewise invested in his family in a healthy way. Whether having fun at home, sailing in the evenings on the Indian River with his children in their little sailboat, or enjoying vacations together, Adrian made quality time and quantity time for his family. Joe Boatright said it well:

> Adrian had an amazing relationship with Joyce and with his family, and he was one of the few people who, on the one hand, had this

enormous responsibility and, on the other hand, had the ability to balance church ministry and family.[17]

KINGDOM-MINDED LEADERSHIP

While Adrian eventually rose to the highest levels of Southern Baptist leadership, his heart was not denominationally myopic. Rather, at Merritt Island he was what we might call today "Kingdom minded"—that is, he truly knew that God's work was broader and deeper than the confines of First Baptist Church and the Southern Baptist Convention. In other words, he appreciated Biblical truth wherever he saw it. Joyce Rogers remembered, "Adrian was not afraid to cross denominational lines at a time when it was not popular to do so."[18]

A Kingdom mindset embraces unity among Evangelicals committed to the inerrancy of the Scripture, the fundamentals of the Christian faith, and personal evangelism. In that regard, Adrian was very much a Kingdom-minded leader—his partnership with the Presbyterian Bill Bright and his key participation in "Dialogue Cape Kennedy" being excellent examples of such:

> I believe in getting together with those who preach the Gospel, regardless of their denomination. Brother, I don't believe we should be so narrowly sectarian that we cannot cooperate with somebody unless they wear the label "Baptist." I believe we ought to love all people everywhere who preach the Gospel of Jesus and who believe the Bible is the Word of God.[19]

This Evangelical flexibility was helpful, not least because of the eclectic nature of Brevard County in the 1960s, to include religious backgrounds. After all, not everyone moving to Brevard was Baptist. Years later, Adrian looked back and said:

> Merritt Island was more or less cosmopolitan, because we had people come from all over to work in the space industry. You are more in the South in Memphis than you are in Florida. Memphis is the Deep South; Florida is more eclectic. We had people come from all over, especially at the space center. The views that I held were not a part of that southern culture…my theological persuasions transcended north, south, east, and west.[20]

In that context, he did not consider First Baptist Church to be in competition with any other Bible-believing, Bible-teaching church in the area, regardless of denomination. In fact, Adrian applauded the efforts of any soul-winning church on Merritt Island: "If anybody can come next door to the First Baptist Church of Merritt Island and reach any soul for Jesus Christ that we can't reach, we ought to be able to say 'Praise God' or else we've got a rotten heart."[21]

Furthermore, Adrian often expressed sympathies for the positive values of other denominations and churches that, while not Southern Baptist, were faithfully preaching the Bible and passionately pursuing God and the Great Commission. For example, he frequently heralded the results that various Independent Baptist churches produced through their bus ministries and other evangelistic initiatives. For example, he said:

> There are churches in America today that are doing a fantastic job—some of which are Independent Baptist churches—going out and winning souls to Jesus Christ and baptizing more people in this day and this age than have ever been baptized by churches in Christendom since the days of the Apostles. And I say, "Whatever they've got, I want some of it."[22]

Specifically, he praised the First Baptist Church of Hammond, Indiana—a fundamental, Independent Baptist church—for baptizing 2,000 people in one year and owning more buses in its bus ministry than were owned by the city of Hammond, Indiana.[23] Not surprisingly, the admiration was reciprocated, such as when Temple Baptist Church in Orlando invited Adrian to speak. The newspaper banner read:

> IT'S NEVER HAPPENED BEFORE...IT MAY NEVER HAPPEN AGAIN! Pastor Jewell E. Smith of Temple Baptist Church, which is an Independent Fundamental Baptist Church, has invited Rev. Adrian Rogers, a Southern Baptist preacher, to speak.[24]

Adrian also did something that was uncommon among Southern Baptist pastors at that time: he admired and followed Independent Baptist John R. Rice and frequently quoted from his publication, *The Sword of the Lord*. Jim Whitmire remembered:

> Adrian frequently quoted John R. Rice, an Independent Baptist. In those days, no self-respecting Southern Baptist quoted John R. Rice or *any* Independent Baptist. But Adrian would unashamedly do it anyway, and I would think, "Oh man, the Convention isn't going to like that!" But Adrian made me love John R. Rice because when he saw truth in a man, he connected with him regardless of his denominational background. He would say, "I'm a Christian first and a Baptist second."[25]

In fact, in the section from *Love Worth Finding* where Adrian listed the names of men who had greatly impacted his life, he first and foremost mentioned John R. Rice:

> I subscribed to Dr. Rice's paper, *The Sword of the Lord*, and was convicted by his clear, courageous stand on the Word of God. At that time, John Rice was criticized and looked down on by [SBC] leadership because he was an independent and not afraid to critique the [SBC] in areas where criticism was justified. Dr. Rice was a tenderhearted man who had a great heart for prayer and evangelism.[26]

Along these lines, in light of Adrian's admiration for those outside of his denomination, Steve Rogers remembered that "my dad was one of the rare people equally loved by both Independent Baptists and Pentecostals."[27]

Indeed, Adrian loved Evangelical unity. However, on the other hand, Adrian adamantly opposed the ecumenical movement that called for unity among churches and denominations when it was accompanied by theological compromise and error:

> We see so many churches today that are merging. They all seem to be on the verge with the urge to merge. They want to come together. And they talk about Southern Baptists and others who will not merge in the ecumenical movement, and they say that we're exclusive and that we're participating in the scandal of denominationalism. But I have the sneaking suspicion that many of these are merging together for survival because of their dwindling numbers....Many of their preachers have stopped preaching the Word of God. They're drying up and dying, and I'll tell you why: they no longer believe that the Bible is the Word of God.[28]

Adrian remarked further on the ecumenical movement—the followers of which he described as "ecumaniacs"—in several messages from Revelation:

> There is a devilish unity. This ecumenical movement is not spiritual, it's devilish because people are not getting together on the basis of the Lord Jesus Christ. They're getting together on the basis of unity and political power. But Jesus said, "My kingdom is not of this world."... People say, "Brother Rogers, are you against unity? Why aren't you Baptists a part of the National Council of Churches and the World Council of Churches?" I say that we believe in cooperation, where we can in the Spirit of Christ. This is the only unity we can have.[29]

Denominational loyalty was not an issue for Adrian, and he had no intention of leading any church other than a Southern Baptist church.

However, if a compromising Baptist church was his only "brand-name" option, he was ready to find an acceptable alternative, and he encouraged his people to consider a similar course:

> I'm Baptist born and Baptist dead—it was a Baptist church that pointed me to Jesus Christ—and when I die perhaps I'll be Baptist dead. But I'd join a church that wasn't a Baptist church quick before I'd join a modern, liberal Baptist church. Don't you get all wrapped up in the name "Baptist." I'm a Christian first....
>
> There are some [Baptist] churches you ought to drive ten miles to get past—I mean that. I'd stay home before I'd go to a liberal, modern church. You start one yourself. Get your neighbor, get your friend, win somebody to Jesus, and say, "We'll start one."[30]

CONTEMPORARY APPLICATIONS

Adrian Rogers had a God-given, special anointing to lead, and that simply cannot be replicated on demand. Yet, a great deal of his leadership principles are very accessible to pastors and other leaders. To be sure, many churches are desperate to be led well by Gospel leaders, and there is no better example of that kind of leadership than Adrian Rogers during his years at First Baptist Church of Merritt Island.

Following our questions in the last chapter about Southern Baptists and the Spirit-filled life, we should address the need for pastors and other church leaders to die to self in every way possible. How many pastors and leaders are ministering and leading in their own strength—in the strength of the flesh? I have admitted in the Preface to this book that initially I was not spiritually ready to tell the story of the Moon Port Pastor precisely because, for many years, I depended on my own strength for ministry and leadership rather than the fullness of the Holy Spirit. More recently, as I knelt and prayed before a service, I heard God say to me, "You have *nothing* to offer these people except my power in and through you—NOTHING." That experience left an indelible impression on my heart that echoes to this day. May God forbid that I ever go back to preaching and ministering and leading in my own strength!

Additionally, every pastor and church leader simply must consider Adrian's powerful example of kindness and humility. Yes, he had a strong personality and, even if not intended, he sometimes led through force of personality. Moreover, his zealous preaching and "bull-dogmatic" stand for the truth could possibly lead someone to miss his kindness and humility. The truth is that Adrian, largely as an overflow of the fullness of the Holy Spirit, possessed mountains of these rare commodities. Regarding the power of apology, we have only included two examples from his 50-plus years of ministry, but they paint a consistent picture of his humility in action at the interpersonal level. My own ministry has been greatly impacted by these examples. In fact, as lead pastor I once brought our entire staff together to offer an apology for the way in which I had admonished a staff member in a meeting the day before. I am not certain I would have done that had I not been influenced by the power of Adrian's apologies. Fortunately, the transparent humility I extended on that day was received positively by all.

If churches today find themselves in an increasingly post-denominational age, then a Kingdom-minded outlook might be considered a foregone conclusion. But even if the average Christian today does not have the same denominational loyalties of 60 years ago, a Kingdom-minded perspective is nevertheless important and needed. For example, local territorialism among pastors is a persistent challenge, but Adrian's example reminds us that evangelical churches in a given community which are faithful to the Word of God are not in competition, but rather are partners in Kingdom work. On a broader scale, denominations and networks that agree on the essentials should likewise understand their Kingdom partnership while refraining from making too much of an emphasis on their differences on secondary issues.

15
RELENTLESS PERSONAL EVANGELISM

It would be good once again to remind ourselves of Adrian's secrets to success: "Let me tell you what has made First Baptist Church of Merritt Island a great church: soul-winning, evangelism, and the Spirit-filled life."[1] Indeed, relentless personal evangelism was a priority that drove nearly every aspect of life and ministry in the Merritt Island years. Adrian frequently likened himself to a man playing a cello who had his finger on one string, repeatedly playing one solitary note. Someone asked, "Why are you only playing one note while the others move their fingers up and down and play on different strings?" The cellist replied, "They're looking for it; I've found it!"[2]

Indeed, Adrian provided both a relentless personal example as well as persistent teaching about personal evangelism. In that regard, the image of the humble Parson in the medieval poem *The Canterbury Tales* comes to mind, especially as he did good works and then taught them to his people:

This fine example to his flock he gave,
That first he wrought and afterwards he taught;
Out of the gospel then that text he caught,
And this figure he added thereunto—
That, if the gold shall rust, what shall the iron do?[3]

To be sure, Adrian provided a powerful, pace-setting example with his own daily witness, making every opportunity and taking every opportunity. He likewise vigorously challenged his people to follow his example, never asking them to do anything that he was not himself doing. Ultimately, through both his example and teaching, he developed a comprehensive culture of personal evangelism at First Baptist Church that transcended any program, sermon series, or campaign.

WHAT HE WROUGHT: ADRIAN'S POWERFUL EXAMPLE

How did Adrian set the example through his own personal witness? First, he possessed a significant "soul consciousness"—that is, he held a deep conviction that every single person he encountered, no matter who they were, no matter where or when, was in one of two categories: saved or lost. There was no third category; there was no in-between category. Second, Adrian never made an assumption about anyone's spiritual condition. Church attendance or religious talk did not necessarily indicate anything regarding a person's salvation. Then, through the power of the Holy Spirit in and through him, Adrian proactively endeavored to find a way into every person's life, in order to first assess their relationship with the Lord and—if lost—to somehow invite the person to "come to Jesus."

In some cases, that meant taking a spontaneous opportunity as he was on his way here or there, not unlike Jesus' command to his disciples: "Go to the lost sheep of the house of Israel. And *as you go*, preach, saying, 'The kingdom of heaven is at hand'" (Matthew 10:6-7). Taking every opportunity meant that any interaction with another person, however unplanned it might be, had been divinely orchestrated by God as an opportunity to share Jesus. At the same time, *making* an opportunity meant Adrian made every effort to fill his calendar with appointments specifically to meet with people and share the Gospel with them. This required a pre-determined purpose and plan, in the same way that Jesus commanded his disciples through a parable:

> Jesus said, "A certain man gave a great supper and invited many and sent his servant at supper time to say to those who were invited, 'Come, for all things are now ready.' But they all with one accord began to make excuses....Then the master said to the servant, 'Go out into the highways and hedges, and compel them to come in, that my house may be filled'" (Luke 14:16-18, 23).

Taking every opportunity and making every opportunity—that is what Adrian Rogers did because that was who Adrian Rogers was.

TAKING EVERY OPPORTUNITY

Examples abound from Adrian's Merritt Island teaching and writing about how he took every opportunity that presented itself to share Jesus. From sharing with a hitchhiker to witnessing to a profane car salesman and everything in between, Adrian always endeavored to get into a person's life and invite them to receive Christ. During a sermon from the late 1990s, Adrian described an incident that had taken place 30 years earlier in Merritt Island:

> A while back I received a letter from a man who said, "Forgive me for not writing you, but I want to tell you what happened to me. Years ago, when you were a pastor in Merritt Island, Florida, I was a long-haired, hippie surfer walking down the street with a surfboard on a hot day.

> You stopped your car and picked me up and shared Jesus Christ with me. I was trying to act cool as if I wasn't paying any attention to you, and I kind of pretended to brush you off. But you witnessed to me, prayed with me, and let me out of the car. Forgive me for not telling you about this sooner, but I never got your witness out of my heart until I gave my heart to Jesus Christ. God saved me and now I'm a preacher of the Gospel of our Savior Jesus Christ." Well, I didn't know that; in fact, I had to think hard to even remember the incident after I got the letter. After all, you're just throwing out the seed. You just don't know what God will do.[4]

On another occasion, Adrian went to buy a car and eventually took an opportunity to share with the salesman:

> I went to buy an automobile one time in Merritt Island. I had the money to buy a brand-new automobile, and I was ready to buy. I even went to the lot and tried not to let any salesman see me until I found the car that I wanted. I had my mind made up, so that when the salesman finally got me, I was already convinced. So we sat down, and I said, "I'm interested in so-and-so." And this man started cursing and using profanity—not swearing at me, but saying things like "It's hotter than blankety-blank" and "G-D this" and "Jesus that" and so forth. So I said, "Sir, just a moment. I came in here to buy a car. I want to tell you about myself. I'm a Christian"—he didn't know that I was a pastor. "And I love Jesus Christ with all of my heart. And I'm grieved to hear his name mixed in the muck and slime that you've mixed it with." And he said, "Well, I can talk any way that I want." And I said, 'Sir, you can talk any way that you want, and I can buy a car anywhere that I want. And I'm not going to buy one here. Goodbye." And I walked out. Later on, he said, "Who was that?" And someone said, "He's the pastor down there at the Baptist Church." And he came down to see me and said, "Sir, I'm sorry. I'm so ashamed." And I led him to Christ.[5]

Adrian would also say that taking every opportunity requires a sensitivity to the Holy Spirit's leadership. Consider this Merritt Island episode:

> My, how God will bless us if we only let him lead us. The other morning I woke up, and my first thought was, "Lord, you take control of me this day. Lord, you fill me with the Holy Spirit this day. I want to give this day to you. You speak to me. Lord, help me to arrange my time to know how best to use it." Well, I had to take the kids to music lessons. Once I got them there, I thought, "This is crazy. By the time I get home, I'll have to turn right around to come back here to get them." So instead of driving back home, I said, "Lord, you show me where you want me to go." Well, I just turned and stopped by King Street Baptist Church to say "Hi" to the pastor. I had never been there to do that before, and I hadn't been sitting down for two or three minutes when two traveling men came in, away from God and away from home. And in less than 10 minutes, I had the sweet opportunity of leading those two men to the Lord Jesus Christ as they got on their knees and prayed with tears, asking Jesus to save them. Now, I don't think that was an accident. The Holy Spirit said, "Turn in here, Adrian." And God said to those men, "You turn in here."[6]

MAKING EVERY OPPORTUNITY

Adrian also met regularly with all kinds of people in his office and elsewhere, and his goal was always to make the most of those opportunities for a Gospel witness. Throughout the Merritt Island years, one particular story involving a senior-level executive at the Cape stands out:

> One day, a man came to see me. He was a big shot at the Cape. He drove a big, white Cadillac; I could see it through my office window. He came in wearing a big gold ring with a big diamond and a very

expensive suit. I had never seen him before. He said, "Mr. Rogers, I need to talk with you. My wife wants to commit suicide, and I don't want her to. Would you talk with her?" I said, "Yes, as long as you come with her." So they showed up in my office, and after talking with her, I found out why she wanted to commit suicide. Her husband was an alcoholic, a gambler, and an adulterer who verbally and physically abused his wife. He humiliated her. He ridiculed her. It was quite easy to see why she was so distraught. So I asked the man—I wasn't asking for information—"Are you a Christian?" He laughed and said, "No, I'm not a Christian. I'm an atheist." And I said, "Oh, you must be a brilliant man. You must know *everything*." He said, "Well, I probably don't know everything." So I said, "But I thought you said you were an atheist." He said, "I am." I said, "An atheist knows that God doesn't exist. Would it be generous to say that you know half of all there is to know?" He said, "Of course." So I said, "Could it be that God might exist outside of your knowledge?" "Oh," he said, "I never thought of that." So I said, "Well, then maybe you're not an atheist; maybe you're an agnostic, which is just a fancy word for 'doubter.'" And he said, 'Yes, I'm a doubter—and a *big* one." I said, "I don't care what size, I want to know what kind. You're either an honest doubter or a dishonest doubter. You say you don't know if there is a God or not, but do you want to know?" Then I told him about John 7:17, which is what Jesus said to the agnostics of his day: "If anyone wills to do his will, he shall know concerning the doctrine, whether it is from God or whether I speak on my own authority." After that, I said, "Would you be willing to sign a statement like this: 'God I don't know whether you exist or not, I don't know whether the Bible is your Word or not, and I don't know whether Jesus Christ is your son or not. But I want to know, and because I want to know, I'll make an honest investigation. And I will follow the results of that investigation, wherever they lead me, regardless of the cost.' An honest man would sign it." He replied, "Well, I'll sign it. I want to be honest. What should I do next?" I said, "I want you to begin to read the Gospel of John, because that book is written that you might

> believe that Jesus is the Christ and believing that you might have life through his name." He said, "But I don't believe that." So I said, "You just make an honest investigation and say, 'God I don't know if this is your Word or not. But if this is your Word, show me. And I make up my mind before the fact that I will obey you if you show me that this is your Word and speak to my heart." And in the matter of a few days, I was on my knees with that man as he wept like a baby and gave his heart to Jesus Christ. The last time I saw that man, he and his wife were sitting in that big white Cadillac holding hands like schoolkids, and she didn't want to commit suicide anymore.[7]

The amazing story did not end there. After several years, the man reached out to Adrian and updated him on his life:

> I got a letter from that man a while back. I had lost track of him. He was up in Bangor, Maine running a tape ministry, working in a Christian school, and serving Jesus in a local church. In his letter, he said, "Let me tell you what's happening in my life," and he gave me a testimony. Then he said, "Brother Rogers, thank you for spending time with this general in the devil's army."[8]

This is just one of many stories that could be told about Adrian's persistent intentionality with the Gospel, all of which remind us of his consistent example of sharing Jesus at every opportunity.

WHAT HE TAUGHT: ADRIAN'S POWERFUL PREACHING

Adrian's preaching about personal evangelism was merely an extension of who he was and what he did, and he rarely preached without in some way including a challenge to his people about sharing the Gospel actively and repeatedly:

> There is one thing that needs to be said over and over and over again to the people of the First Baptist Church of Merritt Island: God has called us and God has commissioned us—every one of us—to be witnesses for him and to be soul-winners. ...The greatest thing that a Christian can do, outside of just knowing and loving Jesus, is to point another soul to Jesus Christ. The Bible says, "He that winneth souls is wise." Jesus Christ is the supreme example, the one of whom it is said we are to walk in his footsteps, and the Bible says in Luke 19:10 that "the Son of Man is come to seek and to save that which is lost."[9]

Some could have used Adrian's powerful example as an excuse: "Brother Rogers, you're so good at winning people to Jesus, but that's not my thing." But he never let the people off that easily, and he often pressed in on the matter:

> It's amazing how God can use one individual. You don't have to be talented. You don't have to have great personality or a flowing tongue. Just let God use you. ...What is the pattern in the Bible? Every member sharing Jesus—all at it and always at it. You are not excused. ...Let me say it again, let me emphasize it, let it burn into your soul. If you are saved and if you know Jesus, you have a mandate from Heaven, God has called you and ordained you and commissioned you—there's no way out of it. Jesus said, "Ye shall be witnesses unto me." When will this get into our souls, that God does not hire preachers and educational directors to do our work for us. Every Christian ought to be a Spirit-filled, empowered, soul-winner.[10]

If each individual Christian is called to witness, Adrian would argue, then entire churches likewise are called to prioritize an evangelistic culture that touches every part of the organization.

> Witnessing is not an option. And a church that is not an evangelistic church has lapsed from the faith. It is an apostate church. The lack

> of witnessing and the lack of soul-winning is a heresy in the church. Sometimes you'll read in a church bulletin, "We will have a week of emphasis on witnessing." That would be like a railroad saying, "We will have a week of emphasis upon transportation." This is our business. We have no other business. Jesus said, "Ye shall be witnesses unto me."[11]

Again, Adrian's priority on an evangelistic culture transcended any program, sermon series, or campaign:

> A church that is not evangelistic and a church that is not missionary has missed the meaning and the message of the Gospel of the Lord Jesus Christ. And anytime we get into anything else that takes away from the preaching of the blood of Jesus Christ and getting men saved from their sin and forgiven, we have missed the message of the old, old book. Sometimes in our churches, we say, "Well, we're going to have a morning service, and that's going to be a worship service. Then we're going to have an evening service, and that's going to be an evangelistic service." My foot! Brother, we need to have an evangelistic atmosphere in the evening service and in the morning service. Do we want souls saved in this church? The early church had a persistent program: "Daily they ceased not to preach and teach Jesus Christ."[12]

Adrian's frequent preaching on personal evangelism contributed greatly to the culture of soul-winning at First Baptist Church. And because there was a culture of personal evangelism, the members proactively visited, witnessed, and led their friends, neighbors, and associates to Jesus Christ. Adrian celebrated this pattern in *The Thrust* on January 25, 1971:

> This is the way it ought to be. Sunday night, I preached on divine healing. This was certainly not an evangelistic message, yet when the invitation was given, the aisles were crowded with those coming forward to profess faith in Christ. There was a young couple, brought

> forward by a businessman, who had won them last Tuesday in visitation. There was a precious little girl, who was accompanied down the aisle by her father, who had led her to Jesus. Two young girls came. The one said concerning the other, "I led my friend to Christ to this afternoon." Then a young housewife brought a sobbing teenager to the front who was saved right there at the altar. The shepherd doesn't give birth to lambs. It is his business to feed the flock. Well-fed, mature, healthy sheep reproduce themselves. It is not the pastor's job to do all the soul-winning. It is his job to preach and to oversee the flock. The members of that flock must be reproducing themselves spiritually by winning souls. No one can do my soul-winning for me, and I can't do yours for you.[13]

THE CHURCH GROWTH ASSUMPTION

First Baptist Church saw phenomenal growth during Adrian's years as pastor, yet the church had no specific "church growth" strategy. In fact, the church growth movement as we have come to know it today was still in its infancy when the Moon Port Pastor led the Merritt Island congregation to become one of the fastest-growing churches in America. Rather, Adrian and the church had what we might call a "church growth assumption," the premise of which was, "If we are faithful as witnesses, our church will grow."

As a Baptist, he sometimes spoke tongue-in-cheek of this church growth assumption: "Someone has said that if we can get two Baptist astronauts to land on the moon, they'd elect one pastor and the other Sunday School superintendent and set a goal for three next Sunday."[14] But on a more serious note, Adrian equated church health with church growth:

> I believe that we as the First Baptist Church of Merritt Island ought to continue to grow. And I believe that when we stop growing, we'll start dying. When a church stops going forward, it starts going

> backward. We must always, constantly day and night, have on our hearts the multitudes."[15]

In Adrian's mind, growth was a forgone conclusion for any church that kept its eyes on "soul-winning, evangelism, and the Spirit-filled life." And he was right. Yes, a modest measure of growth for every church was inevitable in Brevard County in the 1960s, but not the kind of growth that First Baptist Church experienced. Jim Whitmire recalled:

> God's design was this huge influx of people who were coming for the space program, and Merritt Island First Baptist Church played a huge role in the spiritual climate of that whole area. People with all sorts of degrees were coming into the area, visiting the church, getting saved, and joining the church. And, of course, Adrian was the Pied Piper over the whole thing. Other churches in the area grew to a degree, but the wags would say, "First Baptist Church was just growing because of the space industry." Well, that wasn't apples to apples, because ultimately we were growing because of Adrian's evangelistic preaching and leadership. If it was just the space industry, the other churches should've grown at the same speed we did. But Merritt Island became a true megachurch for its day.[16]

At the end of the day, church growth for Adrian was not about the size of the church: "There's nothing wrong with a small church. There's nothing wrong with a big church. But there is something wrong when a church isn't growing when there are lost people around."[17]

CONTEMPORARY APPLICATIONS

In many ways, this chapter on personal evangelism might be considered a subset of the previous chapter on leadership, since church culture is primarily a leadership issue, and developing an evangelistic culture is most certainly a leadership issue. However, given the priority that Adrian placed on personal evangelism, a separate chapter seems warranted. Moreover, this chapter might be considered the culminating chapter of this section, not least because the evangelistic momentum that First Baptist Church experienced could be considered the sum-total of the previous "means" we have highlighted—a high view of the Scripture, the Spirit-filled life, and Gospel leadership.

Also, when talking about the timeless evangelistic principles of the Merritt Island years, it is important to differentiate between the means and the methods. The means remain fundamental and unchanging from one generation to the next. The methods, on the other hand, might not apply equally at all times and in every place. For example, an evangelistic bus ministry worked well in the American culture of the late 1960s and into the 1970s. The simple concept of going into neighborhoods, befriending new children, and giving them rides to church seemed noble and innocent enough. Few parents today, however, would agree. Additionally, a weekly, church-wide evangelistic visitation program such as "God's Invasion Army" proved immensely successful during the Merritt Island years. But that was a time when knocking on someone's door after dark was not outside the realm of possibility. Our culture today, however, presents a different reality: heightened levels of suspicion across the board, a mind-boggling increase in violence, and surveillance cameras on the doorsteps of most homes. Still, our responsibility to embrace the timeless principle of Great Commission intentionality that drove these and other methods 60 years ago remains.

So, what timeless principles do we see in the Merritt Island years? First, we should take note of the obvious: evangelistic churches are led by evangelistic pastors. No church, however blessed here and there with outwardly focused members and staff, will become an evangelistic church without an evangelistic pastor who demonstrates a pace-setting example, persistently preaches about personal evangelism, and promotes a laser focus on winning the lost across the entire organization. To be sure, no pastor can be or will be another Adrian Rogers. But that is not the point.

On the other hand, every pastor should see that his greatest responsibility is to ensure that he is filled with the Holy Spirit, which in turn empowers him with personal evangelism intentionality. Furthermore, God does not need another pastor, however gifted he might be, who ministers and shares the Gospel in his own strength. God needs pastors who are experiencing the Spirit-filled life and who witness day by day as a result.

Second, when it comes to personal evangelism, the Merritt Island years remind us that we are probably not as intentional as we think we are. Adrian taught that evangelistic intentionality begins with soul consciousness—that is, we must first see that every person we meet is in one of two categories: saved or lost. It is very easy for the cares of this world and our busy lives to smother any soul consciousness we might have—we say we're just "too busy" to think along those lines. Moreover, Adrian never made assumptions about anyone's spiritual condition simply because they attended a church service or wore a particular religious or denominational label. Instead, he was very intentional about assessing where each person stood with the Lord by asking some basic inventory questions. Based on that assessment, he always sought a way "in" to the person's life, not a way "out." Again, when we see people as a distraction from our daily agendas, the thought of looking for a way "in" becomes an inconvenience rather than a blessing. The truth is, we have no idea what God will ultimately do when we find a way "in" with the Gospel. I would argue that, while the average Christian is oblivious to these principles, the Spirit-filled Christian will find it hard not to think along these lines.

Third, an evangelistic church will disciple its people in personal evangelism by consistently training them and *sending* them. Adrian made it a point to use what some people have called "the drip method"—that is, he infused personal evangelism training in many different ways at First Baptist Church. From the pulpit, he would share bits and pieces of Bill Bright's "Four Spiritual Laws," which was the default soul-winning curriculum at First Baptist Church. Occasionally, he would not even preach a sermon, per se, but would dedicate the entire sermon to practical aspects of personal evangelism, such as what to do upon entering someone's home and how to transition from talking about a person's background to sharing the Gospel. His "Pastor's Paragraphs" in *The Thrust* was another platform he used effectively to disciple the people about the importance of personal evangelism. Then there were also times, of course, for evangelism training through formal classes, such as during Training Union and later in the University of Christian Education. But Adrian also understood that no amount of training in the classroom could replace the practice of sending people out to make evangelistic visits in a very specific way: each person would go with one or two others, a trained and equipped soul-winner accompanied by someone in need of training. Thus an evangelistic visit had two purposes: share the Gospel with a lost man or women and disciple one or two in soul-winning along the way. Many have pointed out that the majority of churches in the 1990s canceled their weekly "visitation" ministry of training and sending, but those churches never replaced the ministries with another intentional evangelistic emphasis. Perhaps now the time has come to again pursue this level of intentionality, whatever it may look like specifically in any given local church.

Last, numbers represent people, and God's heart is for people. It is true that the emphasis on numbers in the Merritt Island years can be potentially off-putting if viewed through the wrong lens. Yes, it is easy for a numbers-conscious pastor or church to possess the wrong motive and pursue numbers at the expense of authentic disciple making. Adrian knew this and said as much while pastor at First Baptist Church. For example, what Baptist pastor has never been tempted to baptize someone for the sake of the baptism rather than waiting until the person was truly ready to be baptized? That said, we should never judge a philosophy by its abuses. After all, the early church clearly thought numbers mattered when it recorded that "about three thousand souls" were saved on the day of Pentecost, and that subsequently "the Lord added to the church daily those who were being saved" (Acts 2:41,47). In addition, when the disciples returned to Jesus after he sent them out, they gave a report of their ministry results (Luke 9:10). Therefore, as God blesses with increase, we ought to celebrate his goodness and the lives changed by the Gospel. Again, some of the celebratory methods that were common in Merritt Island 60 years ago might not resonate precisely in today's churches. But we should nevertheless celebrate evangelistic wins as often as possible, not least because such recognition of results feeds the evangelistic culture we seek to establish and maintain.

EPILOGUE

September 3, 1972, the first Sunday after Adrian's departure, presented a very different reality for the people of the First Baptist Church of Merritt Island. Their pastor for the last 8 years was gone, whisked away by the will of God for even larger purposes than they could imagine. The previous Sunday night in his last sermon at Merritt Island, Adrian had preached from Philippians 2:12 with the title, "How to Behave When the Pastor is Away." As the Apostle Paul did in his letter, Adrian asked the congregation a pointed question: "Will you serve God in my absence as you have in my presence?" Then he issued this challenge:

> When I leave, I don't want you to just sit around on your thumbs. I'll tell you, there's a lot of work to be done around here. And we can get real sentimental, and we can sing the Hallelujah Chorus, and we can sing "There's A Sweet, Sweet Spirit in this Place," but I'll tell you what I want you to do: I want you to be here next Sunday ready to go to work![1]

In the moment, the hundreds gathered responded with a hearty "Amen!" But one week later, the truth of Adrian's departure provided the congregation a tangible reminder that their dynamic leader was no longer part of the Merritt Island equation. Nevertheless, the following months demonstrated that the church would indeed serve God in Adrian's absence—that the church indeed showed up ready to go to work. Remarkably, the church pressed forward, by God's grace and seasoned by Adrian's example, and baptized upwards of 250 people in the 14-month interim period before a new pastor arrived.[2] If the ultimate test of a pastor's leadership comes after his departure, then that kind of momentum validated the Moon Port Pastor well after he answered God's call to Memphis.

Beyond that affirmation, however, God continued to generate waves of spiritual impact far beyond First Baptist Church, Brevard County, and even the state of Florida. After all, Adrian was not the only person whom God carried away from Merritt Island to new places of service. As we have already seen, the majority of those who came to work in the space industry moved elsewhere after the Apollo Program ended, and those who had seen and heard God's glory at First Baptist Church took that experience with them. Lyvonne Burleson recalled that many found new jobs and contracts in New York, Texas, California, and a host of other states. In what Steve Rogers called "the Merritt Island *diaspora*," those same people went and impacted churches across the country, noting he still receives e-mails and social media messages from random people coast to coast saying, "I got saved under your dad's ministry at Merritt Island," or "Your dad married us at First Baptist Church," or "Your dad baptized me back in Merritt Island."[3] Perhaps Jim Whitmire best summarized the aftermath of Adrian's Merritt Island years in this way:

> The Holy Spirit did a phenomenal work, and when it was all said and done everybody looks back on those years and they know that growing all those people was something special. And when the initial thrust of the space program was over, it was sort of like God pressed down and the people went all over the country. They had seen that glory, and then they went everywhere to serve churches all over the United States.[4]

Truly, the story of the Moon Port Pastor echoes into eternity: God's Word preached powerfully, God's people led well, and thousands saved and discipled—all at the center of an especially-historic season in American history. May God stimulate those who read the story to love and good works, the fullness of the Holy Spirit, Gospel leadership, and personal evangelism.

BIBLIOGRAPHIC NOTE

Numerous primary resources specific to the Merritt Island years are available. First and foremost, upwards of 400 audio recordings of Adrian's sermons from First Baptist Church exist, due in large part to the tireless efforts of Bill Cochran, longtime member and director of the church's tape ministry. Not only did Bill personally record the sermons on reel-to-reel tape, but years later he passed them along to Steve Rogers and the Pastor Training Institute, through which the sermons appeared digitally as *The Merritt Island Years*, a four-disc set that became available in 2011. Since that time, the collection has passed to Love Worth Finding and will soon appear on the ministry's website. The sermons are categorized by Scripture and title, not date; therefore, listeners must rely on incidental references to events or people—for example, revival services with a particular speaker, Apollo 11 moon landing, Jai-Alai vote—in order to determine when the sermon was preached. Overall, these sermons are an incredible resource, not least because of the zeal with which Adrian delivered them, but also because they feature a depth of transparency not as common in Adrian's later preaching.

Norma and Gene Baird, former First Baptist Church historians, as well as Lyvonne Burleson, current First Baptist Church historian, have lovingly preserved and meticulously created several key resources. Roughly fifty percent of the weekly church mailers sent between 1964 and 1972, known in those days as *The Link* and then *The Thrust*, are still extant and provide excellent information, especially the weekly "Pastors Paragraphs" on the last page. A *Book of Memories*, created and printed in 1999 in observance of the church's 50th anniversary, contains many first-hand accounts from those who attended and served during Adrian's pastorate. Lyvonne Burleson has also recorded year-by-year, highly detailed historical notes of church happenings.

The Rogers family donated a number of letters, documents, pictures, and other items to Southwestern Baptist Theological Seminary in 2014, all of which were maintained in the B. H. Carroll Center for Baptist Heritage and Mission. Since conducting research for this book, those items have been relocated to the Mid-America Baptist Theological Seminary in Memphis, Tennessee.

The 1997 biographical video, *Standing on the Promises*, remains difficult to obtain. Love Worth Finding and the Bellevue Baptist Church library both possess copies with undetermined plans for public re-release.

Numerous interviews were conducted as part of the research for this book. These contain first-hand accounts from Adrian's Merritt Island contemporaries, whether family, close friends, First Baptist Church staff, or members. A number of those interviewed have since passed away.

If you would like to hear a collection of
Adrian Rogers' messages while at
First Baptist Church, Merritt Island, Florida,
please follow the QR link below.

NOTES

PREFACE

1. "Adrian Rogers Funeral Service" (Memphis: Bellevue Baptist Church, 2005), 53:50.

2. Jim Whitmire Interview (Jacksonville, Florida, June 19, 2008), 1:01:05.

INTRODUCTION

1. "Remarks to Apollo 11 Astronauts Aboard the U.S.S. Hornet Following Completion of Their Lunar Mission," https://www. presidency. ucsb.edu/documents/remarks-apollo-11-astronauts-aboard-the-uss-hornet-following-completion-their-lunar (accessed May 3, 2023); Adrian mentioned this quote in "A Church Aflame," The Merritt Island Years (Memphis: Love Worth Finding, 2024), 10:50.

2. "Queen Elizabeth's Message to Apollo 11 Crew," https://www.dailymail. co.uk/sciencetech/article-11198037/Queen-Elizabeths-message-Apollo-11-crew-etched-silicon-disc-left-moon-1969.html (accessed May 3, 2023).

3. "Apollo 11: The Greatest Single Broadcast in Television History," https://www.bbc. com/news/world-us-canada-48857752 (accessed May 3, 2023). Cronkite spoke these specific words when the Eagle touched down, but his wonder and amazement lasted throughout the mission.

4. "When I Consider the Heavens," The Merritt Island Years (Memphis: Love Worth Finding, 2024), 2:10.

5. By His Grace and For His Glory (Memphis: Bellevue Baptist Church, 2003), 92-97.

6. "Our History," https://www.lwf.org/about-us/our-history (accessed May 3, 2023).

7. Ibid.

8. Jerry Sutton, The Baptist Reformation: The Conservative Resurgence in the Southern Baptist Convention (Nashville: Broadman & Holman, 2000), 78-87.

9. "Five Lessons I Learned from Adrian Rogers," https://www.namb.net/ send-network/resource/5-lessons-i-learned-from-adrian-rogers (accessed May 3, 2023).

10. Walter B. Sharen and Randy Shepley, *Going for the Jugular* (Macon: Mercer University Press, 1996), 276.

11. "Rogers on Ministry, the SBC, and Post-Retirement," *Florida Baptist Witness* (November 17, 2005), 12.

12. *The Thrust* (August 27, 1972), 4.

13. "Maturity, Ministry, Management," *Pastor Training Institute* (West Palm Beach: PTI, 2005), 2:17.

14. Gene and Norma Baird, Lyvonne Burleson, et al, *A Book of Memories* (Merritt Island: First Baptist Church, 1999), 3,7.

15. John McAleenan, "Rev Rogers and His Island in the Sun," *Today* (May 14, 1972), 4.

16. Joyce Rogers, *Love Worth Finding* (Nashville: Broadman & Holman, 2005).

17. *Standing on the Promises* (Memphis: Bellevue Baptist Church, 1997).

18. "The Battle for Your Mind," *The Merritt Island Years* (Memphis: Love Worth Finding, 2024), 15:20.

CHAPTER 1

1. *Love Worth Finding*, 8,13.

2. "Blessed are the Peacemakers," *The Merritt Island Years* (Memphis: Love Worth Finding, 2024), 2:00.

3. *Standing on the Promises*, 7:15.

4. Ibid, 6:45.

5. "My Private Time with Jesus," *A Legacy of Preaching* (Fort Worth: SBC Tapes, 2005), 2:50.

6. *Standing on the Promises*, 9:58.

7. *What Every Christian Ought to Know* (Nashville: Broadman & Holman, 2005), 54.

8. "The Tragic Story of Saul," *The Merritt Island Years* (Memphis: Love Worth Finding, 2024), 20:10.

9. Ibid, 23:15.

10. Ibid, 25:20.

11. “How to Win Fellow Workers,” *The Merritt Island Years* (Memphis: Love Worth Finding, 2024), 5:00.

12. “A New Testament Church,” (Memphis: Bellevue Baptist Church, 1972), 35:30.

13. Ibid; also “The Power of a Vision,” *The Merritt Island Years* (Memphis: Love Worth Finding, 2024), 22:00.

14. “Our Wonderful Salvation,” *The Merritt Island Years* (Memphis: Love Worth Finding, 2024), 31:00.

15. Ibid.

16. “Spiritual Priority,” *Pastor Training Institute* (West Palm Beach: PTI, 2005), 28:00.

17. “How to Have an Evangelistic Church,” SWBTS Chapel (Fort Worth: SWBTS, 1979), 14:30.

18. “My Private Time With Jesus,” 6:00.

19. *Love Worth Finding*, 157. In Love Worth Finding, Adrian also used the language “filled with the Spirit.” Ibid, 156.

20. Palm Beach High School Year Book, SWBTS Archive Box 13.

21. “Rogers and Herwick Out of Action,” *Palm Beach Wildcats*, November 24, 1958, page 4; SWBTS Archive Box 13.

22. “Thoughts on the SBC,” (Memphis: Bellevue Baptist Church, 1993), 6:58.

23. “My Private Time With Jesus,” 7:45.

24. “Thoughts on the SBC,” 7:30.

25. Certificate of License, SWBTS Archives Box 13.

26. *Standing on the Promises*, 17:30.

27. “Southern Baptists and the Battle for the Bible” (Memphis: Bellevue Baptist Church, 1994), 3:45.

28. “Thoughts on the SBC,” 9:25.

29. Ibid.

30. “Southern Baptists and the Battle for the Bible,” 4:30

31. Adrian Rogers Funeral Service, November 18, 2005; “Revelation 18,” *The Merritt Island Years* (Memphis: Love Worth Finding, 2024), 21:20.

32. “Our Wonderful Salvation,” 31:10.

33. “Maturity, Ministry, Management,” 21:10.

34. *Standing on the Promises*, 16:45.

35. "My Private Time With Jesus," 13:45.

36. *Love Worth Finding*, 28-29.

37. *Standing on the Promises*, 21:00.

38. Ibid.

39. "My Private Time with Jesus," 8:20.

40. *Standing in the Promises*, 21:30.

41. "Faith to Walk with God" (Memphis: Bellevue Baptist Church, 1978), 18:20.

42. *Love Worth Finding*, 43.

CHAPTER 2

1. "Southern Baptists and the Battle for the Bible," 4:30; see also *The Baptist Reformation*, 80-84.

2. *Love Worth Finding*, 34-35.

3. Ibid, 38.

4. Peter Lord Interview (Titusville, Florida; June 18, 2008), 3:30.

5. *Standing on the Promises*, 25:00.

6. "A Cure for Cracked Pots," *The Merritt Island Years* (Memphis: Love Worth Finding, 2024), 21:20; "Maturity, Ministry, Management," 27:00.

7. *Love Worth Finding*, 40.

8. "Maturity, Ministry, Management," 27:00; Joyce Rogers Interview (Memphis, Tennessee; May 5, 2022), 12:15. First Baptist Church of Miami eventually called Junius Foster on July 1, 1958. Interestingly, the church's next pastor was Charles Stanley, who served First Baptist Church of Miami from 1962 to 1968. *Miami News*, May 6, 1961, 5A; *The Miami Herald*, August 24, 1963, 18A; "Miami Church Reverses 5-Year Downward Trend," Florida Baptist Witness, March 19, 1964, 7.

9. *The Bellevue Messenger* (May 16, 1991), 4.

10. *Love Worth Finding*, 43.

11. Joyce Rogers, *Home Life* (October 1961), 15.

12. "My Private Time with Jesus," 16:27.

13. Joyce Rogers, *Home Life*, 16.

14. *Love Worth Finding*, 5.

15. "How to Have an Evangelistic Church," 16:21.

16. *Love Worth Finding*, 159.

17. Ibid, 160; "Blessed are Those Who Mourn," *The Merritt Island Years* (Memphis: Love Worth Finding, 2024), 14:00.

18. "How to Have an Evangelistic Church," 17:00.

19. Ian Thomas, *The Saving Life of Christ* (Grand Rapids: Zondervan, 1961), 68-69.

20. Ibid, 35-57.

21. "Filled with the Holy Spirit," *The Merritt Island Years* (Memphis: Love Worth Finding, 2024), 5:30; also "Spirit vs. Law," *The Merritt Island Years* (Memphis: Love Worth Finding, 2024), 12:30; "A Faithful Teacher," *The Merritt Island Years* (Memphis: Love Worth Finding, 2024), 14:10.

22. *Love Worth Finding*, 161.

23. "New Pastorium is Formally Dedicated," *Fort Pierce News Tribune* (December 22, 1958), 8; *Standing on the Promises*, 30:25.

24. "New Pastorium is Formally Dedicated," 8.

25. "Old Time Religion Sets Record," *Fort Pierce News Tribune* (March 23, 1959), 12.

26. Joe Boatright Interview (Orlando, Florida; June 18, 2008), 17:20.

27. "Meet Your Minister," *Fort Pierce News Tribune* (July 17, 1959), 7.

28. "Parkview Selling Bonds for Church Expansion," *Fort Pierce News Tribune* (June 10, 1960), 5.

29. *Love Worth Finding*, 45.

30. "Reaching Others For Christ" (Memphis: Bellevue Baptist Church, 1996), 22:15.

31. Ibid.

32. Ibid.

33. "A Cure for Cracked Pots," 22:00; Adrian Rogers letter to W. G. Stracener, October 14, 1964 (courtesy of Joyce Rogers).

34. The letter also listed things such as total church membership of 972, Sunday School enrollment of 1,089, and an annual budget of $78,000. Anne Hicks letter to Adrian Rogers, April 22, 1964 (courtesy of Joyce Rogers).

35. Joe Boatright Interview, 19;15; Senior Members Interview (Merritt Island, Florida; June 17, 2008), 12:30; *A Book of Memories*, 27.

36. Senior Members Interview, 15:20; "Christian Homes," *The Merritt Island Years* (Memphis: Love Worth Finding, 2024), 1:30.

37. "A Cure for Cracked Pots," 24:00.

38. Jim Whitmire Interview, 7:30.

39. "A Cure for Cracked Pots," 24:20.

40. Jim Whitmire Letter to Adrian Rogers, June 22, 1964 (courtesy of Joyce Rogers).

41. Robert Pullin Letter to Adrian Rogers, June 25, 1964 (courtesy of Joyce Rogers).

42. Adrian Rogers Letter to First Baptist Church, Merritt Island, June 27, 1964 (courtesy of Joyce Rogers).

CHAPTER 3

1. Jules Verne, *From the Earth to the Moon* (New York: Scribner, Armstrong & Company, 1874).

2. John M. Eriksen, *Brevard County: A History to 1955* (Tampa: Florida Historical Society Press, 1994), 211.

3. Edward Ehrenspeck, *NASA Range Rats: The True Beginnings* (self-published, 2022), 32.

4. "Merritt Island Church to Be Occupied Sunday," *Cocoa Tribune* (April 6, 1950), 6; *A Book of Memories*, 1,5.

5. Jerrell H. Shafner, *History of Brevard County* (Titusville: Brevard County Historical Commission: 1996), 119-129; Erickson, Brevard County, 212-217; William Roy Shelton, *Countdown: The Story of Cape Canaveral* (Boston: Brown, 1960), 32.

6. Senior Members Interview, 3:30.

7. *A Book of Memories*, 2-3,5-6.

8. Shafner, *History of Brevard County*, 126.

9. Eriksen, *Brevard County*, 217.

10. Shafner, *History of Brevard County*, 129-130.

11. Joe Boatright Interview, 8:15.

12. *A Book of Memories*, 24. The Carltons moved their membership in September 1951. Burleson Collection.

13. Senior Members Interview, 10:10.

14. Lyvonne Burleson, ed., *We Pledge Allegiance In His Name* (Merritt Island: First Baptist Church, 2003), 33. Stalag XIII—not to be confused with the fictitious Stalag XIII of "Hogan's Heroes" fame—was also the site of Patton's ill-fated *Task Force Baum* raid in March 1945. Duane P. Schultz, *Patton's Last Gamble* (Mechanicsburg, PA: Stackpole, 2018).

15. "Merritt Baptists to Welcome New Pastor Sunday," *Cocoa Tribune* (October 11, 1957), 8.

16. *A Book of Memories*, 24.

17. Jim Whitmire Interview, 2:20.

18. "Merritt Island Baptists to Occupy New Building Sunday," *Cocoa Tribune* (April 22, 1960), 1,6-7.

19. "Life in Missile Land," *Time* (July 15, 1957), 19-20.

20. Walter A. McDougall, *The Heavens and the Earth—A Political History of the Space Age* (Baltimore: Johns Hopkins University, 1987), 3.

21. "Space: Rendezvous with Destiny," *Time* (April 20, 1959), 5.

22. Lori C. Walters, "Beyond the Cape, 1950-1963," *Florida Historical Quarterly* 87:2 (2020), 252.

23. Charles D. Benson and William Barnaby Faherty, *Moonport: A History of Apollo Launch Facilities and Operations* (Houston: National Aeronautics and Space Administration, 1978), 45.

24. Ibid, 46; Shafner, *History of Brevard County*, 130.

25. Annie May Hartsfield, Mary Alice Griffin, and Charles M. Grigg, eds., *Summary Report* NASA *Impact on Brevard County* (Tallahassee: Florida State University, 1966), 10-11.

CHAPTER 4

1. Arnold Levine, *Managing* NASA *in the Apollo Era* (Washington, DC: NASA, 1982), 17.

2. Roger D. Launius, *Apollo: A Retrospective Analysis* (Washington, DC: NASA, 1994), 1-2.

3. Ibid, 2.

4. *New York Times* (April 17, 1961), 5.

5. Hugh Sidey, "Soviet Traveler Returns from Out of This World," *Life* (April 21, 1961), 20.

6. "Address Before the American Society of Newspaper Editors on April 20, 1961 in Washington, D.C."; https://www.jfklibrary.org/archives/other-resources/john-f-kennedy-speeches/american-society-of-newspaper-editors-19610420 (accessed April 29, 2023).

7. Hugh Sidey, "The Lesson John Kennedy Learned from the Bay of Pigs," *Time* (April 16, 2001), 14.

8. *New York Times*, April 22, 1961, 4.

9. Wehrner von Braun to Lyndon Johnson, April 29, 1961 in Launius, *Apollo: A Retrospective Analysis*, 3.

10. “Special Message to Congress on Urgent National Needs on May 25, 1961 in Washington, D.C.”; https://www.jfklibrary.org/asset-viewer/archives/JFKPOF/034/JFKPOF-034-030 (accessed April 29, 2023).

11. Ibid.

12. Hugo Young, *Journey to Tranquility* (London: Jonathan Cape, 1969), 110.

13. Levine, *Managing* NASA *in the Apollo Era*, 19.

14. “Glenn Orbits Earth Three Times Safely,” *New York Times* (February 21, 1962), 1.

15. “Address at Rice University on the Nation’s Space Efforts,” https://www. jfklibrary. org/learn/about-jfk/historic-speeches/address-at-rice-university-on-the-nations-space-effort (accessed May 2, 2023).

16. “Reflecting on President Kennedy’s Moonshot Speech 60 Years Later,” https://news. rice. edu/news/2022/reflecting-president-kennedys-moonshot-speech-60-years-later (accessed May 2, 2023).

17. Jim Whitmire 2008 Interview, 1:15.

18. Ibid.

19. “Adrian Rogers Funeral Service,” 22:00.

20. “Space: Under Whose Moon,” *Time* (May 31, 1963), 13.

21. “Historical Vignette: The Corps of Engineers Build NASA Facilities,” https://www.usace.army. mil/About/History/Historical-Vignettes/Military-Construction-Combat/050-NASA/#:~:text= The%20mammoth%20structure%20rests%20on, (accessed on May 7, 2023).

22. Lina Mann, “Lyndon B. Johnson: Forgotten Champion of the Space Race,” https://www. whitehousehistory.org/lyndon-b-johnson-forgotten-champion-of-the-space-race (accessed May 7, 2023); Jeff Shesol, “Lyndon Johnson's Unsung Role in Sending Americans to the Moon,” https://www.newyorker.com/news/news-desk/lyndon-johnsons-unsung-role-in-sending-americans-to-the-moon (accessed May 7, 2023).

23. “Space: Under Whose Moon,” *Time*, May 31, 1963, 13.

24. Shesol, “Lyndon Johnson’s Unsung Role in Sending Americans to the Moon.”

25. Michael Marks, “Why Apollo 11 Wouldn’t Have Happened Without Lyndon Johnson,” https://www.texasstandard.org/stories/why-apollo-11-wouldnt-have-happened-without-lyndon-johnson (accessed May 7, 2023).

26. *Florida: Moon port* USA, https://www.loc.gov/item/2021671087 (accessed May 7, 2023).

27. Jim Whitmire 2008 Interview, 4:00.

CHAPTER 5

1. "Cure for Cracked Pots," 25:20.

2. Bill Cochran Interview (Merritt Island, Florida, June 17, 2008), 6:35.

3. Ibid, 7:45.

4. Jim Whitmire 2008 Interview, 15:45.

5. Bill Cochran Interview; 8:30; Gene and Norma Baird Interview (Merritt Island, Florida, June 17, 2008), 3:30.

6. Senior Members Interview, 8:15; Nelson Rutledge Interview (Merritt Island, Florida, June 17, 2008), 14:25; Joe Boatright Interview, 41:10.

7. George Korda Interview (Telephone, April 11, 2022), 4; Jim Whitmire 2008 Interview, 23:15.

8. Jim Whitmire 2008 Interview, 18:15.

9. Steve Rogers Interview (Telephone, April 29, 2022).

10. Adrian Rogers letter to W. G. Stracener; *The Thrust* (December 12, 1965), 4.

11. Steve Rogers Interview, 9:30.

12. Senior Members Interview, 14:10.

13. *Cocoa Tribune* (October 30, 1964), 2B.

14. *Miami Herald* (February 13, 1965), 3B; *Cocoa Tribune* (April 2, 1965), 12; *Cocoa Tribune* (April 9, 1965), 3.

15. Burleson 1965 Notes, 2; Nelson Rutledge Interview, 38:15.

16. Ibid, 3.

17. *The Link* (September 23, 1965), 3.

18. "Space: Closing the Gap," *Time* (June 11, 1965), 6.

19. Ibid, 8.

20. "Moon in Their Grasp," *Time* (December 24, 1965), 9.

21. "New Look at the Cape," *Time* (March 26, 1965), 12.

22. *The Link* (August 8, 1965), 2.

23. Steve Rogers Interview, 42:30.

24. "Things Unshakeable," *The Merritt Island Years* (Memphis: Love Worth Finding, 2024), 5:00.

25. "War," *The Merritt Island Years* (Memphis: Love Worth Finding, 2024), 40:30.

26. *The Link* (November 2, 1965), 1,3.

27. *The Thrust* (November 28, 1965), 1.

28. "The Church at Philadelphia," *The Merritt Island Years* (Memphis: Love Worth Finding, 2024), 17:40, 28:00.

29. Ibid, 30:30.

30. *The Thrust* (December 19, 1965), 4.

CHAPTER 6

1. *The Thrust* (February 13, 1966), 1; *The Thrust* (May 22, 1966), 4.

2. "Merritt Island First Baptist Space Age Church," *Orlando Sentinel* (June 11, 1966), 12; "Merritt Island Church Has Space Age Idea," *Orlando Evening Star* (June 3, 1966), 11A.

3. *The Thrust* (May 29, 1966), 1-3; Burleson 1966 Notes, 2.

4. *The Daily Times* (November 28, 1966), 7.

5. Ibid.

6. *The Thrust* (March 27, 1966), 4.

7. Burleson 1966 Notes, 1.

8. *The Thrust* (March 13, 1966), 4.

9. *The Thrust* (March 20, 1966), 1.

10. Burleson 1966 Notes, 1.

11. *The Thrust* (June 5, 1966), 4; *The Thrust* (June 12, 1966), 4.

12. *The Thrust* (July 31, 1966), 2-3.

13. *The Thrust* (August 14. 1966), 2; *The Thrust* (August 28, 1966), 4.

14. *The Thrust* (September 25, 1966), 4.

15. Ibid.

16. *The Thrust* (October 2, 1966), 4.

17. Ibid.

18. *The Thrust* (October 16, 1966), 4.

19. Nelson Rutledge Interview, 38:30.

20. Jim Whitmire 2008 Interview, 42:30.

21. Ibid, 44:20.

22. Ibid, 44:50.

23. "How to Have an Evangelistic Church," SWBTS Chapel (Fort Worth: SWBTS, 1979), 19:30.

24. Jim Whitmire 2023 Interview; *The Thrust* (December 19, 1965), 2; Steve Rogers Interview, 25:45.

25. Burleson 1966 Notes, 5.

26. Ibid.

27. *The Thrust* (November 6, 1966), 4; *The Thrust* (November 13, 1966), 2-3.

28. *The Thrust* (November 27, 1966), 4.

29. *Cocoa Tribune* (October 27, 1966), 10.

30. *The Thrust* (November 20, 1966), 4; *The Thrust* (November 27, 1966), 4.

31. *Florida Baptist Witness* (November 24, 1966), 3; *Biblical Recorder* (November 23, 1966), 8.

32. *Florida Baptist Witness* (November 24, 1966), 3.

33. *Florida Baptist Annual* 1966 (Jacksonville: Florida Baptist State Convention, 1966), 29.

34. *Florida Baptist Annual* 1966 (Jacksonville: Florida Baptist State Convention, 1966), 29; Biblical Recorder (November 23, 1966), 8.

35. *Standing on the Promises*, 41:00.

36. Steve Rogers Interview, 7:30.

37. Clark Pinnock letter to Adrian Rogers, December 13, 1966 (courtesy of Joyce Rogers).

38. *The Thrust* (December 11, 1966), 1; *The Thrust* (December 25, 1966), 3.

39. *The Thrust* (December 18, 1966), 3.

40. "And Now Apollo," *Time* (November 25, 1966), 8.

CHAPTER 7

1. *The Thrust* (January 1, 1967), 4.

2. *The Thrust* (January 29, 1967), 4.

3. *Florida Baptist Witness* (January 26, 1967), 4.

4. *Florida Baptist Witness* (January 5, 1967), 12.

5. "The Church—A Task Force for Evangelism," *The Merritt Island Years* (Memphis: Love Worth Finding, 2024), 4:30, 18:00, 26:54.

6. *Florida Baptist Witness* (January 26, 1967), 4.

7. Paul A. Meigs letter to Adrian Rogers, January 16, 1967 (courtesy of Joyce Rogers).

8. John Maguire letter to Adrian Rogers, March 3, 1967 (courtesy of Joyce Rogers).

9. *The Thrust* (January 8, 1967), 4.

10. *The Thrust* (January 22, 1967), 4.

11. "Evangelist Eddie Martin Dies of Cancer at Age 81," https://www. baptistpress.com/resource-library/news/5-29-97-evangelist-eddie-martin-dies-of-cancer-at-age-81 (accessed July 8, 2023); Joshua S. Baxter, Justin Cook, Howard Gallimore, and Jonathan Winn, *Inventory to the Edward William Martin Papers* (Nashville: Southern Baptist Historical Library and Archives, 2002), 2.

12. *The Thrust* (January 29, 1967), 4.

13. Ray E. Boothose, *Gus Grissom: The Lost Astronaut* (Indianapolis: Indiana Historical Society Press, 2004), 301.

14. James R. Hansen, *First Man: The Life of Neil A. Armstrong* (New York: Simon & Schuster, 2005), 304; Jim Lovell and Jeffrey Kluger, Lost Moon: The Perilous Voyage of Apollo 13 (Boston: Houghton & Mifflin, 1994), 16.

15. "To Strive, to Seek, to Find, and not to Yield," *Time* (February 3, 1967), 12.

16. *The Thrust* (March 19, 1967), 4.

17. Burleson 1967 Notes, 2; *The Thrust* (April 2, 1967), 2-3.

18. Burleson 1967 Notes, 3.

19. "The World's Most Dangerous Game," *The Merritt Island Years* (Memphis: Love Worth Finding, 2024), 1:00.

20. *The Thrust* (April 2, 1967), 2; "Why Do the Heathen Rage," *The Merritt Island Years* (Memphis: Love Worth Finding, 2024), 4:45.

21. "Jai Alai Issue Debated for Rotary Club," *Orlando Sentinel* (April 20, 1967), B1.

22. "Jai Alai Loses by a Whisker," *Today* (May 3, 1967), 1-2.

23. "The World's Most Dangerous Game," 6:15.

24. "Jai Alai Loses by a Whisker," 1-2.

25. *The Thrust* (April 30, 1967), 2; *The Thrust* (July 9, 1967), 3.

26. Jim Whitmire 2008 Interview, 54:15.

27. *A Book of Memories*, 34.

28. Steve Rogers Interview, 28:30.

29. Nelson Rutledge Interview, 1:05:00.

30. “Rutledge Packs Fun at Merritt Church,” *Orlando Sentinel* (April 25, 1970), B4; Nelson Rutledge Interview, 6:15.

31. *The Thrust* (July 16, 1967), 4.

32. *The Thrust* (March 19, 1967), 4.

33. Steve Rogers Interview, 6:20.

34. Ibid; also Gene and Norma Baird Interview, 8:45.

35. *The Thrust* (August 27, 1967), 4.

36. Jim Whitmire 2008 Interview, 1:20:40.

37. Steve Rogers Interview, 5:00.

38. “Personal Integrity,” *Pastor Training Institute* (West Palm Beach: PTI, 2005), 27:25.

39. Jim Whitmire 2008 Interview, 1:15:30.

40. “Good Reason for Praising the Lord,” *The Evening Tribune* (June 19, 1968), 3B.

41. *The Thrust* (August 27, 1967), 2-3; Burleson 1967 Notes, 4.

42. *The Thrust* (September 10, 1967), 4.

43. “Dialogue Favors Cooperation in Evangelism, Not Structures,” *Baptist Press* (September 11, 1967), 4; “Pastors to Lead National Study,” *Palm Beach Post* (August 26, 1967), 5.

44. “Dialogue Cape Kennedy: Plan Proposed to ‘Win America,’” *Florida Baptist Witness* (September 21, 1967), 2.

45. Ibid.

46. “Dialogue Favors Cooperation in Evangelism, Not Structures,” 4; “Dialogue Cape Kennedy: Plan Proposed to ‘Win America,’” 2.

47. *The Thrust* (October 22, 1967), 4.

48. *The Thrust* (November 26, 1967), 4.

49. Gene and Norma Baird Interview, 12:15.

50. “Pastors Hear Accent on Multi-Sided Responsibility and Joy of Peaching,” *Florida Baptist Witness* (November 23, 1967), 6; *The Thrust* (November 26, 1967), 3.

51. “Life in the Space Age,” *Time* (July 4, 1969), 10-12; Florida: *Moonport* USA, https://www.loc.gov/item/2021671087 (accessed May 7, 2023).

52. Shofner, *History of Brevard*, 207; “Life in the Space Age,” 10-12.

53. "Enoch," *The Merritt Island Years* (Memphis: Love Worth Finding, 2024), 17:30; "Giving Glory to Jesus," *The Merritt Island Years* (Memphis: Love Worth Finding, 2024), 3:30.

54. "What's Wrong with Everybody Anyway," *The Merritt Island Years* (Memphis: Love Worth Finding, 2024), 15:30.

CHAPTER 8

1. *The Thrust* (January 7, 1968), 4.

2. "Elisha: Man of God," A *Legacy of Preaching* (Fort Worth: SBC Tapes, 2005); "A New Testament Church" (Memphis: Bellevue Baptist Church, 1972), 23:20.

3. "Check His Branch Office," *Today* (January 15, 1968), 8A.

4. *The Thrust* (March 17, 1968), 1.

5. *The Thrust* (March 31, 1968), 4; *Love Worth Finding*, 128.

6. *The Thrust* (April 14, 1968), 4.

7. *The Thrust* (April 21, 1968), 1.

8. "Policies for Use of the Activities Building," SWBTS Archive Box 13; Burleson 1968 Notes, 4.

9. "A 4F Family," *The Merritt Island Years* (Memphis: Love Worth Finding, 2024), 24:00.

10. "Policies for Use of the Activities Building," SWBTS Archive Box 13.

11. Burleson 1967 Notes, 4.

12. *The Thrust* (June 16, 1968), 3; Burleson 1967 Notes, 4.

13. "Church Offers Family Program," *Brevard Sentinel* (April 12, 1968), 12.

14. "Baptist Rec Complex Opens," *Today* (June 8, 1968), 3D.

15. "Women's Ministry," *Pastor Training Institute* (West Palm Beach: PTI, 2005), 3:00.

16. A *Book of Memories*, 13.

17. "Women's Ministry," 3:00; Joyce Rogers Interview, 47:15.

18. "Baptists Readying Revival Crusade," *Orlando Sentinel* (May 10, 1968), 8B.

19. *The Thrust* (April 28, 1968), 4.

20. "MI Baptists Slate Revival Crusade," *The Evening Tribune* (May 10, 1968), 4A.

21. Revival Advertisement, *Today* (May 12, 1968), 5B; "Strongest Human Does Lord's Work, *Orlando Sentinel* (May 16, 1968), 2B; "Paul Anderson To Speak," *Orlando Sentinel* (May 15, 1968), 1C.

22. "It's an Old Fashioned Picnic," *The Evening Tribune* (May 20, 1968), 4B.

23. George Korda Interview, 1.

24. *Today* (May 6, 1968), 8B.

25. George Korda Interview, 1.

26. Joyce Rogers George Korda Notes, 2.

27. George Korda Interview, 2.

28. Joyce Rogers George Korda Notes, 3.

29. George Korda Interview, 3; "Battle for Your Mind," 31:00.

30. Joyce Rogers George Korda Notes, 4-5.

31. Ibid, 6-7.

32. *Today* (June 13, 1968), 8B.

33. George Korda Interview, 4; Joyce Rogers George Korda Notes, 7-8.

34. *The Thrust* (June 16, 1968), 3.

35. Burleson 1968 Notes, 2.

36. "Contrasts in Holy Land Impresses Isle Pastor, *The Evening Tribune* (July 12, 1968), 4A; "Good Reasons for Praising the Lord," 3B.

37. *The Thrust* (August 4, 1968), 1; George Korda Interview, 5.

38. "Baptist Overflow New Church," *The Evening Tribune* (August 2, 1968), 3B.

39. *The Thrust* (July 14, 1968), 4; *The Thrust* (July 28, 1968), 4.

40. Gene and Norma Baird Interview, 6:45.

41. "The Bread of Life, Family Style," *All Florida TV Weekly* (December 22, 1968), 12-15.

42. Ibid, 14-15.

43. *The Thrust* (January 5, 1969), 4.

44. *The Thrust* (October 27, 1968), 4.

45. "*Today*'s Women Urged to be Forceful," *The Evening Tribune* (November 10, 1968), 2B; "Campus Crusader's Wife Tells of Experiences," *The Evening Tribune* (November 10, 1968), 3B; Michael Richardson, *Amazing Faith: The Authorized Biography of Bill Bright* (Colorado Springs: Waterbrook Press, 2000), 42-43.

46. *The Thrust* (November 24, 1968), 2-3; *Florida Baptist Witness* (November 21, 1968), 1,3; "Baptist Group Picks Head," *The Evening Tribune* (November 16, 1968), 2B.

47. *The Thrust* (November 17, 1968), 1; "Bertha Smith to be Guest Speaker," *The Evening Tribune* (November 29, 1968), 2B; Bertha Smith, *Go Home and Tell* (Nashville: Broadman & Holman, 1964); Lewis Drummond, *Miss Bertha: Woman of Revival* (Nashville: Broadman & Holman, 1996).

48. *The Thrust* (December 1, 1968), 4.

49. Bertha Smith, *How the Spirit Filled My Life* (Nashville: Broadman & Holman, 1973); "Southern Baptists and the Battle for the Bible," 10:00.

.Steve Rogers Interview, 53:30.

51. "The Last Countdown," *The Merritt Island Years* (Memphis: Love Worth Finding, 2024), 0:45; "Why Do the Heathen Rage," 35:00.

52. "Churches Mark Christmas Season," *The Evening Tribune* (December 20, 1968), 4B.

53. "The Event that Saved 1968," https://www.pbs.org/wgbh/americanexperience/features/moon-event-saved-1968 (accessed August 28, 2023).

CHAPTER 9

1. *The Thrust* (February 9, 1969), 4.

2. "Initial Plans Mapped for Crusade of Americas," *Baptist Press* (July 12, 1966), 1-2; *Crusade of the Americas: 1968, 1969, 1970 Guidebook* (Raleigh, Baptist State Convention, 1967, 1967), 2.

3. "The Associations and Crusade Concern," *Florida Baptist Witness* (November 14, 1968), 4.

4. *The Thrust* (February 9, 1969), 4.

5. *The Thrust* (March 9, 1069), 4.

6. *The Thrust* (March 23. 1969), 4.

7. *The Thrust* (April 27, 1969), 1.

8. *The Thrust* (May 8, 1969), 2-3.

9. "How to Live on the Mountain Top," *The Merritt Island Years* (Memphis: Love Worth Finding, 2024), 6:00.

10. "The Lost Axe Head," *The Merritt Island Years* (Memphis: Love Worth Finding, 2024), 6:45.

11. Ibid, 10:30.

12. *The Thrust* (May 18, 1969), 4.

13. *The Thrust* (June 29, 1969), 4.

14. *The Thrust* (June 1, 1969), 4.

15. *Florida Baptist Witness* (July 10, 1969), 7.

16. *The Thrust* (July 13, 1968), 4.

17. *The Thrust* (July 16, 1968), 4.

18. *The Thrust* (July 13, 1968), 1.

19. "When I Consider the Heavens," 8:30.

20. "Scientific Feats are 'Tribute to God,' *Fort Lauderdale News and Sun-Sentinel* (July 26, 1969), 6B.

21. George Korda Interviev, 4.

22. Jim Whitmire 2023 Interview, 2:15.

23. Burleson 1969 Notes, 5.

24. *The Thrust* (August 24, 1969), 1.

25. *The Evening Tribune* (September 19, 1969), 4B; *Today* (September 20, 1969), 3D; *Orlando Sentinel* (September 16, 1969), 2; *Orlando Sentinel* (September 21, 1969), 6B.

26. Hyman J. Appelman, *The Life Story of Dr. Hyman J. Appelman* (Las Vegas: Solid Christian Books, 1965).

27. "Hyman Appelman," https://www.sbcevangelist.org/hyman-appelman (accessed September 30, 2023).

28. "Blueprint for Victory," *The Merritt Island Years* (Memphis: Love Worth Finding, 2024), 26:00; 31:40.

29. *The Thrust* (August 31, 1969), 4.

30. *The Thrust* (October 12, 1969), 4.

31. *Orlando Sentinel* (November 3, 1969), 3; Evening Tribune (November 14, 1969), 7A.

32. *The Thrust* (November

33. Bill Cochran Interview, 30:20.

34. A *Book of Memories*, 13; "Women's Ministry," *Pastor Training Institute*, 3:00; Lyvonne Burleson Interview, 12:00.

35. *Orlando Sentinel* (November 3, 1969), 2.

36. A *Book of Memories*, 13.

37. *The Thrust* (November 9, 1969), 4.

38. "Pastors Refreshed By Out-of-State Ministers from Varied Backgrounds," *Florida Baptist Witness* (November 20, 1969), 3.

39. "A Moderate Elected By Baptists," *The Miami Herald* (November 12, 1969), 24A.

40. "The World and the Church," *Florida Baptist Witness* (November 20, 1969), 2,6.

41. "A Convention in Tension," *Florida Baptist Witness* (November 27, 1969), 4.

42. "State Southern Baptists Show Signs of Change," *The Miami News* (November 15, 1969), 2A.

43. "A Convention in Tension," 4.

44. *The Thrust* (January 11, 1970), 4.

45. *The Thrust* (December 7, 1969), 4; *The Thrust* (January 11, 1970), 4.

CHAPTER 10

1. David Compton, *Where No Man Has Gone Before: The History of Apollo Lunar Exploration* (Washington: Government Printing Office, 1989), 245.

2. Benson and Faherty, *Moonport: A History of Apollo Launch Facilities and Operations*, 68; "A Ghost Town of Gantries, Time (April 15, 1974), 14.

3. *The Thrust* (March 8, 1970), 4; *The Thrust* (April 5, 1970), 4; *The Thrust* (August 9, 1970), 4.

4. *The Thrust* (January 18, 1970), 4.

5. Burleson 1970 Notes, 1; *The Thrust* (February 15, 1970), 2-3.

6. *The Thrust* (April 5, 1970), 4.

7. *The Thrust* (April 5, 1970), 4; *The Thrust* (August 9), 4.

8. *The Thrust* (March 15, 1970), 4.

9. Ibid, 1.

10. C. E. Autrey letter to Adrian Rogers, August 25, 1967 (courtesy of Joyce Rogers).

11. *The Arizona Republic* (March 14, 1970), 7B; "Southern Baptists Expect 500 at State Sessions," *Tuscon Daily Citizen* (January 16, 1971), 5; George Wilson, "The Evangelism Conference as I Saw It," *Baptist Beacon* (June 28, 1971), 5; "Alexandria Revivals Planned," *Alexandria Daily Town Talk* (March 27, 1971), 4B; Ohio Baptist Messenger (October 14, 1971), 6-7; *The Western Recorder* (December 25, 1971), 16; "Something for Everyone at Elizabethtown," *The Western Recorder* (January 29, 1972), 4; "Rogers Lists Characteristics of an Evangelistic Church," *The Western Recorder* (January 29, 1972), 9.

12. Joyce Rogers Interview, 45:15.

13. Sutton, *The Baptist Reformation*, 7-10.

14. “Five Fundamentals,” *The Merritt Island Years* (Memphis: Love Worth Finding, 2024), 13:30.

15. “Revival,” *The Merritt Island Years* (Memphis: Love Worth Finding, 2024), 8:30.

16. Sutton, *The Baptist Reformation*, 14.

17. Ibid.

18. “Southern Baptists Reject New Commentary,” *The Saline Journal* (June 3, 1971), 2B.

19. “There’s No Magic Formula for Building a Church,” *Today* (May 16, 1970), 5B; “The Church of Jesus Christ,” *The Merritt Island Years* (Memphis: Love Worth Finding, 2024), 10:30.

20. *The Thrust* (August 2, 1970), 4.

21. *The Thrust* (September 6, 1970), 4; Burleson 1970 Notes, 4.

22. *The Thrust* (September 6, 1970), 4.

23. *The Thrust* (October 11, 1970), 4.

24. *The Thrust* (April 18, 1971), 1.

25. Burleson 1970 Notes, 4.

26. “The 5 Ws of the Bus Ministry,” *The Merritt Island Years* (Memphis: Love Worth Finding, 2024), 13:30.

27. Ibid, 13:00.

28. *The Thrust* (January 17, 1971), 1.

29. “Program Jumps with Lively Participants,” *Orlando Sentinel* (July 17, 1971), 5B.

30. “How to Win Family Members,” *The Merritt Island Years* (Memphis: Love Worth Finding, 2024), 8:30.

31. *The Thrust* (June 28, 1970), 4.

32. *The Thrust* (February 28, 1971), 4.

33. George Korda Interview, 3.

34. David Rogers Interview (Telephone, May 2, 2022).

35. *The Thrust* (September 13, 1970), 4.

36. Joyce Rogers Interview, 48:00.

37. *The Thrust* (July 4, 1971), 4; *The Thrust* (October 17, 1971), 4; *The Thrust* (March 26, 1972), 4.

38. Jim Whitmire 2008 Interview, 1:12:20; *The Thrust* (April 28, 1968), 4.

39. *The Thrust* (October 17, 1971), 4; Lyvonne Burleson Interview, 15:15.

40. Jim Whitmire 2023 Interview, 57:00.

41. Jim Whitmire 2023 Interview Burleson 1970 Notes, 2-3.

42. *The Thrust* (September 12, 1971), 2; *Orlando Sentinel* (September 4, 1971), 6B; Burleson 1971 Notes, 3.

43. "Solomon," *The Merritt Island Years* (Memphis: Love Worth Finding, 2024), 2:00.

44. *The Thrust* (September 5, 1971), 4; *Today* (September 6, 1971), 4B.

45. *The Thrust* (October 3, 1971), 2.

46. Senior Members Interview, 36:30.

CHAPTER 11

1. John McAleenan, "Rev Rogers and His Island in the Sun," *Today* (May 14, 1972), 7; "False Prophets," *The Merritt Island Years* (Memphis: Love Worth Finding, 2024), 35:11.

2. *The Thrust* (December 19, 1971), 4.

3. *The Thrust* (December 5, 1971), 4; *The Thrust* (December 12, 1971), 4; *The Thrust* (December 19, 1971), 4; *The Thrust* (January 2, 1971), 4.

4. *The Thrust* (December 12, 1971), 1; Burleson 1972 Notes, 1.

5. *Orlando Sentinel* (January 15, 1972), 4B; *Today* (January 13, 1972), 5A.

6. Freddie Gage, "A Tribute to Adrian Rogers," https://www.baptistpress.com/resource-library/news/first-person-a-tribute-to-adrian-rogers (accessed November 9, 2023).

7. *The Thrust* (January 16, 1972), 1.

8. *The Thrust* (January 23, 1972), 1,4.

9. "Invasion Army Stirred Deep Christian Feelings," *Orlando Sentinel* (January 22, 1972), 6.

10. Ibid.

11. "Israel and Prophecy," *The Merritt Island Years* (Memphis: Love Worth Finding, 2024), 1:00.

12. "Gage Crusade Meant Much to Youth," *Today* (January 18, 1972), 5A.

13. Burleson 1972 Notes 1.

14. *The Thrust* (December 19, 1971), 4.

15. *The Thrust* March 19, 1972), 1.

16. *The Thrust* (April 9, 1972), 4.

17. *The Thrust* (April 16, 1972), 4; "Colonel Jim Irwin Timeless Testimony," https://www.youtube.com/watch?v=-FUS1259dHM (accessed November 8, 2023).

18. *Orlando Sentinel* (April 17, 1972), 4B; "Colonel Jim Irwin Timeless Testimony," https://www.youtube.com/watch?v=-FUS1259dHM (accessed November 8, 2023).

19. *Orlando Sentinel* (April 17, 1972), 4B.

20. "Colonel Jim Irwin Timeless Testimony," https://www.youtube.com/watch?v=-FUS1259dHM (accessed November 8, 2023).

21. "Rev Rogers to Receive Trinity Honorary Degree," *Orlando Sentinel* (May 13, 1972), 6B; "Man of God," *The Merritt Island Years* (Memphis: Love Worth Finding, 2024), 4:30.

22. "Questions from Calvary" (Memphis: Bellevue Baptist Church, 1978), 3:30.

23. "Five Questions Satan Can't Answer" (Memphis: Bellevue Baptist Church, 1992), 5:00.

24. "Questions from Calvary," 4:00; Gayle Rogers Foster Interview (Telephone, March 29, 2022), 1.

25. "Five Questions Satan Can't Answer," 5:30.

26. "Rev Rogers and His Island in the Sun," 5.

27. "Rev Rogers and His Island in the Sun," 4; Questions from Calvary," 4:45.

28. "'New Faces' Featured on SBC Pastors Conference Agenda," http://media.sbhla. org.s3.amazonaws.com/3348,21-Mar-1972.pdf (accessed November 15, 2023).

29. "Elisha, Man of God," A *Legacy of Preaching* (Fort Worth: SBC Tapes, 2005), 6:45.

30. Ibid, 8:00.

31. "How to Please God" (Memphis: Bellevue Baptist Church, 1972), 52:30.

32. "The Story Behind the Jesus Revolution Cover and Where the Movement Stands a Half-Century Later," *Time* (July 26, 2023), 10-15; "Youth and the Jesus Movement," *The Merritt Island Years* (Memphis: Love Worth Finding, 2024), 10:00.

33. Michael Richardson, *Amazing Faith: One Man Who Spent His Life Taking God at His Word* (Colorado Springs: Waterbrook Press, 2000), 155-156.

34. "Youth and the Jesus Movement," 10:00; "How to Have an Evangelistic Church," 20:30.

35. "Reverend Rogers to Lecture at 'Explo 72' Conference," *Orlando Sentinel* (May 6, 1972), 6.

36. Ibid.

37. "Youth Leaving for Explo," *Orlando Sentinel* (June 10, 1972), 6.

38. Amazing Faith, 156.

39. *The Thrust* (June 25, 1972), 4.

40. *Love Worth Finding*, 54-55.

41. *Standing on the Promises*, 35:00; Love Worth Finding, 56.

42. "Bellevue Baptist to Hear Prospective Pastor Sunday," *Commercial Appeal* (August 12, 1972), 15.

43. "How to Please God," 55:00.

44. *The Thrust* (August 27, 1972), 1.

45. Ibid, 4.

CHAPTER 12

1. "The Book that Built a Church," *The Merritt Island Years* (Memphis: Love Worth Finding, 2024), 2:45.

2. Ibid, 4:00.

3. "False Prophets," *The Merritt Island Years* (Memphis: Love Worth Finding, 2024), 50:20.

4. "The Book that Built a Church," 21:30.

5. Ibid, 29:00.

6. Ibid, 32:20.

7. Ibid, 34:45.

8. "How to Have a Growing Church," *The Merritt Island Years* (Memphis: Love Worth Finding, 2024), 3:00.

9. Ibid, 8:15.

10. "The Book that Built a Church," 35:30.

11. "It Costs to Serve Jesus," *The Merritt Island Years* (Memphis: Love Worth Finding, 2024), 19:00.

12. "False Prophets," 6:15.

13. Ibid, 6:50.

14. "How to Have a Growing Church," 4:30; "False Prophets," 28:30.

15. "False Prophets," 15:00.

16. Ibid, 16:30.

17. Ibid, 18:45.

18. "How to Have a Growing Church," 11:30.

19. "False Prophets," 30:20.

20. Ibid, 10:20.

21. Ibid, 24:00.

22. Ibid, 14:30.

CHAPTER 13

1. "Who Is the Holy Spirit," *The Merritt Island Years* (Memphis: Love Worth Finding, 2024), 1:15.

2. We use "Pentecostal" to refer to a Christian of any denomination that officially identifies itself as "Pentecostal," and we use "charismatic" to refer to a Christian of any other denomination who embraces doctrines or practices typically associated with a Pentecostal denomination. See C. Douglas Weaver, *Baptists and the Holy Spirit* (Waco: Baylor University, 2019), 208.

3. *Love Worth Finding*, 156.

4. "Gifts of the Holy Spirit," *The Merritt Island Years* (Memphis: Love Worth Finding, 2024), 19:00; "If Any Man Thirst," *The Merritt Island Years* (Memphis: Love Worth Finding, 2024), 13:30.

5. "Filled with the Holy Spirit," *The Merritt Island Years* (Memphis: Love Worth Finding, 2024), 6:30; 13:30.

6. Ian Thomas, *The Saving Life of Christ* (Grand Rapids: Zondervan, 1961), 68-69.

7. "Sin Against the Holy Spirit," *The Merritt Island Years* (Memphis: Love Worth Finding, 2024), 11:30.

8. J. Oswald Sanders, *The Holy Spirit and His Gifts* (Grand Rapids: Zondervan, 1970); J. Oswald Sanders, *The Pursuit of the Holy* (Grand Rapids: Zondervan, 1972).

9. "Filled with the Holy Spirit," 20:15.

10. Ibid, 21:30-24:00.

11. "The Tragic Story of King Saul," *The Merritt Island Years* (Memphis: Love Worth Finding, 2024); "The Lost Axe Head," *The Merritt Island Years* (Memphis: Love Worth Finding, 2024).

12. "How to Live on the Mountaintop," *The Merritt Island Years* (Memphis: Love Worth Finding, 2024), 5:45.

13. Ibid, 6:00.

14. “Going Deeper,” *The Merritt Island Years* (Memphis: Love Worth Finding, 2024), 2:00.

15. Ibid, 30:45.

16. Ibid, 35:00.

17. “Deacon Ordination,” *The Merritt Island Years* (Memphis: Love Worth Finding, 2024), 15:00.

18. “The Lost Axe Head,” 11:15.

19. “The Man of God,” *The Merritt Island Years* (Memphis: Love Worth Finding, 2024), 31:00; also “How to Have an Evangelistic Church,” SWBTS Chapel (Fort Worth: SWBTS, 1979), 13:30.

20. “Possessing Our Possessions,” *The Merritt Island Years* (Memphis: Love Worth Finding, 2024), 5:00.

21. “The Blessing of Being a Branch,” *The Merritt Island Years* (Memphis: Love Worth Finding, 2024), 2:00.

22. “The Blessing of Being a Branch,” 21:00; also, “If Any Man Thirst,” *The Merritt Island Years* (Memphis: Love Worth Finding, 2024), 8:00.

23. “Deacon Ordination,” 15:30.

24. “What Kind of Church,” *The Merritt Island Years* (Memphis: Love Worth Finding, 2024), 5:00; “Deacon Ordination,” 16:30.

25. “A Class for Cowards,” *The Merritt Island Years* (Memphis: Love Worth Finding, 2024), 30:00.

26. “Deacon Ordination,” 5:30.

27. “Gifts of the Holy Spirit,” 26:30.

28. *The Thrust* (May 2, 1971), 4.

29. “Gifts of the Holy Spirit,” 15:15.

30. Jim Whitmire 2023 Interview, 36:00.

31. Weaver, *Baptists and the Holy Spirit*, 209, 214-215.

32. “Who is the Holy Spirit,” 33:15.

33. “Possessing Our Possessions,” 4:00.

34. “Six Little Words,” 32:30; “How to Have a Growing Church,” 18:15.

35. “How to Live on the Mountain Top,” 8:30.

36. “The Power of the Holy Spirit,” 23:00.

37. *Baptists and the Holy Spirit*, 207-227; Stanley N. Gundry, *Five Views of Sanctification* (Grand Rapids: Zondervan, 1987), 151-183; Andrew Naselli, *No Quick Fix* (Bellingham: Lexham Press, 2017), 13-27.

38. Joyce Rogers Interview, 8:30.

39. Steve Rogers Interview, 19:00.

40. Michael Catt Interview (Telephone, April 15, 2022), 3.

41. "Filled with the Holy Spirit," 5:30.

42. "Who is the Holy Spirit and What Does He Do?" *The Merritt Island Years* (Memphis: Love Worth Finding, 2024), 11:00.

CHAPTER 14

1. "Island Pastor is True Leader," *Cocoa Tribune* (August 9, 1968), 5B.

2. "The Tragic Story of King Saul," 42:00.

3. Joe Boatright Interview, 20:45.

4. Gayle Rogers Foster Interview, 1.

5. Joyce Rogers Interview, 2:00.

6. Joe Boatright Interview, 45:30.

7. David Rogers Interview, 1.

8. Peter Lord Interview, 11:45.

9. Jim Whitmire 2008 Interview, 25:00; Joyce Rogers Interview, 15:30.

10. Jim Whitmire 2008 Interview, 27:30.

11. Ibid, 28:00.

12. "A Tribute to Adrian Rogers," *Chris Fabry Live*, https://www.youtube.com/watch?v=BFdrAl7k07E (accessed December 23, 2023).

13. "False Prophets," 42:10.

14. Jim Whitmire 2008 Interview, 33:15.

15. Joe Boatright Interview, 35:00.

16. "Blessed are Those Who Mourn," *The Merritt Island Years* (Memphis: Love Worth Finding, 2024), 20:30.

17. Joe Boatright Interview, 42:30; also Adrian Rogers Funeral Service.

18. Joyce Rogers Interview, 55:30.

19. "The Return of the Redeemer," *The Merritt Island Years* (Memphis: Love Worth Finding, 2024), 15:15.

20. "Oral Memoirs of Adrian Rogers: Interviewed by Barry Hankins, August 18, 1997" (Waco: Baylor University, 2003), 3.

21. "The 5Ws of the Bus Ministry," 21:00.

22. "Let the Fire Fall," *The Merritt Island Years* (Memphis: Love Worth Finding, 2024), 18:15.

23. "The 5Ws of the Bus Ministry," 21:30.

24. *Orlando Sentinel* (August 21, 1971), 6A.

25. Jim Whitmire 2008 Interview, 17:30.

26. *Love Worth Finding*, 123. Adrian mentioned eleven men in that section: John R. Rice, Hyman Appleman, Billy Graham, Robert G. Lee, W. A. Criswell, Gray Allison, Vance Havner, Ian Thomas, Stephen Olford, J. Sidlow Baxter, and Bill Bright.

27. Steve Rogers Interview, 1:07:00.

28. "Revelation 16," *The Merritt Island Years* (Memphis: Love Worth Finding, 2024), 26:30.

29. "Earth's Golden Age," *The Merritt Island Years* (Memphis: Love Worth Finding, 2024), 21:00; "How to Have a Growing Church," 6:00; also "Tower of Blunders," *The Merritt Island Years* (Memphis: Love Worth Finding, 2024), 29:00.

30. "False Prophets," 34:00.

CHAPTER 15

1. "The Battle for Your Mind," 15:20.

2. "Task Force for Evangelism," 3:00.

3. "General Prologue," https://chaucer.fas.harvard.edu/pages/general-prologue-0 (accessed December 27, 2023).

4. "Learning to Share Jesus" (Memphis: Bellevue Baptist Church, 2003), 27:00.

5. "Maturity, Ministry, Management," 35:30.

6. "The Tabernacle," *The Merritt Island Years* (Memphis: Love Worth Finding, 2024), 33:00.

7. "Jacksonville First Baptist Church 1999 Pastor's Conference," https://www.facebook.com/watch/?v=576592789717039 (accessed December 27, 2023), 33:00; "Righteousness of God," *The Merritt Island Years* (Memphis: Love Worth Finding, 2024), 36:30; "No Other Way to Heaven Except Through Jesus" (Memphis: Bellevue Baptist Church, 1996), 30:00.

8. “Jacksonville First Baptist Church,” 39:00; “Righteousness of God,” 38:00.

9. “Called to Win Souls,” *The Merritt Island Years* (Memphis: Love Worth Finding, 2024), 1:00.

10. “Prove Your Love,” *The Merritt Island Years* (Memphis: Love Worth Finding, 2024), 21:00.

11. “Dedicated Discipleship,” *The Merritt Island Years* (Memphis: Love Worth Finding, 2024), 25:00.

12. “The Theology of a Thief,” *The Merritt Island Years* (Memphis: Love Worth Finding, 2024), 9:00; “Task Force for Evangelism,” 27:00.

13. *The Thrust* (January 25, 1971), 4.

14. “Blueprint for Victory,” 5:45.

15. “How to Have a Growing Church,” 1:00.

16. Jim Whitmire 2008 Interview, 8:00.

17. “Maturity, Ministry, Management,” 1:30.

EPILOGUE

1. “How to Behave When the Pastor is Away,” *The Merritt Island Years* (Memphis: Love Worth Finding, 2024), 5:00.

2. Burleson 1973 Notes, 3.

3. Steve Rogers Interview, 1:17:00.

4. Jim Whitmire 2008 Interview, 1:00:40.

Printed in the USA
CPSIA information can be obtained
at www.ICGtesting.com
JSHW012229150624
64787JS00007B/21